THE CHILDREN OF HENRY VIII

John Guy is a Fellow of Clare College, University of Cambridge, and also teaches on the Yale in London programme at the Paul Mellon Centre for Studies in British Art. He read history at Cambridge and has held academic positions in Britain and the United States throughout his career, specializing in the Tudor period. His books include the bestselling *Tudor England*, *The Tudors: A Very Short Introduction*, *A Daughter's Love: Thomas and Margaret More*, *Thomas Becket: Warrior, Priest, Rebel, Victim: A 900-Year-Old Story Retold* and *'My Heart is My Own': the Life of Mary Queen of Scots*, which won the Whitbread Biography Award, Marsh Biography Award and was a Finalist for the National Book Critics' Circle (USA) Biography/ Autobiography of the Year Award. He appears regularly on BBC radio and has presented five documentaries for BBC2 television. He also writes and reviews for national newspapers and magazines, including *The Sunday Times* and *The Literary Review*.

the CHILDREN *of* HENRY VIII

JOHN GUY

OXFORD
UNIVERSITY PRESS

OXFORD

UNIVERSITY PRESS

Great Clarendon Street, Oxford, OX2 6DP,
United Kingdom

Oxford University Press is a department of the University of Oxford.
It furthers the University's objective of excellence in research, scholarship,
and education by publishing worldwide. Oxford is a registered trade mark of
Oxford University Press in the UK and in certain other countries

First Edition published in 2013
First published in paperback 2014

Impression: 1

British Library Cataloguing in Publication Data

Data available

ISBN 978-0-19-284090-5 (Hbk.)
ISBN 978-0-19-870087-6 (Pbk.)

Printed in Great Britain by
Clays Ltd, St Ives plc

Praise for *The Children of Henry VIII*

'With the panache for which Guy's work has become known, The Children of Henry VIII portrays the childhood nightmares of Britain's most celebrated dysfunctional family… [It] is a portrait miniature of a book, skilfully portraying the character of an age, yet managing to do so with enough detail and care to bring its subjects to life.'

Times Literary Supplement

'[A] smart, lively little book enriched by the reliable pleasure of Guy's prose, his pen dancing as deftly about his compact historical portraits as Horenbout's brush once did over his stunning miniatures.'

The Sunday Times

'Guy, whose prose is commendably readable, has a real gift for bringing Tudor history to life for 21st-century readers…'

The Independent on Sunday

'This may be a well-known story, but Guy presents it with typical narrative flair and attention to detail, producing a book with obvious appeal.'

BBC History Magazine

'The stunning psychodrama that was the Tudor court is brilliantly evoked in John Guy's little book.'

The Lady

'Well-written, well-researched and a lot of fun.'

The Glasgow Herald

'John Guy is that rare cross: a scholar who also writes for the popular market. It shows here, as he sketches with verve and fluency the education and the beliefs, as well as, briefly, the reigns of these last Tudors. But where he excels is in illuminating the relationships between the squabbling siblings. They say if you've got lemons, make lemonade, and in Guy's hands the story of The Children of Henry VIII is fresh, sparkling and sharp.'

The Literary Review

'John Guy has written an admirable account…the result is a minor masterpiece.'
Jonathan Sumption, *The Spectator*

'[Guy's] absorbing, thoroughly researched book does justice to two exemplary women—and reminds us that history is full of ironies.'
Claire Tomalin, *The New York Times*

'Compelling…Guy's scholarship is irreproachable.'
The Independent on Sunday

'Carries its learning lightly…this warm and vivid portrait of the most attractive father and daughter relationship in English history will reward the specialist as well as the general reader.'
Eamon Duffy, *The Independent*

Praise for *Thomas Becket*:

'It is to Guy's immense credit that he has written such a lively, effortlessly readable biography—a book that not only corrects many historical errors and uncertainties, but merits reading more than once, for the sheer joy of its superb storytelling.'
The Times

'…breathes new life into an oft-told tale of throne and altar antagonism, with its complex undercurrents of money, politics, religion and shocking violence. However well you think you know the story, it is well worth the read.'
Financial Times

'Guy deftly sets a timeless and all-too-familiar emotional tussle…against the less familiar social and political landscape of medieval Europe.'
The New York Times

'A compelling read… [Guy] knows how to take the familiar and shape it into a narrative that both improves our historical knowledge and is entertainingly astute, and in places positively moving.'
Peter Stanford, *The Independent*

'Guy wears his learning lightly, and this is undoubtedly the most accessible Life of Thomas Becket to be published in recent years.'
Katherine Harvey, *Times Literary Supplement*

'Magnificently successful… John Guy deserves both our thanks and our admiration.'
Nicholas Vincent, *The Tablet*

ACKNOWLEDGEMENTS

I gladly acknowledge the generosity and kindness of the many archivists and librarians who have helped to smooth my path, chiefly at the British Library, the National Archives at Kew, the Fellows' Library at Clare College, the Bodleian Library, Cambridge University Library, the Bibliothèque Nationale de France, and especially the London Library. The genealogical tables were drawn and digitized by Richard Guy of Orang-Utan Productions from my rough drafts.

I've nothing but thanks and admiration for Peter Robinson, my agent, for his constant encouragement and for giving helpful advice on the manuscript. I owe an immense debt to Luciana O'Flaherty at Oxford University Press, whose idea the book was, and who edited it with astonishing speed and efficiency. She was ably assisted by Matthew Cotton, whom I thank especially for his tact when the manuscript arrived a few weeks later than I had predicted. Alan Bryson was generous with advice and suggestions and I am indebted to him for showing me some newly discovered letters of the young Elizabeth that he is currently co-editing for publication. I express heartfelt thanks to my students at Cambridge, especially those from Clare and Gonville and Caius Colleges, whose supervisions on the Tudors unaccountably strayed on several occasions into territory discussed in this book. Julia, as ever, was a tower of strength and read the complete manuscript several times, making a number of invaluable suggestions.

I also warmly thank David and Frances Waters, whose astonishing talent for booking opera tickets ensured that Julia and I were able to go to Bayreuth immediately after I had done the final revisions to the book.

London
August 2012

CONTENTS

LIST OF ILLUSTRATIONS

LIST OF COLOUR PLATES

NOTE ON UNITS OF CURRENCY

In citing units of currency, the old sterling denominations of pounds, shillings and pence have been retained. There are twelve pence (12d.) in a shilling (modern 5p or US 8 cents), twenty shillings (20s.) in a pound (£1 or US $1.60), and so on. A mark is 13s. 4d. (66p or US $1.05). Rough estimates of modern values for sixteenth-century figures can be obtained by multiplying all the numbers by a thousand. Equivalents for European denominations, where possible, are worked out from 'Money and Coinage of the Age of Erasmus', in *Collected Works of Erasmus*, 76 vols (Toronto, 1974–), I, pp. 311–47, and P. Spufford (ed.), *Handbook of Medieval Exchange* (London, 1986).

GENEALOGICAL TABLES

THE TUDOR SUCCESSION

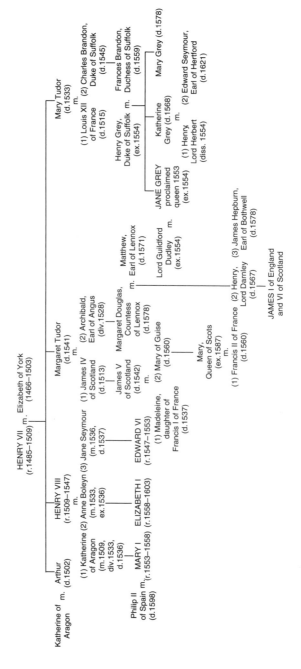

THE BOLEYNS

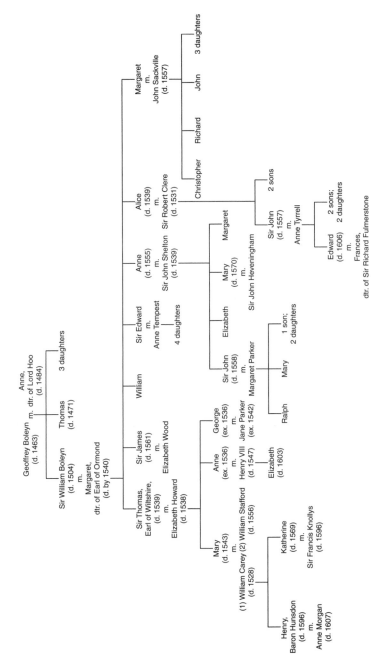

THE HOWARDS

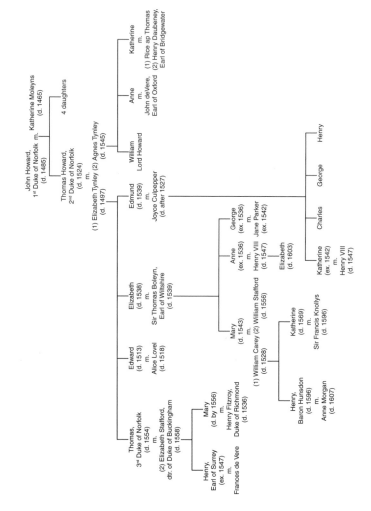

John Howard,
1ˢᵗ Duke of Norfolk m. Katherine Moleyns
(d. 1485)   (d. 1465)

Thomas Howard,   4 daughters
2ⁿᵈ Duke of Norfolk
(d. 1524)
m.
(1) Elizabeth Tynley (2) Agnes Tynley
(d. 1497)   (d. 1545)

Edmund   William   Anne   Katherine
(d. 1539)   Lord Howard   m.   m.
m.   John deVere,   (1) Rice ap Thomas
Joyce Culpepper   Earl of Oxford (2) Henry Daubeney,
(d. after 1527)   Earl of Bridgewater

Thomas,   Edward   Elizabeth
3ʳᵈ Duke of Norfolk (d. 1513)   (d. 1538)
(d. 1554)   m.   m.
m.   Alice Lovel   Sir Thomas Boleyn,
(2) Elizabeth Stafford, (d. 1518) Earl of Wiltshire
dtr. of Duke of Buckingham   (d. 1539)
(d. 1558)

Henry,   Mary
Earl of Surrey   (d. by 1556)
(ex. 1547)   m.
m.   Henry Fitzroy,
Frances de Vere Duke of Richmond
                 (d. 1536)

Mary   Anne   George
(d. 1543)   (ex. 1536)   (ex. 1536)
m.   m.   m.
(1) William Carey (2) William Stafford Henry VIII Jane Parker
(d. 1528)   (d. 1556)   (d. 1547) (ex. 1542)

                                Elizabeth
                                (d. 1603)

Henry,   Katherine
Baron Hunsdon   (d. 1569)
(d. 1596)   m.
m.   Sir Francis Knollys
Anne Morgan   (d. 1596)
(d. 1607)

Charles   Katherine   George   Henry
                 (ex. 1542)
                 m.
                 Henry VIII
                 (d. 1547)

Prologue

O N Saturday, 2 April 1502, Arthur, Prince of Wales, the elder son
of the king of England, Henry VII, died at Ludlow Castle on the
Welsh borders, aged just 15. The young prince, married less than five
months before at St Paul's Cathedral to the Spanish princess, Katherine of Aragon, had first felt unwell at Shrovetide in early February.[1]
On Easter Day (27 March), his condition rapidly worsened, 'at the
which season [there] grew and increased upon his body... the most
pitiful disease and sickness, that with so sore and great violence had
battled and driven [itself] in[to] the singular parts of him inward.'
Finally, 'that cruel and fervent enemy of nature, the deadly corrup-
tion, did utterly vanquish and overcome the pure and friendful
blood, without all manner of physical help and remedy.'[2]

The causes of Arthur's death are keenly debated. A credible
hypothesis is that he died of bubonic plague, which returned to
the West Country in 1502. If that was so, little could have been done
for him, for the best that medical science could offer at this time

was to tuck the patient up warmly in bed and dose him with a cocktail of white wine mixed with the powder of dried ivy berries ground in a mortar, failing which he should have the anus (or 'vent') of three or four partially plucked hens pressed against his buboes (or sores) to draw out the infection, after which the buboes were to be rubbed with treacle.[3]

The 'sweating sickness' and tuberculosis are also regularly suggested.[4] A viral pulmonary disease, the 'sweating sickness' or 'sweat' had first reached England with the French mercenaries fighting alongside Henry VII's troops at Bosworth in 1485 when, as Earl of Richmond, he had captured the crown in battle from Richard III, the last of the Yorkist kings. Its usual victims were not children or teenagers, but the middle-aged; the classic symptoms were myalgia and headache, accompanied by 'a deadly and burning sweat', leading to abdominal pain, vomiting, increased headache and delirium, followed by cardiac palpitations, paralysis and death. Dreaded for its 'sudden sharpness and unwonted cruelness', the 'sweat' normally took less than twenty-four hours to kill: those who lasted that long were almost certain to survive the attack.[5]

Since Arthur had felt unwell for two months, and even after the onset of his final decline took almost a week to die, his illness would seem to be different. Only one historian makes a positive claim for the reappearance of the 'sweat' in 1502, and no evidence is cited to substantiate the assertion.[6] Moreover, while the 'sweat' returned to England in 1506 and 1508, these outbreaks are known to have been mild.

Tuberculosis is improbable, since the condition develops very slowly and Arthur was considered to be a fit and healthy teenager before he fell ill. The idea that he was generally 'weak and sickly' derives from a nineteenth-century misreading of a letter, written in

FIGURE 1   Prince Arthur, from a stained-glass window in the north transept of Great Malvern Priory, attrib. Richard Twygge and Thomas Wodshawe.

Latin, that his father sent to Katherine's parents, King Ferdinand of Aragon and Isabella of Castile, a few weeks after their daughter's wedding. In it, Henry explained that Katherine had been allowed to accompany her young husband to Wales even though many people had advised against it, 'because of the tender age of our son'.[7]

Arthur was nine months younger than his wife, and Henry had been warned against the perceived dangers of allowing a 15-year-old boy to enjoy unlimited sex—a risk particularly feared by the Spanish ambassador in London, Don Pedro de Ayala, since it was commonly believed in Spain that 'an undue indulgence' in 'the pleasures of marriage' had caused the death of Katherine's elder brother Juan, who died aged 19 in 1497, six months after marrying Margaret of Burgundy.[8]

A further possibility is testicular cancer, perhaps suggested by the phrase 'the singular parts of him inward'.[9] If correct, this diagnosis would not merely establish the cause of death but could conceivably explain the protestations of Katherine's first lady of the bedchamber, Doña Elvira Manuel, in a letter to Queen Isabella sent shortly after Arthur's funeral that, although Katherine was a widow, she was still a virgin. For if the prince had testicular cancer, a disease most frequently found in men aged between 15 and 44, the pains and the damage to his reproductive system could have resulted in an impaired sexual function. Although Doña Elvira's letter can no longer be traced in the archives, its contents are known because Isabella quoted them on 12 July in a letter written at Toledo, saying, 'It is already known for a certainty that the said Princess of Wales, our daughter, remains as she was here, for so Doña Elvira has written to us.'[10]

◆　◆　◆

FIGURE 2   The gatehouse at Ludlow Castle, Shropshire. Prince Arthur and Katherine of Aragon passed through it when they arrived at Ludlow in 1502.

Barely was Arthur's body cold than Sir Richard Pole, the lord chamberlain of the prince's household, sent letters announcing his death to the king's councillors at Greenwich Palace. As the messenger arrived during the night of Monday, 4 April, when the king was in bed, the councillors decided to break the news to him early the next morning through his confessor, a Franciscan friar.[11] Knocking at Henry's chamber door 'somewhat before the time accustomed', the friar was admitted and asked all the servants to leave. Once he and Henry were alone, the friar quoted a text from the Book of Job, using the version from the Latin Vulgate Bible. 'If we have received good things from the hand of God', he solemnly intoned, 'why should we not endure bad things?'[12]

Henry knew instantly that he was about to receive a devastating blow. When the friar blurted out that his 'dearest son was departed to God', the king at once sent for his wife, Elizabeth of York, saying that 'he and his queen would take the painful sorrows together'. As soon as she arrived 'and saw the king her lord and husband in that natural and painful sorrow', she—using 'full, great and constant comfortable words'—besought him 'that he would first, after God, remember the welfare of his own noble person, the comfort of his realm and of her.' The living, said Elizabeth, had to take priority over the dead.

In a valiant effort to comfort the husband whom she seems genuinely to have loved, and for the moment concealing the true extent of her own grief, Elizabeth reminded him that his own mother, Lady Margaret Beaufort—married to King Henry VI's half-brother, Edmund Tudor, at the age of 12—had been able to have only one child. Quickly made pregnant, she had been left with a serious gynaecological impairment after her son's delivery. Despite this, Elizabeth recalled, Henry had survived through innumerable tribulations to manhood and won the crown. He also still had a healthy young son and two daughters. And she quickly added, were they themselves not still both young enough to have more children?[13]

It was not to be. With Arthur's younger brother, Henry, Duke of York, still not quite 11 when his elder brother died, his father naturally feared for the dynasty's security and the succession. Arthur's death changed things for ever, for it would now be the younger Henry who would inherit the throne and make Katherine of Aragon his bride.

The royal couple did try almost immediately for another baby in the fervent hope that they could have a male heir in reserve, and within a couple of months Elizabeth was pregnant again. On 12 December, ahead of her accouchement at the Tower of London, she was rowed there along the Thames from Westminster in the royal barge for the day to oversee the preparation of her apartments.[14]

Returning to the Tower on 26 January 1503, the queen and her attendants first took wine and spices in the Presence Chamber before ceremonially processing to her lying-in chamber, which was hung from floor to ceiling with Flemish tapestries and equipped with a 'rich bed' with the finest embroidered coverlets and the most expensive linen sheets.[15] At the door of the chamber, her attendant lords and councillors departed, leaving only the queen and her ladies to enter the room.

On 2 February, the Feast of Candlemas, in the middle of the night, Elizabeth 'travailed of a child suddenly'.[16] She was successfully delivered of a baby girl by the same midwife who had delivered Arthur, but the birth had been a difficult one, and shortly after dawn the child was hastily christened Katherine in the Church of St Peter ad Vincula at the Tower.[17] Soon the queen herself became alarmingly ill and Henry sent for Dr Halesworth, a physician from Kent, who travelled night and day by road and river to reach her bedside.[18] Whether he arrived in time is not recorded, but if he did, he was unable to save Elizabeth, who died on the morning of Saturday, 11 February, her thirty-seventh birthday.[19] Her baby was still alive the next day, when four yards of flannel were purchased for her, but she died shortly afterwards.[20]

With both Arthur and Elizabeth gone, the king was an altered man. Always cautious to the point of obsession about money and his prerogative rights, he became increasingly suspicious, reclusive and rapacious. He withdrew into his Privy Chamber, where he put a ring of steel around himself, tormented by fears for his dynasty's security and over-protective of his surviving son, whom he rarely allowed out of his sight.[21] When information reached him that several 'great personages' considered other candidates more suitable to succeed him than Prince Henry, arrests were made and steps taken to counter the threat of rebellion and internal lawlessness by extreme and sometimes illegal methods.[22] In readiness for a possible dynastic crisis, the king also spent liberally on improving the country's defences, seeking to deter foreign powers from attempting to intervene in the succession.[23]

Henry was noticeably jumpy in July 1506, after one of the galleries closest to the royal apartments at his favourite palace at Richmond collapsed during major construction works less than an hour after he and Prince Henry had been walking in it. Fortunately no one was injured, but the carpenter responsible for the shoddy work was sent to prison.[24]

The king's health, meanwhile, collapsed. His eyesight began to fail, he appears to have suffered a minor stroke and he found writing difficult. Not long after he became a widower, it was reported that 'the king's grace is but a weak man and sickly, not likely to be no long lived man'.[25] He survived, but visiting him in late March 1507, another Spanish envoy, Dr Roderigo de Puebla, found him confined to bed, unable to eat or drink for six days and receiving almost no one. By then, he would regularly fall sick during the early months of each year, rallying in the summer. In 1507, his condition was complicated by 'a quinsy', an acute, pustular tonsillitis that made it painful to eat or speak.[26]

◆　　◆　　◆

Henry VII died at 11 p.m. on Saturday, 21 April 1509. For two days, his trusted privy chamber servants kept the news a closely guarded secret while, Kremlin-style, they jockeyed for position in the new reign. Only on the afternoon of the 23rd were the king's councillors informed. Later that same evening, the whole Court was told. Next day, while heralds proclaimed the accession of the younger Henry in the streets of London, two of the most hated of the old king's ministers were arrested and sent to the Tower in a carefully planned *putsch*. At the same time, several illegally held prisoners were released from the Tower and other prisons.[27]

The atmosphere in these days was highly charged, for by no means was it a foregone conclusion that the transition would be smooth. The elder Henry had possessed the flimsiest of claims to the throne when, against all the odds, he defeated Richard III in battle. He had won the crown only because the lack of a fixed law of succession enabled him, by force of arms, to proclaim himself king and because Richard III had become so hated that even a man with Henry's dubious claim was preferable.[28]

Henry VII had first arranged for his younger son's betrothal to Katherine of Aragon in June 1503, and a year later the young prince was formally married to her after Pope Julius II issued a dispensation allowing him to wed his elder brother's widow. Of course, this so-called 'marriage' had been just one move on the chessboard of the king's diplomacy and was not consummated. Only 13 when he took his vows, the bridegroom was below the lawful age of marriage, and on the eve of his fourteenth birthday, he repudiated the wedding, as canon law entitled him to do, once more at his father's behest.[29]

But after Henry VII's death, the question of the marriage arose again. Clearly the new king, then approaching his eighteenth birthday, was in two minds about it, at one moment claiming (according to a report of one of his councillors) that 'it would burden his conscience to marry his brother's widow', and at another professing that his dying father had ordered him to marry Katherine as soon as possible to consolidate the alliance with Spain.[30]

When, however, Henry VIII decided to do something, he did it with gusto and because he believed it to be right. So it was that, declaring himself to be deeply in love and sweeping aside the objection that his bride-to-be was nearly six years older than he was, he astonished his councillors by marrying Katherine for a second time on 11 June 1509 in his late mother's oratory at Greenwich Palace. When he then ordered a magnificent joint coronation ceremony for himself and his wife to take place barely a fortnight later on Midsummer Day, it seemed as if the dynasty was indeed secure at last.

Not so. For in his final years, Henry VII had become deeply resented by his subjects for his summary justice and extortions, not least in London. By creating an atmosphere of fear and coercion, he had reopened dynastic wounds and would come to be regarded by many with old Yorkist allegiances as a false king and a usurper. To counter this, his son unashamedly set out to court popularity, to build a reputation for honour and magnificence and to usher in a new golden age. As a delighted courtier exclaimed, 'Our king's heart is set not upon gold or jewels or mines of ore, but upon virtue, reputation and eternal fame.'[31]

But monarchies and dynasties are not built on virtue or reputation alone. They are rooted in families, marriages and the birth of legitimate heirs and successors. Only when the new King Henry had fathered children of his own might it be said with any real confidence that the dynasty was stable. Nobody in 1509 understood this better than Thomas More, already rising fast in his career as a London lawyer. In a handwritten set of verses presented to Henry to celebrate his glorious coronation, More declared that, while the new king 'has banished fear and oppression' by his affirmations of respect for justice and the rule of law, and his determination to arrest and imprison informers and anyone else 'who by plots or conspiracies has harmed the realm', what really matters is that Katherine should become the 'mother of kings'. 'Fecund in male offspring', More confidently avowed, 'she will render your ship of state stable and enduring for all time.'[32]

It is quite possible that Henry, in his euphoria at becoming king and his first flush of love for Katherine, never bothered to read More's verses before placing them on the shelves of the royal library. And yet, More, who was already a keen student of history and would shortly become the author of an unpublished *History of King Richard III*, had grasped the essential point. A few years later, Henry would come to know it, and in due course More would himself become a casualty of the intense family drama that would ensue as the king struggled to produce a legitimate male heir.

The story of Henry VIII's children, therefore, is not simply a tale of royal personalities and their foibles set apart from the grand narrative of political and social change. It is also the dynastic history of England.

CHAPTER 1

In the Beginning

CHRISTMAS 1510 was a time of joyous celebration for Henry VIII, his wife Katherine of Aragon and their Court. Not only would the second anniversary of their marriage and coronations soon be approaching, but more significantly Katherine was heavily pregnant.

Nothing mattered more in a dynastic monarchy than that the queen should give birth to a legitimate son and heir to settle the succession. So when, on the morning of New Year's Day 1511, Henry VIII, not yet 20, heard the news that Katherine, who had celebrated her twenty-sixth birthday only a fortnight before, had been delivered of a healthy son at Richmond Palace, he was exultant. As the gunners of the Tower fired salvoes in salute, he ordered bonfires to be lit in the streets of London and free wine to be distributed to the citizens to drink his health and that of his wife and child.[1]

On Sunday, 5 January, the baby was christened Henry after his father and grandfather in the Franciscan friary church beside the privy garden at the palace. The ceremonies, similar to those at Henry's own baptism, followed to the letter the handbook, first devised by the Lancastrian kings and handed down by the Yorkist Edward IV, known as the *Royal Book*. Wrapped in a tiny mantle of cloth of gold lined with ermine, the infant was carried by his god-mother from the great hall of the palace to the friary church along a neatly gravelled path protected from the cold and rain by a covered walkway. Inside the church, the west door, walls and ceiling were draped with fine tapestries and cloth of gold, with carpets laid under foot. The heavy solid silver font, brought in specially from Canterbury on a cart, stood on a raised temporary platform, three steps high, that was overlaid with crimson fabric and hung about with cloth of gold. Suspended above it was a canopy of crimson satin fringed with gold. Beside it, concealed behind a screen, a bra-zier burned sweet-smelling herbs to purify the air. Along the side walls of the nave 200 esquires and yeomen stood holding torches, poised to light them as soon as the child was baptized.[2]

The next day was the Feast of the Epiphany, more colloquially known as Twelfth Night, the final climax of the Christmas festivi-ties. Like his father before him, Henry put on his imperial crown and purple robes and sat in state in his Presence Chamber dressed almost exactly as he had been at his coronation with an orb and sceptre in his hands. Thus arrayed, he solemnly processed with his nobles and courtiers to the Chapel Royal, where he offered gifts of gold, frankincense and myrrh like the Three Kings at the very first Epiphany, afterwards presiding at spectacular candlelit revels and a banquet in the great hall of the palace, surrounded by statues of eleven of his most revered ancestors.[3]

With the celebrations over, Henry went on a pilgrimage to the shrine of the Blessed Virgin Mary at Walsingham in Norfolk to give thanks for the birth of his son.[4] On his return, he ordered a tournament to be held on 12–13 February in the tiltyard at the palace of Westminster, where he meant to put his jousting skills and masculinity on show as one of the four challengers. Katherine, rested and recovered from the ordeal of childbirth and attended by her ladies, presided serenely over this glittering and expensive piece of theatre from the vantage point of a newly constructed gallery.

♦　　♦　　♦

Henry in his youth was the personification of monarchy, the fount of honour; his only flaw was his inability, like his father before him, to look people straight in the eye.[5] Six feet two inches tall and with a thirty-five-inch waist, he was as lean as he was fit before gluttony caused him to bulge.[6] Calling himself 'Loyal Heart', he and his companions first entered the lists at the Westminster tournament on horseback, hidden inside an elaborate mock forest resting on a huge chariot that was pulled by mules disguised as a lion and an antelope. When the chariot stopped before Katherine, actors dressed as foresters blew their horns, the signal for Henry and his fellow challengers to burst out of a golden castle at the centre of the forest, each brandishing a spear. When the jousting began, Henry hogged the limelight by running twenty-five courses, far more than anyone else.

Once the jousting was over on the second day of the tournament, Katherine presented the prizes, her prestige as the mother of an heir to the throne indicated by the fact that she did not have to declare her husband to be the champion.[7]

But on 23 February, joy turned to sorrow. Prince Henry, just seven weeks old, suddenly died.[8] Katherine was distraught. As the chronicler Edward Hall records, 'like a natural woman [she] made much lamentation'. Henry, it seemed at the time, was less troubled than he would be later, believing that since he and his wife were still young, they would have many more children together. According to Hall, he took the calamity 'wondrous wisely', selflessly hiding his pain in order to console his wife. Perhaps, but knowing Henry, it is more likely that Hall's report is the equivalent of a modern press release, designed to portray the king as a model husband. What his private feelings were, we can only imagine.[9]

Swaddled in a pall of black velvet, the tiny coffin of the young prince was carried along the Thames from Richmond to Westminster Abbey in a cortege of three black-draped barges. By tradition, members of the royal family did not attend funerals, so neither Henry nor Katherine was present in the abbey to see their son interred in a tomb to the left-hand side of the high altar near to the shrine of the abbey's founder, St Edward the Confessor. But if the dead prince's parents were absent, the leading nobles and courtiers and more than 400 others were in the abbey, including a contingent of 180 poor men, clad in specially tailored black gowns and hoods. Later, the poor men, who were doubtless selected from among the occupants of the abbey's almshouses or those who had received Maundy money, were handsomely rewarded for bearing wax torches in the funeral procession and praying for the child's soul.[10]

◆　　◆　　◆

This would be neither the first nor the last reproductive tragedy to befall Katherine. Her earliest known pregnancy had ended in a miscarriage on 31 January 1510, when she had 'brought forth prematurely a daughter'.[11] At the time it was routinely assumed that

Henry and Katherine's inability to have a living son was her fault. The stereotype was that if a woman failed repeatedly to produce living offspring, it was the result of her gynaecological or obstetrical difficulties.

Thus Andrew Boorde, an experienced physician who wrote several medical treatises and claimed to have attended Henry VIII, believed that a woman's inability to conceive was the result of 'too much humidity' in the womb. The result was that when 'the seed of man is sown', 'the woman cannot retain it'. She should avoid laxatives, declared Boorde, and try crushed mandrake apples mixed with rose water and sugar, eat plenty of peaches and (if she were fat) scatter pepper liberally on her food. If she had menstrual pains, she might ease them by taking the juice of St John's wort mixed with red wine. In the 'unlikely' event that the man was at fault, he should eat only wholesome food, try such remedies as 'a confection of ginger' and avoid sex immediately after meals.[12]

Tudor medicine had scarcely advanced since the time of the ancient Greeks. Now modern experts argue that Katherine's pregnancy mishaps fit the symptoms of haemolytic disease of the newborn caused by a genetic incompatibility between the blood groups of the parents. In this situation, a couple will rarely be able to produce successfully more than one living child. In other instances, the foetus or newborn infant will develop severe, often fatal anaemia, jaundice or heart failure caused by the destruction of its red blood cells. In a newborn child, death will typically occur within a few weeks.[13]

Henry would have been responsible for the couple's problems if he were positive for a blood group antigen known as Kell and his partner—like 90 per cent of Caucasian populations—was negative. In those circumstances, a high proportion of the foetuses he

FIGURE 3 Lady Margaret Beaufort, Henry VIII's grandmother, from a nineteenth-century engraving.

fathered would die because his partner would make antibodies to the foetal red blood cells. And the genetic mismatch, in Katherine's case, would have been this way round, because her sisters, Juana of Castile and Maria of Portugal, each produced living children with consummate ease and are therefore likely to have been Kell negative.

In 1513 Katherine was pregnant again, but in September or October she was delivered of a premature son who died within hours. Another boy was stillborn in November or December 1514.

At last, and to the royal couple's considerable relief, on Tuesday, 18 February 1516, at about 4 a.m., the queen produced a healthy daughter, who was christened Mary. Katherine doted on her and at first was eager to bring up and educate the child herself, but Henry was determined to follow royal protocol. As revised and updated by his grandmother Margaret Beaufort in 1493, this specified that—once the christening was past—the baby should be put in a royal nursery under the charge of a 'lady mistress' or governess, who was to be assisted by a nurse and four female chamber assistants known as 'the rockers', who took it in turn to rock the royal cradle. A physician was to be in regular attendance and was to supervise every aspect of the infant's diet.

The child's everyday cradle was to have 'four pommels of silver and gilt' and other suitable decorations. And a 'cradle of estate' was to be available when ambassadors or visitors were present, covered by a quilt of ermine and a canopy of crimson cloth of gold and blazoned with the royal arms. Yeomen, grooms and a laundress were appointed to perform menial duties in the nursery at the direction of the governess. Lastly, generous supplies of mattresses, sheets, blankets and swaddling bands were to be requisitioned as well as eight large carpets to cover the floor to exclude draughts.[14]

Put in charge of Mary's nursery on the eve of her mother's accouchement in 1516 was Elizabeth Denton, none other than Henry's own governess when he was a boy. Appointed when he had been about 5, she was the most important figure in his childhood apart from his mother, Elizabeth of York, and he retained the fondest memories of her.[15] Long in receipt of a generous pension from the king, she was brought out of retirement, but either she became ill or clashed with Katherine, since Margaret, Lady Bryan, mother of one of Henry's cronies and the sister of Lord Berners (a distinguished translator of romances and chivalric histories including Froissart's *Chronicles*), was appointed to replace her.

Marked out by Henry as Denton's successor even before the latter had officially vacated the post,[16] Lady Bryan took up her new role in 1518 when—perhaps to strengthen her hand in dealing with Katherine—the king created her a baroness. Bryan then served as Mary's governess until the early summer of 1519, when she moved elsewhere.

◆   ◆   ◆

Henry boasted that his daughter's birth was a portent of better things to come, but it was not. Katherine was said to be pregnant again by August 1517, but no announcement was made. Her final pregnancy ended in November 1518, when she gave birth to a stillborn girl. Her difficulties encouraged Henry's serial infidelities, which may have begun as early as 1510 when he first looked, or perhaps more than looked, at another woman. She was one of the sisters of Edward Stafford, Duke of Buckingham, Anne, Lady Hastings, to whom Henry would later offer an expensive gift.

Katherine first heard of the scandal when Anne's sister, Elizabeth, complained on her behalf to the duke. But when Buckingham indignantly confronted Henry, the king retaliated by rusticating Elizabeth from Court. She chiefly blamed William Compton, Henry's 'groom of the stool' (chief body servant) for her banishment. A backstairs politician more infamously known as Henry's 'ponce', Compton was the man who arranged the king's sexual intrigues.[17] Twenty years later, when Henry had designs on Mistress Amadas, the wife of Robert Amadas, sometime master of the jewelhouse, it was Compton who organized their liaisons at his house in Thames Street, London.[18]

When, in the summer of 1515, Katherine was pregnant with Mary, Henry began a clandestine liaison with Jane Popincourt. A high-spirited Frenchwoman who had come to England as a French tutor to the king's younger sister Mary and afterwards joined Katherine's household, Jane danced before the king in the Twelfth Night revels of 1515 at Greenwich Palace as one of 'six ladies richly apparelled'.[19] When, by the following May, Henry had grown tired of her, she was shipped off home to France with a payoff of £100.[20]

By then, Henry had begun a more serious affair with Elizabeth Blount, whom he first encountered when he danced with her at a Court mummery on New Year's Eve in 1514. Clad in blue velvet and cloth of silver, his face hidden by a masking visor, Henry was clearly enjoying himself, since the dancing lasted for 'a great season'.

A daughter of one of the king's men-at-arms, Elizabeth (better known to her friends as 'Bessie') had become a gentlewoman to Katherine a year or so before. Already spotted by the king's favourite jousting partner, Charles Brandon, Duke of Suffolk, as an exceptional beauty, she was well connected, a kinswoman of at least two of the most senior officials of Katherine's side of the household.[21]

By the time the queen's final pregnancy began early in 1518, Elizabeth was Henry's mistress, and in or around June 1519 she gave birth to their son, christened Henry and afterwards known as 'Henry Fitzroy'.

Estimates of how long their affair lasted vary from around six months to several years. Most likely the liaison started in earnest in the summer of 1518, when Cardinal Wolsey, the king's chief minister, was busy negotiating a landmark pan-European peace accord known as the Treaty of Universal Peace.[22] At a sumptuous entertainment that Wolsey organized in October for the French ambassadors, 'the like of which'—says one of the Venetian negotiators—'was never given either by Cleopatra or Caligula', Elizabeth once again took a leading role as a dancer. But by then, she was visibly pregnant. To spare Katherine's feelings, Elizabeth was partnered in these revels not by Henry, but by Sir Francis Bryan, Lady Bryan's son, but nobody was deceived.[23]

As her lying-in approached, Henry sent Elizabeth to a secluded manor house adjacent to St Lawrence's Priory at Blackmore, near Ingatestone in Essex. Wolsey took charge of all the details, enabling the king to keep his distance while his mistress gave birth.[24] For his part, Henry pretended to know nothing of her accouchement until he knew for sure from Wolsey's investigations that the child was his—and was a boy.

In June, the king amused himself at Windsor Castle and Richmond. In July he hunted in Surrey and Sussex. Only at the end of August did he venture into Essex.[25] Wolsey, meanwhile, handled the baby's christening, at which he stood as the infant's godfather.[26]

Despite acknowledging her son as his own, Henry quickly ended his affair with Elizabeth once her child was delivered. Seeking to be rid of her, he married her off to Gilbert Tailboys, the young heir of George, Lord Tailboys of Kyme and his wife

Elizabeth Gascoigne, the sister of Sir William Gascoigne of Gawthorpe, one of Wolsey's most trustworthy retainers. No doubt Wolsey had first recommended Gilbert as a suitable husband. A royal ward after his father was declared insane in 1517, Gilbert could offer Elizabeth respectability and security, although she continued to receive presents from Henry for the rest of her life.[27] In 1523, Wolsey even engineered a special act of Parliament in her favour, ensuring she would live as a wealthy widow should Gilbert unexpectedly die.[28]

◆ ◆ ◆

Fitzroy's birth would present Henry with a potential opportunity, but also a stark dilemma. The king needed a son. Fitzroy was illegitimate, but bastardy need not be a bar to the succession. Henry already had a tangible example in his own family of how things could be made to play out. Had not his own Lancastrian great-great-grandfather, John Beaufort, Earl of Somerset, the eldest son of John of Gaunt by his long-standing mistress, Katherine Swynford, been retrospectively legitimized by Parliament and a papal bull? True, Henry IV had specifically barred Beaufort and his brothers from the succession in 1407, but such a bar could easily be removed by Parliament and it was mainly as a claimant through his Beaufort mother by descent from John of Gaunt that Henry VII staked his claim to the throne.[29] Who was king, constitutionally, was a question of whom Parliament (or in the Middle Ages the 'estates of the realm') would recognize as king, a point that Thomas More could readily concede when asked the question directly.[30] Could Henry therefore treat his daughter and her half-brother as equal contenders?

Almost no one outside Italy believed that rank could trump gender in the sixteenth century. The prospect of a woman ruler was considered abhorrent and unsafe: England had never known one, since Matilda, Henry I's daughter to whom he had tried to leave the crown in 1135, was forced to flee from London on the eve of her coronation and ended up designating her eldest son as her heir after a long civil war.

Henry VIII from the beginning was deeply sceptical of allowing Mary to be recognized as his successor. While necessarily secretive in his early dealings with Fitzroy for fear of antagonizing Katherine, he would be careful to keep all his options open.

◆　　◆　　◆

Lady Bryan was replaced as Mary's governess in the early summer of 1519 by Katherine's confidant and close ally, Margaret Pole, Countess of Salisbury, one of Mary's godmothers. The daughter and only surviving child of George, Duke of Clarence, a younger brother of Edward IV, she was also the widow of Sir Richard Pole, one of the pillars of Henry VII's regime and the man the king had chosen to be lord chamberlain to his son, Arthur, when he had first created his princely household at Ludlow. She brought the highest social status to the post of governess. To reflect her high standing, Mary's household staff was increased to include a chamberlain, a treasurer, a chaplain, a gentlewoman and twenty or so male servants.[31]

But all was not what it appeared to be. Drafted in at the highly sensitive moment when Elizabeth Blount was about to give birth to Fitzroy, Pole was placed at the centre of what was made to look like a princely establishment to enable Henry to deceive Katherine into believing that their daughter would become his heir should the couple have no more children.[32]

Historians usually explain Bryan's disappearance from Mary's household by reference to her marriage to David Zouche after her first husband, Sir Thomas Bryan, suddenly died. But the chronology does not fit. Sir Thomas, Katherine's vice-chamberlain, was already dead by 1 January 1518, when Elizabeth Denton was still governess. And Lady Bryan had almost certainly married Zouche before she left Mary's household.[33]

In reality, Henry had Lady Bryan earmarked for another role in the summer of 1519, sending her to take charge of Fitzroy. Most likely she looked after him at a number of royal manor houses within easy reach of London. In a letter to Thomas Cromwell, Wolsey's successor as Henry's chief minister, written soon after Anne Boleyn's fall in 1536, Bryan explains, 'When my Lady Mary's grace was born, it pleased the king's grace to appoint me "lady mistress" and make me a baroness, and so I have been a m[other] to the children his grace has had since.' The original letter was partially burned in a fire in 1731, but fortunately the words 'to the children his grace has had since' are intact and fully legible.

When this letter was written, Prince Edward, the child of Henry's third wife, Jane Seymour, was not yet born. The only other child the king fathered after Mary besides Elizabeth, his daughter by Anne Boleyn, was Fitzroy. So logic dictates that when Bryan spoke of being 'a m[other] to the *children* his grace has had since', she must have been including him.[34]

◆　◆　◆

Before Margaret Pole took charge of Mary, the young princess had a smaller, more rudimentary household. At first, her nursery was housed in Katherine's apartments, but as Mary became a toddler and more staff were needed, space became a problem. Protocol allocated Mary two rooms for herself—an inner one where she lived and slept in her everyday cradle, and an outer one where visitors could be received. The governess needed her own room, while the 'rockers' and other female servants shared a dormitory.[35]

Few of Katherine's apartments at the royal palaces could meet such requirements. Problems of space were even more acute if the royal couple were travelling around the countryside. In consequence, Mary regularly found herself traipsing around the home counties in her parents' footsteps, staying at manor houses a few miles' distance from them or else at other lodgings where she could conveniently be visited.[36]

In December 1517, for example, her household lodged at Ditton Park, a refurbished royal manor house on the north bank of the Thames in Buckinghamshire, chosen because it was just two miles from Windsor Castle, where Henry and Katherine planned to spend Christmas. Although Windsor was on the south bank of the river, a ferry operated at Datchet nearby, and Mary and her servants were twice rowed over for 20 pence a time. Sitting up in bed on New Year's Day, Mary received gifts of a gold cup from Wolsey, a pomander of gold from her aunt, Henry's sister Mary, and a primer or first reading book from Agnes Howard, Duchess of Norfolk, another godmother.[37]

Over the next couple of years Mary lodged at places such as Bisham Abbey in Berkshire, where many of Margaret Pole's ancestors were buried, The More (now Moor Park) in Hertfordshire, one of Wolsey's larger houses, and Richmond, where in June 1520—following Henry's and Wolsey's diplomacy with Francis I at the Field of Cloth of Gold—a party of French gentlemen came to visit her as part of an escorted tour of the sights of the metropolis organized by Wolsey.

Under the watchful eye of her governess and half a dozen other noble ladies, Mary—rising four and a half—welcomed the Frenchmen and their official minders, who were led by Thomas Howard, Duke of Norfolk, and Richard Fox, the septuagenarian, almost blind bishop of Winchester. As the duke informed Henry afterwards, Mary greeted her visitors 'with [a] most goodly countenance, proper communication and pleasant pastime in playing at the virginals'.[38]

By then she had some thirty menservants in addition to her female staff, all of whom functioned within a fully fledged household with its own chamber and service departments such as the wardrobe, bakehouse, pantry, buttery and stables. Henry allocated an adequate, but not especially generous budget of £1,100 a year to Mary's treasurer. Frequent purchases recorded in his accounts, apart from recurrent expenditure on salaries, food, drink and clothing, and special items such as New Year's gifts, included large quantities of strawberries and cherries, which Mary particularly enjoyed, and 'hippocras', a cordial drink made of wine flavoured with spices, for the entertainment of guests.[39] After Mary had performed on the virginals for her French visitors, she played host, offering them 'strawberries, wafers, wine and hippocras in plenty'.[40]

Mary spent Christmas 1520 with her parents at Greenwich, staying until mid February when Henry rode with Katherine into Hertfordshire and Cambridgeshire on the initial stages of another pilgrimage to Walsingham. Among the gifts offered to the princess at this New Year were a second gold cup from Wolsey; two silver-gilt flagons from the princess's third godmother, Katherine Courtenay, Countess of Devon; a pair of candle-snuffers from the Duke of Norfolk; bags containing a variety of nuts, grapes, oranges and cakes from local well-wishers; 'rosemary bushes with

gold-painted spangles' (presumably used as decorations) from 'a poor woman of Greenwich'; as well as a small purse made of 'tinsel satin', a costly silk fabric incorporating tiny brocading wefts of gold, silver or silver-gilt metal, given by 'Mother Margaret', Mary's nurse.[41]

◆   ◆   ◆

FIGURE 4   Edward Stafford, Duke of Buckingham, whom Henry VIII executed for treason in 1521, from a nineteenth-century engraving by R. Ackermann.

Henry was now approaching 29 and Katherine 35. It was 'to fulfil a vow', as the Venetian ambassador reported, that the queen now headed with Henry for Walsingham—a vow plainly connected to her desire to conceive a son before she reached the menopause.[42] But when Henry was within sight of Walsingham, if he even got that far, he abruptly left his wife and returned alone to Essex, perhaps to see Fitzroy.[43] Then, alerted to imminent danger by Wolsey, he hastened back to Greenwich, where he planned to strike against the Duke of Buckingham, the most important and the richest nobleman in the country.

By mid April 1521, Henry had decided to put Buckingham on trial at Westminster Hall on a charge of high treason. He accused Buckingham of plotting to depose him, claiming that the duke had listened to the prophecies of Nicholas Hopkins, a Carthusian monk. According to these, Henry 'would have no issue male of his body' and Buckingham 'should get the favour of the commons and he should have [the] rule of all'. The duke also stood accused of slandering Wolsey, calling him 'the king's bawd' for arranging the lying-in of Elizabeth Blount and keeping a watchful eye over Fitzroy. Making matters worse for himself, Buckingham had declared that the death of Prince Henry in 1511 was divine vengeance for Henry VII's execution in 1499 of the Earl of Warwick, Margaret Pole's brother, by then the only remaining direct male descendant of Edward III and the strongest Yorkist rival for the throne.

After a show trial in which Henry selected the judges and coached the prosecution witnesses, the duke was found guilty. Sentence of death was pronounced by his fellow peer, the Duke of Norfolk, who was barely able to control his tears as the verdict was delivered. Buckingham's end was brutal. He died in agony, beheaded on 17 May by a bungling executioner who took three strokes of the axe to sever his head.[44]

No sooner was Buckingham condemned than, to Katherine's dismay, Henry dismissed Margaret Pole as Princess Mary's governess. As a prominent former Yorkist, she had fallen under suspicion for several reasons: the strongest in Henry's eyes was that, three years before, Buckingham's heir, Henry, Lord Stafford, had married her daughter Ursula, and as part of the nuptial settlement, the duke had contracted to pay Margaret the colossal and unexplained sum of £2,000.[45] Pole's best friends were all from prominent Yorkist families such as the Courtenays (the Countess of Devon was one of Edward IV's daughters), and with Wolsey—the duke's avowed enemy—constantly privy to the king's thoughts and urging him on, Henry believed he had detected the beginnings of a menacing dynastic conspiracy of the sort that had scarred his father's reign.[46]

Almost fifteen years later, when Mary was ill and at loggerheads with her father, refusing to give him the obedience that he believed to be his due, the Spanish ambassador would remind Henry that she continued to hold Margaret Pole in the greatest affection 'as her second mother'. When the ambassador asked whether, in the interests of a reconciliation and his daughter's health, he would consider restoring Pole to her old position, Henry called her 'an old fool' and a woman 'of no experience'. If Mary 'had been under her care during this illness', he said, 'she would have died.'[47]

By then, the battle lines would be irrevocably drawn over Henry's break with Rome and divorce from Katherine. But Pole's removal as Mary's governess was also a watershed in 1521. Besides reflecting Henry's enmity to those noble families he suspected of plotting against him, it also signalled the beginning of his rift with his queen. From now onwards, their lives would gradually drift apart.

CHAPTER 2

Smoke and Mirrors

WITH Buckingham dead, Henry spent much of the summer of 1521 redistributing the duke's confiscated lands and supervising the search for Mary's new governess. While he did so, the 5-year-old princess was brought to Windsor Castle to live with her parents. Bewildered by why a woman she accounted as a 'second mother', someone she clearly adored and looked up to had suddenly been taken from her, Mary must also have been perplexed as to why a dozen or so tapestries seized by Henry's henchmen from the Duke of Buckingham's castle at Thornbury and still bearing his insignia, should suddenly have arrived to decorate her bedroom.[1]

Henry's search ended on 24 July, when he instructed one of his secretaries, Richard Pace, to ask Wolsey to recruit Elizabeth de Vere, Dowager Countess of Oxford, if he could twist her arm. If not, Jane, Lady Calthorpe was to be approached and her husband, Sir Philip, offered the post of princess's chamberlain. Although active on and off at Court for fifteen more years, the dowager countess suffered from bouts of ill health and respectfully refused the offer.[2] Wolsey therefore engaged the Calthorpes. By October everything was settled and they were appointed at a joint salary of £40 a year.[3]

Once the new governess and her husband were safely in charge, Mary left Windsor, parting from her parents, who travelled in the royal barge to Greenwich for Christmas, and returning to Ditton Park, where she stayed until the end of January.[4] This year, for the first time, Mary—as her sixth birthday fast approached—was to spend the festive season entirely alone. For a royal child, this was part of growing up.

To compensate, the Calthorpes commissioned a full quota of entertainments between Christmas Eve and Twelfth Night, mimicking on a smaller scale her father's 'goodly and gorgeous mummeries' at Greenwich.[5] The hall at Ditton Park was decorated with a boar's head, and one of Mary's chamber servants, John Thurgoode, was chosen as 'Lord of Misrule' to preside over her revels. He, in turn, hired a part-time actor to play a friar, another to play a shipman, another dozen or so to stage a 'disguising' involving a hobby horse and Morris men. Props requisitioned included two tabors (or drums), a stock of visors, coats of arms, hats, gold foil, rabbit skins and tails for mummers, coats and pikes for the Morris men, a dozen 'clattering staves', bells, frankincense, and a small quantity of gunpowder, possibly for fireworks.

On Christmas Day, the clerks of St George's Chapel, Windsor, crossed the Thames by ferry to sing a selection of songs and carols for the little princess.[6] And on 1 January, one of Henry's servants arrived to present the king's New Year's gift of a heavy solid silver cup filled with money.[7] For Katherine, however, the separation from her daughter was too painful to bear, and she stole briefly away from Greenwich to present her own gift in person.[8]

In February 1522, Mary moved to Hanworth in Middlesex, a beautiful moated manor house in an idyllic rural setting, where she made an offering on Candlemas day.[9] But, to her sheer delight, by the middle of the month she was unexpectedly back at Greenwich and Richmond palaces, reunited with her mother with whom she stayed for the rest of the spring and early summer.

Not just this, but also the Calthorpes, who hitherto had been sufficiently, but not extravagantly provided with furnishings and effects for her, suddenly found Henry willing to give them everything they felt they needed to equip Mary's household in a manner fit for a princess. Items loaned from Henry's collections included costly sets of Flemish tapestries on classical or religious themes, such as the labours of Hercules or Christ's Passion. A 'bed of estate' was supplied for Mary's bedchamber along with multiple sets of bed hangings, canopies and quilts, some of crimson satin embroidered with hearts, lions and falcons, others of cloth of gold or crimson and blue velvet. A 'chair of estate' with a canopy was provided for her Presence Chamber so she could sit in state to receive visitors, complete with a 'cloth of estate of blue cloth of gold' emblazoned with the royal arms to hang behind the chair beneath the canopy.[10]

◆　◆　◆

A hidden agenda lay behind this outward show. Henry and Wolsey's diplomacy in 1521 and 1522 was an elaborate exercise in smoke and mirrors as they busily put the finishing touches to a treaty of alliance with Katherine's 22-year-old nephew, the Holy Roman Emperor and king of Spain, Charles V, son of the queen's sister Juana. The treaty would mark a major shift in Henry's and

Wolsey's priorities in foreign policy, which since 1514 had been largely pro-French.

Following a secret meeting with Charles at Bruges in 1521, Wolsey sought to detach England from the obligations to Francis I that had been agreed at the Field of Cloth of Gold. Instead, Henry committed himself to joining Charles in what the emperor called his 'Great Enterprise'—a joint invasion of France by himself and Henry.[11] Their plan was to encourage the Duke of Bourbon, the constable of France, to rebel and then to invade Francis's territories from the north and south in a pincer movement, enabling the victors to divide the spoils.

Linked to the treaty was to be a dynastic marriage alliance with Charles by which Mary and her cousin were to be betrothed. The idea was that she should marry him when she was 12—the minimum age allowed by the Church for a woman to marry—and Henry would pay Charles a dowry amounting to almost half a million crowns.[12]

Henry, therefore, had not recalled his daughter to Court out of parental affection; she was brought there to be told that she would shortly become engaged to one of the most powerful rulers in Europe, and to learn how to play her part. To this end, she was given a gold brooch to wear on her bosom with her cousin's name picked out in jewels. She was encouraged to believe she had fallen in love with him, taking him as her 'valentine' on St Valentine's Day. And when wheeled out to meet one of Charles's ambassadors sent ahead to agree draft terms for the treaty, she duly complied, questioning him 'not less sweetly than prudently' about her future husband while ostentatiously wearing her gold brooch.[13]

To ratify the treaty, Charles undertook a state visit to England lasting a month. On Sunday, 25 May 1522, the Marquis of Dorset met him at Gravelines and escorted him into Calais, from where he was to embark for England. Next day, the emperor arrived at Dover where Wolsey greeted him to the accompaniment of a deafening salute from the castle guns. A week later, Charles and Henry rode side by side into Gravesend, where thirty barges awaited them, ready to transport them and their courtiers along the Thames to Greenwich in a spectacular river pageant.[14]

This was not the first time that Henry and Wolsey had sought to extort an advantage from Mary's future marriage. When she was two and a half, and Wolsey had been brokering the Treaty of Universal Peace, the king had affianced her to the Dauphin of France.[15] The cardinal's revels at which Henry's mistress, Elizabeth Blount, had partnered Sir Francis Bryan had been arranged to celebrate this betrothal. Katherine, who was Spanish through and through, had never approved of Wolsey's pro-French diplomacy in those years. She was overjoyed when Charles, already king of Spain, was elected to the imperial throne in 1519, for his election dramatically shifted the balance of power in Europe, making him a better ally and marital prospect than his great rival Francis I of France.

After Wolsey's secret diplomacy with the emperor at Bruges in 1521, Mary's betrothal to the Dauphin could be quietly forgotten.

♦   ♦   ♦

When Charles arrived at Greenwich at the start of his state visit in 1522, Katherine and Mary were waiting for him at the door of the palace's great hall. As described by Edward Hall, Charles 'asked [for] the queen's blessing, for that is the fashion of Spain between the aunt and the nephew. The emperor had great joy to see the queen his aunt, and especially his young cousin…the lady Mary.'[16] Charles was lodged in Henry's own riverside apartments at the palace which were so splendidly furnished and hung with fine tapestries, that even the worldly Spaniards were impressed.

During the festivities and sports over the next three days, Henry showed off his jousting skills while Charles and Katherine watched from a special pavilion, and in the evenings the queen banqueted with her nephew, while her ladies danced for them. Brushing aside the criticism of some of his stuffier advisers, Charles overcame his natural shyness and entered into the spirit of the occasion by joining in one of Henry's jousts, riding a 'richly trapped' charger. Katherine could watch contentedly as the two most important men in her life behaved like kinsmen and allies.[17]

On 6 June, while Katherine and Mary stayed behind at the palace, Charles and Henry, dressed identically in cloth of gold, made a triumphal entry into London, riding side by side. After hearing Thomas More, now employed as Henry's principal secretary, deliver a Latin oration praising them and the bond of friendship between them, the two kings processed through the city, entertained by a series of tableaux laid on by the citizens and merchants, the finest of which was choreographed by More's brother-in-law, John Rastell, a well-known printer and theatrical impresario.[18]

The centrepiece of these tableaux was an island representing England set in a silver sea surrounded by waves and rocks surmounted by the stars, planets and a depiction of heaven. Woods and mountains, flowers, birds, animals, ponds and fish could be seen on the island, where statues of Charles and Henry stood immobile, carrying unsheathed swords. It all looked predictable enough, until the astonished spectators saw that the whole scene was a complex mechanical contrivance. As the real Charles and Henry approached, the contraption burst into life. Clockwork birds sang, toy fish leapt from their pools, the animals moved and the statues turned towards each other, first casting away their swords and then embracing 'in token of love and peace'.

Rastell's tableau was a masterpiece of invention and imagination. Except there was no mention of Mary or her betrothal.[19]

On Whitsunday, 8 June, Wolsey celebrated a special high mass before the two kings at St Paul's, assisted by twenty mitred prelates. Henry and Charles then travelled by barge to Wolsey's palace of Hampton Court and onwards to Windsor Castle, where on the evening of the 15th, the theme of 'love and peace' was clumsily rammed home again to the visitors in a long, excruciatingly boring play—supposedly a farce ridiculing 'the king of France and his alliances' and likening Francis to a wild and unruly horse whom only Charles and Henry were able to bridle.[20]

The private reaction of one of the imperial delegation, Martin de Salinas, was deep cynicism. With another six years to wait before Mary was 12 and with Charles eager to secure his own dynasty in Spain, it seemed likely that the plan for her marriage was going nowhere. The tell-tale sign at the St Paul's service was that 'no betrothal ceremonies were performed, no oath sworn'.[21]

At Windsor on the 16th, Charles and Henry concluded a general offensive and defensive alliance. Three days later, they swore to observe this treaty before the altar in St George's Chapel and *Te Deum* was sung. They then signed a secret subsidiary treaty. At last Charles promised to marry Mary as soon as she was 12, Henry promised not to marry her to anyone else, and both promised to invade France before the end of May 1524.[22] But by article 28, the terms of the subsidiary treaty were never to be published. And still no formal act of betrothal took place. Everything relating to Mary's marriage rested on promises and fair words, for Charles too was an expert at diplomacy.

◆   ◆   ◆

Katherine bade her nephew a fond farewell at Windsor, but within three years things would look very different. In particular, her pilgrimages to Walsingham and her hopes for a miracle such as that granted to the post-menopausal St Elizabeth when her prayers were answered and she gave birth to John the Baptist, were destined to come to nothing. For even as Charles and his entourage set out with their vast baggage train to Winchester on their way to board their fleet at Southampton, Henry had found himself another mistress.

Mary Boleyn had first been invited into Henry's bed shortly after she appeared in a glittering candlelit masque laid on by Wolsey for the ambassadors sent ahead to finalize the arrangements for Charles's state visit. Held on the evening of Shrove Tuesday, 4 March 1522, at York Place, the cardinal's principal London home, the masque entitled 'the assault on the *Château Vert*' was preceded by a tournament on the theme of 'unrequited love'. Mary Boleyn and her sister Anne, the talented and precocious daughters of Sir Thomas Boleyn and his wife Elizabeth, played two of the eight leading female roles in the masque. Mary was cast as 'Kindness' and Anne as 'Perseverance'—prophetically as it turned out.

The masque began after supper, when Henry and Wolsey led the ambassadors into a 'great chamber' richly hung with tapestries reflecting the theme of the action, at the far end of which was an elaborate timber castle with battlements covered in green tinfoil. The castle boasted three green towers, each surmounted by a faux-heraldic banner showing the power that women could have: one depicted three broken hearts, one a man's heart being gripped by a woman's hand and the third showed a man's heart being turned upside down. Standing on the towers were eight damsels, including Mary and Anne, guarded by a posse of choirboys dressed as evil women—the enemies of love—who garrisoned the castle.

After a narrator called 'Ardent Desire', dressed in crimson satin embroidered with burning flames in gold, had made a speech, Henry ordered the attack. To the sound of off-stage cannon, he and his companions, dressed in cloaks of blue satin and cloth of gold caps, bombarded the castle and its defenders with dates, oranges and 'other fruits made for pleasure' while the boys responded with a desperate hail of rosewater and comfits. Once the damsels had been rescued, everyone danced until the end of the evening when the participants removed their disguises and all 'were known'.[23]

As a teenager Mary Boleyn had gone to Paris in the retinue of Henry's younger sister 'to do service' for her (as contemporaries quaintly put it) when she married the decrepit 52-year-old Louis XII, returning with her when Louis died only eighty-two days after the wedding. If a later taunt by Francis I is to be believed, she also 'did service' to Louis's courtiers, earning a reputation as 'una grandissima ribalda et infame sopre tutte' ('a very great bawd and infamous above all').[24] On her homecoming, she was found a place in Katherine's household. On 4 February 1520, Henry attended her wedding to William Carey, one of his gentlemen of the Privy Chamber.[25]

After her return from Paris, Mary's morals had not been called into question. And it was not until two years later, after she danced with Henry at Wolsey's masque, that she became the king's mistress. Thereafter, the gossip began and William Carey, who prudently chose to lay down his wife for his king, found himself the recipient of a shower of royal patronage, amassing an enviable haul of lands and perquisites.[26]

◆　◆　◆

Henry's latest affair became public knowledge when a royal navy ship was named the *Mary Boleyn*.[27] Katherine's outward reaction was one of stony silence. As with Elizabeth Blount, she believed that Henry would soon tire of his amour. Although finding the liaison a blow to her pride, she did not envisage it encroaching on her own position or her daughter's inheritance, especially now the princess was pledged to marry the most powerful ruler in Europe.

In private, Katherine threw all her energy into directing Mary's upbringing, a role her husband had once sought to limit, but was now prepared to tolerate if it stopped his wife from interfering elsewhere. Besides, Henry had so far overlooked his daughter's education, not regarding it as much of a priority. Convention dictated that, by the age of 6 or 7, a child considered to be next in line for the succession should be given a professional schoolmaster.[28] Henry had sent his daughter a goshawk in the summer of 1522 in an attempt to encourage her to take up the princely sport of falconry, but that was all.[29]

While Margaret Pole—an educated woman and a patron of scholars—had been her governess, Mary had started to learn to read.[30] When reciting the ABC, she would have begun by making the sign of the cross and then saying, 'Christ's cross me speed', as all children were taught to do. And if Pole followed the example of Thomas More, who had become famous throughout Europe for giving his daughters the best education that money could buy, she would have read aloud to Mary from books such as William Caxton's famous translation of Aesop's *Fables* with its graphic woodcut illustrations, 'sounding and saying' the individual vowels and letters to build simple words and phrases, and pointing to the pictures in the way children were taught then.[31]

As one of Mary's godmothers, Pole had promised at her baptism to help with her religious education. The primer (or early reading book) that another godmother, Agnes Howard, had sent as a New Year's gift would typically have contained the Lord's Prayer, the *Ave Maria*, the Creed and the Ten Commandments—the texts considered to lay the foundations of a Christian education, which children were expected to learn by heart. Often included in such primers were model graces for use before and after meals, an almanac for calculating the date of Easter and a calendar of saints to whom intercessions might be made.

A talented musician who in later life owned three pairs of virginals, Pole must also have arranged for Mary's earliest music lessons, because the princess was proficient at the virginals by the time she played host in the summer of 1520 to the party of French gentlemen.[32] So much so that when Charles's diplomats who had watched 'the assault on the *Château Vert*' said their farewells in 1522, Katherine, determined to display her daughter's talents, would not allow them to leave until they had seen her dance and play the clavichord. As the envoys dryly remarked, Mary 'did not have to be asked twice.'[33]

It may also have been Pole who taught Mary how to write with a quill-pen. Whoever taught her was not versed in the latest techniques, for among the literary *cognoscenti* fine penmanship was much more than a mere technique of communication.[34] Whereas More's daughters learned to shape their letters at an early age, using the clear, bold italic script originating in Italy that was iconic of the educational values of the Renaissance and in which each letter is generally formed with at least one separate pen stroke and

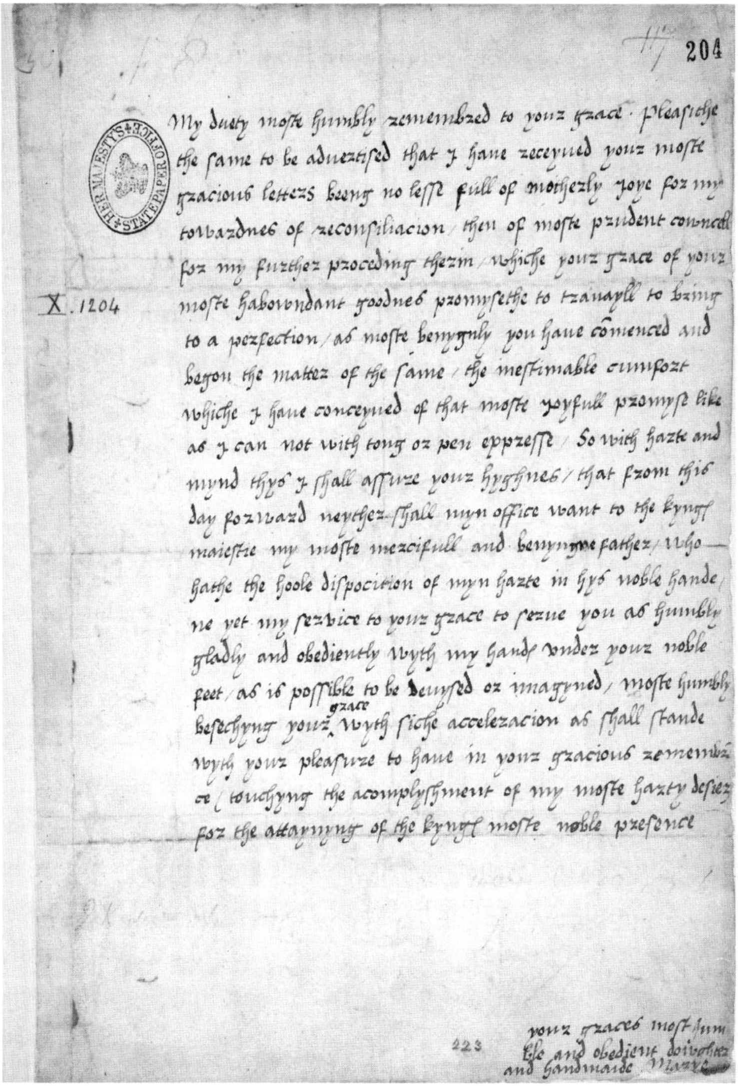

My duety moste humbly remembred to your grace. pleasithe the same to be aduertised that I haue receyued your moste gracious letters beeng no lesse full of motherly ioye for my towardnes of reconsiliacion then of moste prudent councell for my further proceding therin which your grace of your moste habowndant goodnes promysethe to trauayll to bring to a perfection as moste benyngnly you haue comenced and begon the matter of the same the inestimable cumfort whiche I haue conceyued of that moste ioyfull promyse like as I can not with tong or pen expresse So with harte and mynd thys I shall assure your hyghnes that from this day forward neyther shall myn office want to the kyngs maiestie my moste mercifull and benyngne father who hathe the hoole disposicion of myn harte in hys noble hande ne yet my service to your grace to serue you as humbly gladly and obediently wyth my hande under your noble feet as is possible to be deuysed or imagyned moste humbly besechyng your grace wyth suche acceleracion as shall stande wyth your pleasure to haue in your gracious remembrance touchyng the acomplyshment of my moste harty desier for the attaynyng of the kyngs moste noble presence

your graces most humble and obedient doughter and handmaide Marye

Figure 5 A letter to Queen Jane Seymour in 1536 from Henry's elder daughter, Mary, illustrating the more conventional, cursive, idiosyncratic handwriting that she was taught to use as a child in preference to the new bold italic script.

sometimes with two, Mary was taught to write in the more conventional, cursive, idiosyncratic style familiar to her parents' generation (see Figure 5).

◆   ◆   ◆

Where Pole had begun until Henry dismissed her from her position, Katherine continued, largely bypassing the Calthorpes. To do so, she would regularly have to commute the fifteen or so miles between the royal palaces and the manor houses where Mary's household was stationed.

Katherine, we know, began teaching her daughter Latin, because in a letter she wrote to her when she was 9, shortly after Henry *had* at last found her a proper schoolmaster, the queen explains, 'As for your writing in Latin, I am glad that ye change from me to Master Fetherstone, for that shall do you much good, to learn by him to write right'.[35]

Her mother also introduced Mary to elementary French and of course to Spanish, her own native tongue. Her preference for all things Spanish can be observed at close quarters early in 1523, when the child was 7. Then, Katherine offered her patronage to Juan Luis Vives, a Spanish-born scholar living in the Low Countries, whom Thomas More had recommended to her. For seven or eight years now, More's three daughters had been studying Latin and Greek, moral philosophy, mathematics, music and astronomy. So able was his eldest child, Margaret, that she could identify mistakes in the Latin of More's best friend Erasmus of Rotterdam, the most distinguished Renaissance scholar and translator outside of Italy.[36]

Vives had first met More in Bruges in 1521, when More had gone as Wolsey's understudy for the secret diplomacy with Charles.

Born in Valencia around 1492, the Spaniard was a brilliant rhetorician also trained in medicine, descended from a family of *converso* Jews. Educated at Valencia and then in Paris and afterwards briefly a teacher at the University of Louvain where Erasmus had lectured, he sought a new appointment and a salary after his young Flemish patron was killed in a riding accident, leaving Vives penniless.[37]

More acted as an intermediary for Katherine, who commissioned Vives to write a book on women's education. When, in April 1523, the Spaniard submitted his draft, his hopes were set on an appointment as Mary's schoolmaster. Travelling to England to deliver his manuscript entitled *De Institutione Feminae Christianae* ('The Education of a Christian Woman'), he secured an audience with Wolsey, who snatched him away to Oxford to fill a prestigious post. Visiting More's house four or five months later, Vives corrected the proofs of his book and inserted a brief eulogy of Margaret More and her sisters.[38]

But unlike More, who (after early reservations) allowed his eldest and ablest daughter to read any book she wanted, including oratorical works otherwise allowed only to male students, Vives severely curtailed his reading list for women. Quoting St Jerome, he urged that a woman should hear and speak only 'what pertains to the fear of God'. Selected books of the Bible and the moral writings of Plato, Tertullian, Cicero, Seneca and Boethius he considered appropriate. Romances and other fashionable literature were banned. Such works, Vives protested, were 'pernicious', written by 'the slaves of vice and filth'. It would be better that a young woman should lose her eyes than read such enticements to lust.[39]

Vives, like most of his Spanish contemporaries, was always more concerned with what a girl should not read than with what she should. Unlike More and Erasmus, he was a decidedly reluctant champion of women's education.[40]

In October 1523, Vives sent Katherine a more detailed syllabus for her daughter.[41] Advising Mary to work at her Latin in company with other girls of the same age, he said that she should begin by mastering the eight parts of speech and five declensions. If a word or phrase caught her imagination, she should write it down and memorize it. Once she had a grasp of Latin syntax, she should 'turn little speeches from English into Latin, easy ones at first, gradually more difficult ones' as a way of beginning to converse in Latin.

But—ever the reactionary—he reminded Katherine that, though fluency in Latin and English was the ultimate goal, in the case of a woman it could only be to improve her linguistic skills, not to equip her to make public speeches, least of all to rule, since that was men's work. His further book recommendations for Mary, which he later published, came revealingly with others for Charles Blount, the son of the queen's chamberlain. And whereas the boy's reading list included oratorical works, Mary's merely added More's *Utopia* and Erasmus's *Education of a Christian Prince* to some more of Plato's moral dialogues.[42]

Here was the rub. For while the king's new mistress would indeed turn out to pose no real threat to either Katherine or her daughter, someone else did. It was not yet even Mary Carey's sister, Anne. It was Henry Fitzroy, the king's child by Elizabeth Blount, now approaching 5 years old. Over the next couple of years, he was to step out of the shadows. Henry soon would be declaring that he loved him 'like his own soul'.[43] And he was about to prove it.

CHAPTER 3

Prince or Princess?

I N the last week of May 1525, shocking news began to filter through to Katherine. At Henry's request, Wolsey had ordered his newly promoted chamberlain, Richard Page, to design a royal coat of arms for the king's 'entirely beloved son the lord Henry Fitzroy'.[1] News also leaked out that John Palsgrave, a former tutor to Henry's younger sister Mary and a champion of Renaissance values in education second only to Thomas More and his innermost circle of friends, was to be made the boy's schoolmaster.[2]

Just where Fitzroy had been living for the last five years will always remain a mystery. Perhaps he was still with Lady Bryan, perhaps he had rejoined his mother after her marriage to Gilbert Tailboys, to be brought up in Lincolnshire with his half-sister. One of Palsgrave's letters to the child's mother complaining of the difficulties he had to overcome in tutoring him appears to cast some of the blame on to her—'insomuch', he wrote, 'that not so little as six sundry matters have been contrived against me, whereof yourself were as guilty in any of them as I was'.[3] This might suggest that

Fitzroy had gone to Lincolnshire at least occasionally. In 1525, however, he was suddenly brought out of obscurity to Court.

On Wednesday, 7 June, at an election of new knights to the coveted Order of the Garter in St George's Chapel, Windsor, Fitzroy was declared the unanimous first choice to fill one of two vacant places. At his installation on the 25th, he was placed in the second stall on the sovereign's side, the most exalted position after his father's, after which his banner, helm and crest were set up over his stall and his new coat of arms embossed on the roof of the chapel above the organ gallery, clear for all to see.[4]

On Sunday, 18 June, an investiture still more astonishing and far-reaching in its significance took place. At Bridewell Palace on the Thames, Henry's principal London residence following a disastrous fire which had destroyed much of the old palace of Westminster in 1512, Fitzroy was raised to the foremost rank of the peerage.

As the trumpets sounded, the 6-year-old boy—first dressed in the robes of an earl—was escorted through the long gallery by the Earls of Arundel and Oxford and led into Henry's Presence Chamber, its walls resplendent with tapestries and cloth of gold. When he drew close to his father, who stood in majesty before a golden throne, flanked on either side by Wolsey and a galaxy of lords and prelates, he knelt.

Henry then ordered his son to stand up, the cue for Thomas More to read out (in Latin) the child's letters patent creating him Earl of Nottingham. After his investiture, the new earl withdrew, only to reappear a short while later, dressed this time as a duke and led in by the Dukes of Norfolk and Suffolk. Once more the boy knelt before his father, this time to be invested as Duke of Richmond and Somerset.[5]

These dignities were not chosen at random. Henry VII's father, Edmund Tudor, had been created first Earl of Richmond by his half-brother Henry VI. Even more to the point, the dukedom of Somerset was the one inherited from Henry VIII's Beaufort ancestors, the progeny of the illicit relationship between John of Gaunt and Katherine Swynford. As to the earldom of Nottingham, its last incumbent was Richard, Duke of York, the younger son of Edward IV.

To give substance to his son's position, Henry granted the boy castles, lordships and lands valued at £4,845 per annum, making him one of the wealthiest nobles in the kingdom. Scattered across England and Wales with the lion's share in Lincolnshire, Somerset and Devon, the new ducal estates included many properties traditionally associated with the titles he now held.[6] A jewel in his crown was the manor of Collyweston in Northamptonshire, one of Henry's grandmother's favourite houses, which she had expensively remodelled as a secondary royal palace. The king even gave his son a privy apartment at St James's Palace.[7]

And Henry's bounty did not stop there. On Sunday, 16 July, Henry nominated Fitzroy as Lord Admiral of England, one of the greatest offices of state.[8] To contrive the necessary reshuffle, he risked a quarrel with Thomas Howard, Duke of Norfolk, whom the king had originally appointed Lord Admiral for life, but now displaced. Since a child of 6 could hardly discharge the duties, they were reassigned to Viscount Lisle, who was made Vice-Admiral.[9]

In official documents Fitzroy was to be addressed as 'the right high and noble prince Henry...Duke of Richmond and Somerset.'[10] Katherine, increasingly protective of her daughter's status and dignity, did not flinch in expressing her sense of outrage to her husband. All she did was infuriate him.[11] Quick to nose out a scandal, the Venetian ambassador told a friend that three of the queen's Spanish gentlewomen had encouraged her to speak her mind. The king, in retaliation, 'has dismissed them [from] the Court—a strong measure, but the queen was obliged to submit and to have patience.'[12]

Once Henry had been careful to appease his wife in everything, but those days were over. Now, her position was seriously weakened and by other factors than the king's liaison with Mary Boleyn, which had largely fizzled out. Forty, fat, with no son and seemingly little chance of conceiving one since she was said to have passed the menopause, the queen's hold on Henry had become tenuous. By the end of 1524, the royal couple had stopped sleeping together.

Foreign affairs further undermined Katherine. A fortnight or so after Henry had commissioned Fitzroy's coat of arms, her nephew Charles repudiated his promise to marry Mary. His move was part of a drastic upheaval in diplomacy begun when his armies had routed the French at the battle of Pavia on 24 February 1525 in the biggest slaughter of Frenchmen since the battle of Agincourt. Francis I had been captured and taken to Madrid. His captivity would last just over a year.

Henry was at first overjoyed. The 'Great Enterprise' he had planned with Charles in 1522 had come unstuck the following year, when the Duke of Suffolk marched to within fifty miles of Paris, but failed to capture the city. After Pavia, it briefly seemed that France, after all, would be partitioned by the two allies.[13]

But it was not to be. For instead, the victorious Charles decided to marry his cousin Isabella, the infanta of Portugal, and ditch his agreement with Henry.[14] He may have been unnecessarily provoked, since Henry too had attempted to vary the terms of the earlier treaty, even suggesting that, in exchange for delivering Mary to him in marriage, Charles should send the captured Francis to England, or else meet Henry in Paris and watch while he was crowned king of France.[15] Whoever was more to blame, the marriage treaty was in tatters, putting an end to Katherine's dreams for her daughter of a Spanish match.

◆   ◆   ◆

Around the Court an explosion of speculation greeted Fitzroy's ennoblement. Some thought the king planned to declare Fitzroy to be his heir; others that he would be made king of Ireland.[16]

Whether Henry had decided to make Fitzroy his successor ahead of Mary is difficult to judge. He was certainly considering it, even if he was dithering.[17] His views on female succession are known to be extremely close to those expressed in 1531 in the preface to a pamphlet entitled *A Glasse of the Truthe*, the contents of which he vetted himself.[18] With his divorce from Katherine and quest for a legitimate male heir then topping the agenda, the *Glasse* cautioned that if a woman 'shall chance to rule, she cannot continue long without a husband, which by God's law must then be her governor and head, and so finally shall direct the realm.'[19]

Henry feared that a woman successor was a recipe for civil war, and when later in his reign he did finally concede that circumstances could arise in which a woman might succeed, he attempted to dictate precisely how she would be permitted to marry.[20]

But Henry had a more immediate objective in mind by ennobling Fitzroy. On Wolsey's advice, a radical reorganization of regional government was about to begin. For ten years, the cardinal had been planting his own 'new men' into key positions in the outlying regions as part of a deliberate policy aimed at diluting the influence of the traditional nobility and centralizing state control.[21]

By late 1523, government in the far north had all but collapsed after Wolsey lost patience with the two leading northern magnate families, the Percies and Dacres, for their flagrant abuses of power. He ousted them from their entrenched positions, and in despair at the resulting chaos the Duke of Norfolk resigned as Warden-General of the Marches (i.e. borderlands) against Scotland.[22] Wales too was in radical need of reform. Crime went unpunished in a society riddled with different lordships, customs and laws. In particular, conflicts of jurisdiction enabled criminals to escape trial by fleeing from one lordship to another.[23]

On 22 July 1525, Henry and Wolsey made Fitzroy the titular head of a revived Council of the North and appointed him Warden-General, following a precedent set by Richard III when he had declared his son's household at Middleham to be his Council in the North.[24]

The move explains why, within a few days of Fitzroy's investiture, a large and luxurious princely household was recruited for him with a full complement of thirty or so bureaucrats and councillors, backed up by over a hundred lesser officials and servants. According to Wolsey's estimates, the annual cost of food, fuel and clothing alone for such an establishment would leave only small change out of £2,500.[25]

A scribbled list of the furnishings needed just for Fitzroy's chambers and those of his head officers includes two 'cloths of estate', four 'great carpets' and twenty smaller ones, four chairs including one of cloth of gold and one of velvet, enough wall hangings, stools and cushions for up to eight rooms, twenty-one beds, and several dozen sets of bed hangings, quilts, pillows, linen and blankets to put on them.[26]

In effect, the councillors and officers of Fitzroy's household had become the new northern administration, acting in the boy's name. Along with the young duke, who was given yet more commissions as Chief Justice of the Forest beyond the Trent and Lieutenant-General in the North, they were sent to live at the castle of Sheriff Hutton, thirteen miles north of York.[27] Wolsey must have regarded their departure as urgent, since they left London a mere four days after the boy was appointed Warden-General.[28] This was possible because almost all the new councillors and officials were already in Wolsey's service in one way or another. The overwhelming majority were churchmen or lawyers, and none was above the degree of a knight. They were typical of the 'new men' the cardinal had already been positioning around the regions.

Katherine, meanwhile, muffled her opposition to Fitzroy's honours after Henry issued supplementary letters patent declaring that, although his son's ducal rank was to be superior to that of all other dukes, it was not to take precedence over 'the offspring of our own body and heirs and successors'.[29] Such a formula implied that Mary was *not* excluded from the succession—or at least not in so many words—although curiously this document was never copied into the official series of Chancery enrolments and so lacked legal force.

◆　◆　◆

The point quickly became irrelevant. For on the same day as Henry proclaimed Fitzroy to be Warden-General, Wolsey announced similar instructions and ordinances for the government of Wales that had Mary as their focus. He had, it seems, been working on this all along while the king was dithering. And now Henry decided to implement it.[30]

The result was that, in mid August, the 9-year-old princess found herself riding in a horse litter to the Duke of Buckingham's former castle at Thornbury on her way to Ludlow on the Welsh borders, where she was to become the titular head of a new Council in the Marches of Wales. Her existing household at Ditton Park was dissolved and a new one recruited.[31]

And to Katherine's delight, her daughter's new household and councillors vastly outshone Fitzroy's. Whereas none of his officers had ranked above a knight, Mary's chamberlain and steward were peers, the head of her household and president of her Council was John Veysey, a leading courtier-bishop, and sixteen ladies and gentlewomen, many of the highest rank, were recruited to her Privy Chamber.[32] Even Margaret Pole was recalled as a sop to the queen, in case she worried that her daughter was being sent 150 miles away.[33]

Overall, 300 officials and servants gained places in Mary's new household.[34] So ruinously expensive was it, bills amounting to £5,900 were run up in its first eighteen months of operation.[35] Building repairs alone cost £500. Both Ludlow Castle, which Edward IV had rebuilt for his eldest son, and its associated manor house at Tickenhill, near Bewdley, which Henry VII had refitted for Prince Arthur who spent much of his time there, needed refurbishment. Tickenhill especially had fallen into severe disrepair.

Katherine's one remaining concern was that, while the small print of Wolsey's instructions clearly identified her daughter as the 'Princess of the Realm' and she would from now on be colloquially known as the 'Princess' or 'Princess of Wales', her father never officially invested her with either the title or the lands associated with it, as he clearly had done for Fitzroy.[36] He had allowed her to assume the title most closely associated since Edward I's reign with the succession, but had failed to back it up with a more tangible form of recognition.

Was such ambiguity an oversight, or had Henry deliberately recognized his son as a *de facto* prince while allowing Mary to build up false hopes?

◆　　◆　　◆

With each of Henry's children now living in the regions, their educations began in earnest. Palsgrave, a graduate of the University of Paris and an expert in languages including Greek, seemed to be an ideal choice as Fitzroy's tutor. His pupil, however, was more problematic. A healthy, active boy, tall and red-haired like his father and with a love of outdoor sports, he proved headstrong and unruly. No sooner had his entourage travelled four miles out of London on its journey north than he refused to ride in the horse litter provided for him, demanding instead to mount his own pony. And when the cavalcade reached Collyweston, an anxious Palsgrave wrote to inform Wolsey that the child had insisted on hunting in the park, killing a buck.[37]

Once at Sheriff Hutton and Pontefract Castle, where Fitzroy increasingly preferred to live, Palsgrave settled down to instruct his charge, using a distinctive method of teaching French that he claimed to have invented for Henry's younger sister and a new and simpler way of teaching Latin.[38] After learning the basic rules of Latin grammar, Fitzroy began reading some elementary Latin poetry such as Virgil's *Eclogues*.[39] And as a way of better understanding the meaning of the texts, Palsgrave set him short 'themes' or essays (sometimes in Latin) on topics encountered during his reading.

Fitzroy, unfortunately, was weak at mastering vocabulary. It was holding him back, so Palsgrave asked Henry to send his son a painter to illustrate the words being taught. 'It shall', he told the king, 'be to him [Fitzroy] a great furtherance in learning as well to know the names of things as the things themselves by their pictures.'

But when Henry discovered which artist the tutor had his eye on, he employed him elsewhere, leaving Palsgrave to complain how the want of a painter was causing both master and pupil to struggle.[40] Wolsey's response was to send him a classroom assistant, who was also to teach the boy singing and the virginals.[41] It was hardly satisfactory, but Palsgrave was unable to obtain more.

In what was tantamount to an end-of-term report to Henry, the thwarted Palsgrave decided to lie. He declared himself extremely fortunate to be charged with training 'so excellent' a young mind. There had been difficulties, but he felt confident that he could overcome them. He and his pupil, he continued, soon hoped to embark on Greek, a decision taken after Henry had consulted Thomas More.[42] Himself the beneficiary of an expensive classical education after Prince Arthur's death in 1502, but never having studied Greek, Henry wanted to hear the pros and cons. Before finally making up his mind, he sent for More's daughters, who all knew Greek, and who displayed their prowess before the whole Court at Richmond Palace to the astonishment of their audience.[43]

As Palsgrave privately briefed More, Fitzroy had some ability, but he was surrounded by philistines who constantly distracted him, 'some to hear a cry at a hare, some to kill a buck with his bow, sometime with greyhounds and sometime with buckhounds... some to see a flight with a hawk, some to ride a horse.'[44] Schoolmasters, he knew, regularly beat their lazy or disobedient pupils into compliance, but Palsgrave hesitated to touch a prince. 'To make the child love learning', he declared wistfully, 'I never put

[him] in fear of any correction, nor never to suffer him to continue at any time till he should be wearied.'[45]

To help motivate his pupil, Palsgrave found him classmates as study companions, just as Vives had recommended. But since those he recruited were either much older or younger than Fitzroy and not, as Vives had suggested, of the same or a similar age, this was far from ideal.[46]

•   ◆   •

Palsgrave's career as a royal schoolmaster came to an abrupt end in February 1526, when through Wolsey's patronage he was replaced by Richard Croke. An internationally renowned scholar and Reader in Greek at Cambridge University, Croke was a difficult, self-righteous character who could quarrel with anyone and left Cambridge under a cloud. He was hardly likely to succeed where Palsgrave had failed.[47]

Soon Croke was accusing one of the boy's gentlemen-ushers, Sir George Cotton, of luring the child away from his books. Spurred on by Cotton—as the hapless schoolmaster claimed in a graphic litany of complaints to Wolsey—Fitzroy ducked his lessons to practise archery or to ride, hunt and hawk. He refused to get up at six in the morning to study before attending mass as Croke demanded, and refused to write anything before dinner (which then was eaten between 12 noon and 2.30 p.m. depending on the season). When in the late afternoon he did finally saunter into the schoolroom, he was too tired to study.

Cotton, it seems, also made a fine art of ribbing or humiliating Croke in front of the prince and his fellow pupils. Should the tutor criticize the boy's work, Cotton would say, 'The passage is too difficult: he made a mistake. What can you expect?' And if Croke lost

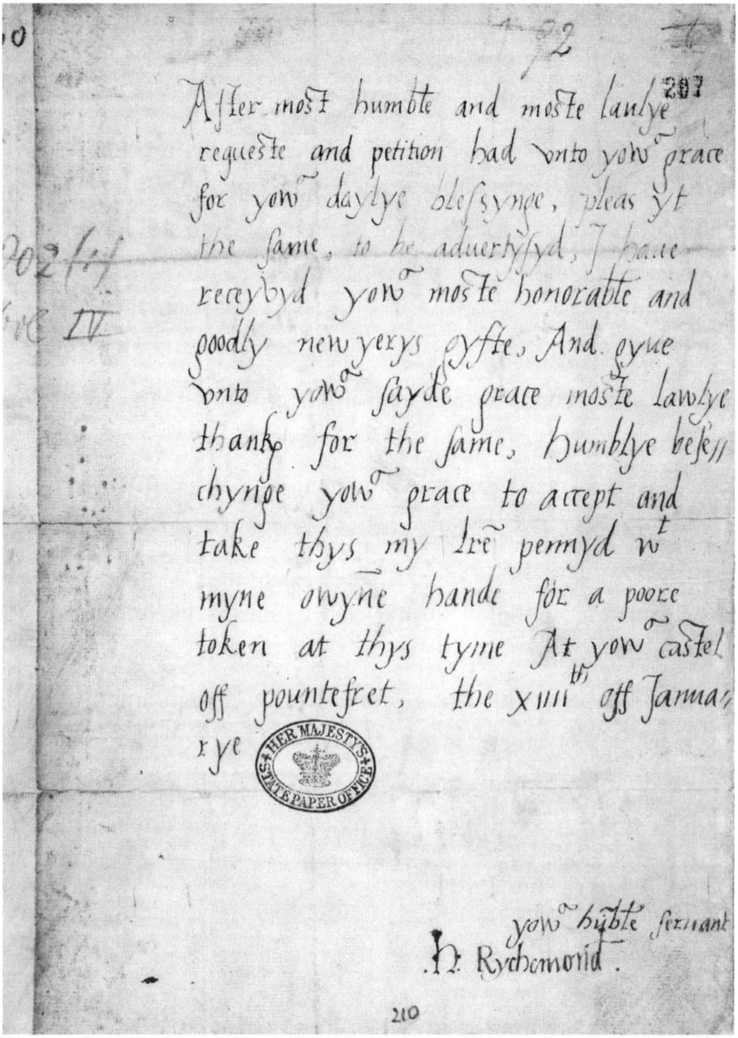

After most humble and moste lawlye requeste and petition had vnto yowr grace for yowr daylye blessynge, pleas yt the same, to be aduertyssyd, I haue receyvyd yowr moste honorable and goodly new yerys gyfte, And gyue vnto yowr sayde grace moste lawlye thanks for the same, humblye besechynge yowr grace to accept and take thys my lre pennyd wt myne owyne hande for a poore token at thys tyme At yowr castel off pountefret, the xiiiith off Januarye

yowr hūble seruant
H. Rychemond.

FIGURE 6 Henry Fitzroy's earliest letter to Henry VIII, thanking him for a New Year's gift, 14 January 1527. The letter was the 7-year-old boy's first attempt at the fashionable italic script favoured by the champions of Renaissance values in education.

his temper, Fitzroy—incited by Cotton—would taunt him, saying, 'Master, if you beat me, I will beat you!' When Cotton finally invited 'players and minstrels' into the boy's Privy Chamber for a recital of bawdy songs, Croke's patience snapped.[48]

What stung Croke most was that, having successfully taught Fitzroy how to write using the italic hand so favoured by the champions of Renaissance values in education, Cotton had gone out of his way to teach him the old-fashioned, cursive, idiosyncratic script that Croke especially reviled.[49] That Croke was teaching Fitzroy to write in an italic hand is conclusively proved by the boy's earliest surviving letter to his father from Pontefract on 14 January 1527, thanking him for a New Year's gift (see Figure 6).[50]

After a stand-off lasting several months, Croke managed to agree with Fitzroy that the prince would pay more attention to his studies if, in return, he was allowed to concentrate on texts that captured his imagination. So Croke reluctantly dropped Latin poetry and moral philosophy. And in an inspired move, he encouraged his pupil to dip into the eight books of Julius Caesar on the Gallic Wars, an action-packed narrative full of battles, fire and slaughter, written for the general reader in a simple style that avoids difficult syntax or vocabulary. Depicting Caesar as a loyal patriot and incorporating some of the most vivid descriptions of military strategy ever written, the books clearly struck a chord with a student as eager to imitate the victories of Edward the Black Prince at Crécy and Henry V at Agincourt as his father had been at a similar age.

A year later almost to the day, the 8-year-old wrote separately to his father and Wolsey in a now nearly perfect italic hand, asking for a child's suit of armour. As he assured his father, 'I effectually give my whole endeavour, mind, study and pleasure to the diligent application of all such science and feats of learning as by my most loving councillors I am daily advertised to stand with your most high and gracious pleasure.' Therefore, he continued, 'remember me your most humble and lowly servant with a harness for my exercise in arms according to my learning in Julius Caesar.' And the boy signed off, 'Trusting in God as speedily and profitably to prosper in the same as your grace shall perceive that I have done in all mine other learnings.'[51]

The effect would have been greatly spoiled had Henry known that, for almost a year, the prince had been corresponding cheerfully with James V of Scotland, seeking his advice about the best kind of hunting dogs. When Fitzroy sent the Scottish king a gift of six or eight dogs 'for hunting the fox and a couple fit for the leash', James—who addressed the boy as 'our tender cousin'—reciprocated with 'two brace of hounds for deer and smaller beasts'. And if he enjoyed hawking (as he already knew he did), he would send him at the right season 'some of the best red hawks in the country'.[52]

◆   ◆   ◆

Mary, by comparison, showed every sign of being a serious and dedicated student. Wolsey's ordinances for her household had laid down that, 'first, principally and above all other things', Margaret Pole, 'according to the singular confidence that the king's highness hath in her'—the cardinal surely had a glint in his eye when he said that—shall 'give most tender regard to all such things as [may] concern the person of the said princess, her honourable education, and [her] training in all virtuous demeanour.'[53]

Pole was to ensure that her young charge 'at seasons convenient' was to 'use moderate exercise for taking open air in gardens, sweet

and wholesome places and walks'. Mary was to continue practising the virginals, but not so excessively that it interfered with
learning Latin and French. She was to improve her dancing and
learn deportment, and even how to make sure her servants washed
and dressed her properly.[54]

Mary's first official schoolmaster, Richard Fetherstone, a
staunch Catholic, who now took over from Katherine as her
daughter's Latin teacher, also doubled as her chaplain. Plainly her
religious education was to be as central to her studies as it had
always been to her Spanish mother's. Already one of Katherine's
inner circle and soon to become one of her legal advisers, Fetherstone's views on education were conveniently close to those of
Vives. It was in these years that the devout Catholic beliefs that
were later to become the defining principles of the young princess's life were instilled into her.

Within two years she would be able to translate the prayer of St
Thomas Aquinas from Latin into English well enough to win plau-
dits from Lord Morley, a noted scholar and translator. 'I do well
remember', he later wrote in the front of a New Year's gift to her,
'that scant you were come to twelve years of age, but that you were
so ripe in the Latin tongue... that your grace not only could per-
fectly read, write and construe Latin, but furthermore translate
any hard thing of the Latin in to our English tongue.'[55]

To improve Mary's French conversation, Wolsey assigned her
an experienced French tutor, the Fleming Giles Duwes. A lutenist
and a fluent French speaker who doubled as a royal librarian,
Duwes had previously been Prince Arthur's 'schoolmaster for the
French tongue' and Henry's own lute teacher. Sent by Wolsey to
join the princess at Ludlow as a gentleman-waiter along with his
wife, Duwes possessed a renowned collection of music books and

instruments, including clavichords, virginals and regals (small portable organs), all of which Mary was allowed to play.[56]

As the author of a French grammar that would be published in 1533, *An Introductory for to Learn, to Read, to Pronounce and to Speak French Truly*, a work most valuable for its advice on pronunciation and glossary of useful words, Duwes set out the manner 'by the which I have so taught and do teach daily'. If this was indeed how Mary learned to speak French, she would have begun by practising how vowels should be pronounced, then (as in Latin) how to distinguish and use nouns, pronouns, adverbs and participles, and finally how to use and conjugate verbs.

Once the basics were mastered, Duwes expected his pupils to begin to converse, starting by learning model texts by heart. In a number of these, Mary would engage in polite conversation with fictive messengers sent by her father or another foreign prince, who brought a gift or news for her. Other set texts included mock 'letters' addressed to her by her officials at Ludlow, along with poems and sample 'conversations' on topics with which she was generally familiar, such as 'the ceremonies of the mass'. Finally, Mary was to speak her lines from the scripts of model 'dialogues' after learning them by heart, usually on topics chosen from moral philosophy.[57]

◆   ◆   ◆

By April 1527, the 11-year-old Mary had been recalled from Ludlow to Greenwich, where she was visited by French ambassadors as a central plank of one of Henry and Wolsey's many plans during these years to negotiate another pan-European peace accord. Charles V had released Francis I from captivity in Madrid, but part of the price was that the French king should marry Eleanor, the

Dowager Queen of Portugal, Charles's sister.[58] To counter the threat of a Franco-imperial dynastic alliance, Wolsey boldly proposed that Mary should marry Francis instead. Only if Charles agreed to bind himself to a fresh Treaty of Universal Peace, he argued, should Henry stand by idle if Francis married Eleanor, and if such a marriage took place, then to ensure that England was not isolated from the new European order, Mary should marry the French Dauphin and Fitzroy be betrothed to Eleanor's daughter, the Infanta Maria of Portugal.[59]

On St George's Day (23 April), according to an account of the visit now in Paris, Henry led the French ambassadors into the great hall at the palace, where Katherine and Mary were waiting to greet them. The king then asked them to speak to Mary in French, Latin and Italian, 'in all which languages she answered them'. She then played proficiently on the virginals.[60]

Just how skilled Mary really was in Italian is open to doubt.[61] Other visitors believed she had little more than a smattering, picked up from her mother's servants. A similar uncertainty surrounds her mastery of Spanish, a language she is known to have spoken, but in which she was never completely fluent, despite learning the basics from her mother. And, unlike in Fitzroy's case, Henry never provided his daughter with a Greek teacher.[62]

After weeks of diplomatic haggling, a treaty with France was finally agreed by which Mary would marry either Francis himself or (more likely) his second son, Henry, Duke of Orléans, then a child of 7.[63] But the treaty still had to be ratified, and by the time it was, the princess's world had started to implode. Long before the time of the French ambassadors' visit, Henry and Katherine were mainly living apart. Soon after Mary had departed with her entourage for Ludlow in 1525, her mother was complaining to her, 'I am in that case that the long absence of the king and you troubleth me.'[64]

Worse was to come. Soon Henry would completely dismiss Fitzroy from his thoughts, something which in other circumstances would have caused Katherine's heart to rejoice. No longer would her fears that her husband's illegitimate son could oust her daughter from her rightful place in the succession appear justified.

But the reason devastated her. Henry had concluded that his marriage to Katherine was not simply in trouble; he decided that it was 'incestuous' and invalid. That explains why Fitzroy was so suddenly dropped from his agenda. Bizarre as it may sound to modern ears, by canon law an illegitimate child could not inherit from a parent living with a wife or husband in an incestuous marriage. In a few special cases, the children of princes were exceptions, but in no circumstances could an exception apply if the *father's* marriage was incestuous—even though the child was by his mistress—because the father was an 'unnatural' person living in sin in defiance of God.[65]

A crisis in Katherine's relationship with Henry was about to begin, and all his children would be casualties.

CHAPTER 4

Sons and Lovers

ENRY fell in love with Anne Boleyn during 1526. As with Elizabeth Blount, he finished his affair with Mary Carey as soon as he knew she was pregnant. Since Mary's son was born on 4 March 1526, this must have been by the late summer of 1525, when Henry travelled around the south-east for several months with a few chosen intimates, restlessly moving between his houses and hunting lodges, rarely staying at any of them for more than a week.[1] The child was christened Henry, and inevitably Katherine's supporters darkly insinuated that he was the king's and not William Carey's, but no proof exists.[2] Henry never acknowledged the boy, and if the younger Carey knew he had royal blood in his veins, he took the secret to the grave.

The king's new love's looks were surprisingly unconventional. As the Venetian ambassador observed, 'Madame Anne is not one of the handsomest women in the world; she is of middling stature, swarthy complexion, long neck, wide mouth, bosom not much raised, and in fact has nothing but the English king's great appetite, and her eyes, which are black and beautiful.'³ A natural brunette with an unremarkable figure, she lacked the pale, translucent beauty and blonde hair then in vogue. One of her protégés, when asked to compare her to Elizabeth Blount, said that Anne was 'very eloquent and gracious, and reasonably good looking', but Blount was prettier.⁴

What Anne had in spades was French *chic* together with wit, vivacity, intelligence and a quick tongue—all combined with a sophistication gained through her nine years of training at the Court of Margaret of Burgundy, Charles V's aunt, and afterwards in France as a gentlewoman attending first on Henry's younger sister and then Queen Claude, wife of Francis I.

Not that Anne had lacked suitors since her return from Paris in 1521 to become one of Katherine's gentlewomen. The poet Thomas Wyatt—married at 15 on his father's decree to a woman he detested—started wooing her within the accepted limits of courtly love, only to find himself emotionally smitten. Another suitor, Henry Percy, heir to the vast northern earldom of Northumberland, was a more realistic proposition. He first encountered Anne around 1522 when, as one of Wolsey's servants, he resorted 'for his pastime unto the queen's chamber and there would fall in dalliance among the queen's maidens'. Soon he found himself 'more conversant with Mistress Anne Boleyn than with any other' and the couple considered themselves betrothed.⁵

Percy's father, however, had very different plans. His son, he decided, would marry Mary Talbot, the Earl of Shrewsbury's daughter, a far better catch than Anne. But if Wolsey's gentleman-usher and earliest biographer, George Cavendish, is to be believed, it was the cardinal who finally ended the betrothal, acting on Henry's orders—he 'practised nothing in the matter, but it was the king's only device'.[6] And the anecdote rings true, because Percy reluctantly married Mary Talbot somewhere between the summer of 1525 and September 1526, so the chronology fits.[7]

Anne 'smoked' at Wolsey's interference, 'for all this while she knew nothing of the king's intended purpose'.[8] Henry's courtship, therefore, had not yet begun. But when it did, he was quickly besotted. He bombarded Anne with gifts and wrote her love letters, seventeen of which have survived and are kept in the Vatican Library, perhaps filched from Anne's cabinet around the time of her fall by one of Katherine's sympathizers and secretly kept within the Catholic community until they could be taken to Rome.[9]

In these extraordinary outpourings Henry calls Anne his 'darling', his 'own sweetheart', the woman he 'esteems' most in the whole world.[10] Her prolonged absence, he insists, will be 'intolerable'.[11] And in an ironic role reversal, he casts himself as her 'true servant', gently chiding her for not writing to him as she has promised, for, he says, 'it has not pleased you to remember the promise you made me when I was last with you—that is, to hear good news from you.'[12] He sends a gift of a buck he has killed himself, 'hoping that when you eat of it you may think of the hunter'.[13] He even sends her what he says is the 'nearest thing' to himself: his 'picture set in bracelets' and with a 'device', possibly based upon their intertwined initials.[14]

But Anne, who was clearly flattered but probably not in love with the king, refused to submit like her sister. 'Since my parting from you', Henry then writes, 'I have been told that the opinion in which I left you is totally changed'. This, he declares, will be 'a very poor return for the great love which I bear to you'. He cannot understand why, if she loves him, it is not 'a little irksome' to her 'to keep me at a distance'. His letter unsubtly hints that his patience is limited. Anne needs to decide, for if she 'voluntarily' sought their separation, Henry 'could do no other than mourn my ill-fortune, and by degrees abate my great folly'.[15]

Since all of Anne's replies are lost, what she said to Henry can only be conjectured. She must have continued her delaying tactics, since the king tried again. He has been, he says, 'for above a whole year stricken with the dart of love, and not yet sure whether I shall fail or find a place in your heart and affection'.[16] Does Anne love him 'with an ordinary love' or a 'singular love'? He demands to 'know expressly your whole mind as to the love between us two.' If she will surrender herself 'both body and heart' to him, she will be his 'only mistress'; he will think of no one else and 'serve' her alone. So desperate is he for an answer that if she does not want to reply in writing, he is ready to go wherever she wishes to 'have it by word of mouth'.[17]

At last Anne yielded, but ambiguously. She wrote to Henry, probably at the beginning of 1527, enclosing a New Year's gift.[18] This must have taken a good deal of careful planning, involving her ambitious father, Sir Thomas Boleyn, whom Henry had made Viscount Rochford on the same day as he had ennobled Fitzroy. Anne's gift was an expensive jewel, a ship set with a 'fine diamond' in which a 'solitary damsel is tossed about'. As the means to convey a message, it was brilliantly choreographed and Henry instantly grasped its 'fine interpretation'. Anne, the damsel, was safe in the ship just as she was safe in his arms.[19] Since she could not herself have afforded such an item, her father must have agreed to buy it for her. And a payment is indeed recorded in her father's accounts to Cornelius Hayes, 'the king's goldsmith'.[20] Although too small to pay for the whole gift, it might well have been a first instalment.

Henry was jubilant. He promised Anne his eternal love, pledging himself 'for ever to honour, love, and serve you sincerely'. But he laments that Anne is not yet ready to sleep with him. 'Assuring you', he writes, 'that henceforward my heart shall be dedicated to you alone. I wish my body was so too.'[21] In other words, Anne's surrender was conditional.

So infatuated was Henry that he allowed Anne to bargain with him. She would not become his mistress like her sister; she would be his wife and his queen. With Katherine several years past the menopause, Anne played her ace of trumps, daringly vowing to give the king a legitimate male heir, one who—unlike Fitzroy—could be certain to succeed to the throne, because she and Henry would be married.

Henry, for his part, seems to have believed that an annulment of his marriage to Katherine would be straightforward, or perhaps the pious queen could be persuaded to take religious vows and retire to a nunnery, in which case he would be free to marry again. It was a breathtaking gamble on both sides and the question was how to win it.

◆　◆　◆

Henry sprang into action, informing Wolsey around Easter 1527 that he had deep 'scruples' about the validity of his marriage to Katherine, but at this stage concealing his intention to make Anne his wife rather than his mistress. He did so not because his chief minister could be predicted to oppose a divorce, but because he knew the cardinal would do all he could to dissuade him from marrying a subject. Many of Wolsey's later difficulties with Henry would spring from this initial deception. At a stroke, the king deprived his most trusted servant of the essential facts he needed to fulfil his master's desires, because if Henry was to marry Anne, the king was in almost exactly the same predicament as he had been in 1503 when his father had first decided to betroth him to his dead brother's widow. Besides an annulment of his marriage to Katherine, he would *also* need a papal dispensation allowing him to marry a woman to whom he was already related in the first degree of affinity, i.e. Anne, because of his earlier sexual relationship with her sister.[22] And that would not be easy.

In May 1527, Wolsey secretly summoned Henry to appear before a special church court at York Place to answer matters affecting the 'tranquillity of consciences' and the salvation of the king's soul. What Henry said there will never be known, but shortly afterwards he claimed his conscience had been most recently 'pricked' by questions asked by the ambassadors sent to discuss Princess Mary's betrothal to the Duke of Orléans.[23]

Wolsey's stage-managed proceedings came to nothing. His secret court had to be abruptly adjourned after the appalling news arrived that a mutinous imperial army led by the Duke of Bourbon—its soldiers starving and unpaid—had besieged Rome and sacked the city. Pope Clement VII was forced to flee along the secret tunnel connecting the Vatican to the Castel Sant'Angelo, where he signed a truce, making himself Charles V's prisoner.[24]

With the pope now firmly under the thumb of Katherine's nephew, Wolsey knew that the queen would be certain to win if she appealed for justice in her case to Rome. When he left with Thomas More for Amiens in July on a mission to ratify the French alliance, the cardinal had the seeds of a daring plan germinating in his mind. He would convene a powerful group of cardinals at Avignon and take over the government of the Church while the pope was incapacitated.[25] He would then meet Charles at Perpignan and attempt to strike a deal on the divorce in Henry's favour. He had French support, but was strongly opposed by the Italian cardinals and by Clement himself.[26] The plan came to nothing. Henry, meanwhile, impatiently took command of his divorce campaign.

◆   ◆   ◆

From this point onwards, the king consistently voiced two arguments. One—chiefly used at Rome—was that he had never been legally married to Katherine, because the bull of dispensation granted by Pope Julius II that had first allowed him to marry his elder brother's widow had contained serious flaws. The other— mainly used for whipping up support in England—was more far-reaching, denying that the pope had ever had sufficient authority to allow the marriage in the first place.[27]

As Henry scribbled eagerly to Anne, he was himself writing a book on his 'great matter'. 'I am right well comforted', he explained, 'in so much that my book maketh substantially for my matter; in looking whereof I have spent above four hours this day, which caused me now to write the shorter letter to you at this time, because of some pain in my head.'[28]

Several versions of this 'book' in all its different drafts and incarnations have survived. Henry insisted that the Old Testament prohibition on marriage to a brother's wife (Leviticus 20:21) was a precept of divine law binding on Christians. He rejected a seemingly contrary text (Deuteronomy 25:5), denying its relevance on the grounds that it merely reflected a Jewish tradition known as the 'levirate' by which the brother or next of kin to a deceased man was bound to marry the widow.

Determined to prove that the Levitical law meant that Pope Julius's dispensation had been improperly granted, Henry summoned

Robert Wakefield, a distinguished Hebraist from Cambridge University, who advised him that the divine retribution threatened against illicit marriage partners according to Leviticus—'they shall be childless'—was to be understood solely in the male gender. The biblical text, said Wakefield, should correctly read: 'If a man shall take his brother's wife, it is an impurity. He hath uncovered his brother's nakedness: they shall not have sons.' This, at a stroke, removed a major stumbling block from Henry's case as his daughter Mary was alive and well.[29]

Soon afterwards, the king went further, claiming that sexual intercourse with a brother's widow was both 'incestuous' and 'contrary to the law of nature'—it was an 'abominable' act condemned by God as much as if it had been forbidden by the Ten Commandments, which no pope could dispense. Henry's opinion had its supporters, but a majority of the most learned theologians and canon lawyers disagreed.[30]

Wolsey schemed tirelessly to secure the divorce, but became increasingly desperate as Anne Boleyn's father and brother George began taking charge of the king's diplomacy and issuing threats that the pope was not the true 'vicar of Christ'.

At last and after months of negotiation, the beleaguered cardinal obtained a commission from Pope Clement allowing him to hear the king's suit jointly with Cardinal Campeggio at a second special court to be convened at Blackfriars, a Dominican monastery a stone's throw from the Thames.

On 31 May 1529, the two cardinals summoned Henry and Katherine to appear before them on Friday 18 June.[31] Campeggio, however, had already received secret instructions from the pope, ordering him not to proceed to judgment without a further express commission. And at a Consistory at the Vatican on 16 July, the case was revoked to Rome. Two days later, the embattled Clement wrote letters of apology to Henry and Wolsey claiming that his hands were tied, but his regrets were hollow.[32]

* ◆ ◆ ◆

When the pope's letters arrived, Wolsey's fall was inevitable. In August, Henry summoned Parliament, which assembled on 3 November and passed a series of anticlerical acts to which he assented. On 9 October, Wolsey was indicted in the Court of King's Bench for *praemunire* (i.e. illegally exercising papal jurisdiction). He wisely pleaded guilty, and was replaced as Lord Chancellor by Thomas More.[33] But More had a battle on his hands as long as Henry was listening to the Boleyns, who had recruited a think tank to investigate the divorce and find a way to avoid a trial of the case at Rome. Led by Edward Foxe, Provost of King's College, Cambridge, Thomas Cranmer, a theologian at Jesus College, Cambridge, and Nicholas de Burgo, a Florentine Franciscan teaching in Oxford, they made their initial report in the autumn of 1530.

Henry was delighted with their findings, which he annotated in forty-six places. For, after investigating the king of England's lawful powers and prerogatives from first principles and ranging historically as far back as 187 AD, they argued that Henry and his royal ancestors had always been endowed by God with an 'imperial' and sacred authority, part of which had been 'lent' to churchmen over the centuries, but which could be resumed at will.

According to this (often specious) research, the pope was merely the 'bishop of Rome' whose power was limited to his own diocese, whereas the king was a 'sacral emperor' in his kingdom. In short, Henry was now said to be (as it were) a second King David or King Solomon as described in the Old Testament, or else like a great

Christian Roman Emperor such as Constantine or Justinian. On this assumption, he might lawfully prescribe the articles of faith for his subjects and legislate for both Church and State—just as those regal prototypes had done.[34]

Soon Henry would be found jotting down a note that papal jurisdiction had been exercised in England 'but only by negligence or usurpation as we take it and esteem'.[35] If he were to put such revolutionary ideas into practice, they could be used to justify a break with Rome and to declare Henry to be the Supreme Head of an autonomous Church of England. That would make the divorce as easy as the ABC, because if the king was the true head of the English Church and not the pope, then he might lawfully empower the archbishop of Canterbury or a panel of bishops to investigate his troubled 'conscience' and report their findings to him, a verdict which could then be enforced by the authority of Parliament.[36]

◆   ◆   ◆

It is a measure of Henry's innate conservatism that he waited almost three years before taking the plunge. Despite Anne's constant badgering—which included showing him selected passages from William Tyndale's writings and led to two famous Lutherans being invited to England with safe conducts to advise on the divorce—the king continued to seek an annulment of his marriage through negotiations at Rome. Every possible trick and feint was used there to secure a hearing of his case at home, or failing that on neutral ground. His chief agents in this diplomacy were the Boleyns. Anne's father, whom Henry made Earl of Wiltshire, was sent to Bologna and Rome to bribe the cardinals. Her brother, who succeeded his father as Viscount Rochford, went to Paris to champion the divorce there.[37]

Spurred on by Anne, Henry also turned his venom on to Katherine in a renewed attempt to persuade her to enter a nunnery, but she remained defiant. In August 1531, she was exiled to The More, Wolsey's former house in Hertfordshire, while Mary stayed at Richmond with Henry. Katherine would never see her husband again.

And Anne made quite sure that the queen would never again set eyes on her beloved daughter either.[38] The pressure took its toll on Mary, who could not keep food down.[39] Now 15, she had to cope with the onset of puberty as well as stress, suffering menstrual difficulties besides feverish illnesses and bouts of depression and insomnia.[40] Henry allowed Katherine's physician to attend her, but when Mary begged him to let her visit her mother, the king refused—at Anne's insistence.[41]

Henry, meanwhile, hunted with Anne, who rode pillion with him through the countryside to the amazement of gawping villagers.[42] And to reassure her that she really would soon be queen, he remodelled the privy apartments at several of the principal royal palaces with her tastes and comforts uniquely in mind.

At Hampton Court, an entirely fresh range of lodgings was begun at astronomical cost. At York Place, Wolsey's London home, which Henry had seized along with all the former minister's other property and turned into the palace of Whitehall, similar additions and improvements were made.[43] Anne was given Hanworth, where boxes, cupboards, desks, chests, tables, doors and other joinery were fitted out for her, and some of the exterior walls and chimneys redecorated in the latest and most fashionable Italian style.[44] Even the royal lodgings at the Tower of London were rebuilt in readiness for the ceremonies on the eve of her anticipated coronation.[45]

◆   ◆   ◆

In May 1532, Thomas More resigned as Lord Chancellor after losing out to Thomas Cromwell in a parliamentary battle to defend the Church from Henry's predations. At the time More resigned, Henry promised to respect his former secretary's conscience, but under pressure from Anne he broke his promise three years later, putting him on trial for his life and executing him.

For Katherine, More's resignation was a disaster, since Cromwell—Wolsey's old fixer and solicitor, who filled the vacuum—was allied to the Boleyns. He was not yet the king's chief minister, but would soon make himself indispensable.

The turning point in the divorce campaign was a rendezvous at Boulogne between Henry and Francis I the following October, arranged as the sequel to the ratification of a new Treaty of Mutual Aid between the two kings.[46] Anne, whom Henry made Marquis of Pembroke in her own right at a ceremony at Windsor Castle in readiness for the visit, accompanied Henry as far as Calais, where he escorted her to mass and everywhere else as if she was already queen.[47]

After the two kings talked at Boulogne, they returned to Calais, where Francis was lodged in splendour at the Staple Hall. There, after supper on the 27th, Anne partnered Francis in a spectacular masque, a supreme recognition of her status as a future queen and a public demonstration of what she and Henry believed to be the French king's promise to back their case at Rome.

Henry's ambassador at the Vatican, Gregorio Casale, also attended the summit as an observer. And to make quite sure that a divorce would soon be granted, Henry allocated him another 3,000 ducats from the pensions he and Wolsey had been granted by France over the years, so that he could bribe the cardinals into submission. If necessary, Casale was even empowered to throw in an English bishopric or two.[48]

So confident of success were Anne and Henry after the summit that she at last agreed to sleep with him, either at Calais or on their leisurely journey home. A mutual exchange of vows took place in November, and by December Anne was pregnant.[49]

Henry was at last galvanized into action, and on 24 or 25 January 1533 the couple were secretly (and bigamously) married at Greenwich Palace.[50] As soon as the writs for a new session of Parliament could be issued, Cromwell set about drafting an Act in Restraint of Appeals to Rome, which passed in April. This prohibited all appeals on whatever grounds from the church courts to the pope, stopping Katherine in her tracks.

And when Henry gave his royal assent to this legislation, he finally made his break with the past.

◆　◆　◆

While Parliament debated the Act of Appeals, the bishops ruled Katherine's marriage to be unlawful. On 23 May, Cranmer—whom Henry rewarded with the archbishopric of Canterbury—annulled it and pronounced Anne's marriage valid. Her coronation festivities began on 19 May and lasted more than a fortnight.[51]

And unlike Katherine, who had been crowned with Queen Edith's crown, Anne was anointed with holy oil and chrism and then crowned with St Edward's crown—the one reserved for kings, not for consorts. She even sat on St Edward's chair while she was crowned, the chair kept for sovereigns.[52] Now pregnant with the child that Henry felt certain would be a son, she believed she had won. For according to canon law, a second marriage contracted during annulment proceedings was valid if the first marriage was subsequently dissolved. Likewise, if a child was conceived outside wedlock, the baby was legitimate in the eyes of the Church if a lawful marriage between the parents was solemnized before he or she was born.

Since English secular law differed in several crucial respects from canon law over illegitimacy and inheritance, Cromwell over the next eighteen months steered further measures through Parliament, guaranteeing that the succession would pass to Anne's children, first to her male issue, and if there were none surviving to her 'issue female'. These acts also ensured that Henry's second marriage would be judged lawful both by Parliament and the courts, and they provided that anyone who denied the validity of his marriage to Anne or the legitimacy of their children would be tried for treason. Soon another act would declare that the king, not the pope, was Supreme Head of the Church of England.[53]

Anne's baby was born shortly after 3 p.m. on Sunday, 7 September 1533 at Henry's favourite palace of Greenwich. Edward and Henry had already been mooted as the child's names and dozens of open letters to the nobility and leading gentry announcing the 'deliverance and bringing forth of a prince' were prepared from stock lists in the office of the queen's secretary.

When the news broke that the child was female, all these documents had to be altered one by one.[54] They still managed to go out on the day of the birth as Anne had intended. But because insufficient space had been left between the words to cram in more than one extra literal, 'princess' had to be spelled with only one 's'.

To celebrate, *Te Deum* was sung in the Chapel Royal and at St Paul's, but the customary bonfires in London to mark a royal birth were few and far between.[55] Preparations then began for the christening three days later. For the moment Henry continued to follow the *Royal Book*. For while Anne's failure to produce a son was a crushing blow, something he had never dreamed could happen to him, he was still infatuated by his new queen and standing by her.

The baptism, therefore, was meant to be a very public event—the two French ambassadors were the guests of honour. But Henry cancelled the two-day tournament he had originally been planning, for only a son was worthy of that.

Charles V's ambassador, meanwhile, gloated in triumph over the royal couple's discomfort. He enraged Anne by refusing to attend the baptism, telling anyone who would listen that her child was a 'bastard' and mocking the physicians and astrologers who had predicted a boy.[56]

The christening was held at the Franciscan friary church at Greenwich, where Henry had himself been baptized. The mayor and aldermen of London led the procession from the great hall of the palace in their scarlet robes, followed by the king's councillors, the gentleman and children of the Chapel, and then the barons, bishops and earls. Next came the Earl of Essex, the Marquises of Exeter and Dorset carrying the taper and salt to be used at the service, followed by Mary Howard, the Duke of Norfolk's younger daughter, who bore the chrism. Finally, Agnes Howard, one of the godmothers, carried the baby enveloped in purple cloth of gold with a long train lined with ermine.

Since protocol prevented kings from attending their children's baptisms and a newly delivered woman was forbidden by canon law from entering a church until she had been ritually purified, the Duke of Norfolk, Anne's uncle, presided. The christening itself was performed by John Stokesley, bishop of London, who named the child Elizabeth after Henry's own mother whom he still greatly revered.

Once the baptism was over, the esquires and yeomen who lined the side-aisles lit their torches. The sudden blaze of light was the

cue for a herald to cry out, 'God of his infinite goodness send pros-
perous life and long to the high and mighty Princess of England,
Elizabeth'.

The trumpets blew, after which Archbishop Cranmer, who
was the baby's godfather, carried her to the high altar, where he
confirmed her. The procession then made its way back to the palace, where gifts were offered to the queen and the child, and a
message came from Henry ordering sweet wine and comfits to
be served.[57]

◆   ◆   ◆

In December 1533, Henry decided that Elizabeth should be sent
with her nurse to a recently appropriated royal manor at Hatfield
in Hertfordshire, some twenty-five miles north of London. Put in
charge of her nursery was the inveterate Lady Bryan, whom Henry
recalled to royal service as his daughter's first governess.[58]

Elizabeth travelled to Hatfield in a horse litter, lodging overnight
at Elsings in Enfield, Middlesex, a palatial manor house once
belonging to the wealthy courtier Sir Thomas Lovell, who
bequeathed it to the Earl of Rutland. Both Hatfield and Enfield were
places Elizabeth would come to know well and to love. In 1539,
when Henry decided that he wanted Elsings mainly for his children's use, the earl surrendered it to him in exchange for a generous grant of ex-monastic lands in the Midlands.

Although now separated from her daughter, Anne took the
closest possible interest in her welfare, ordering her the most fashionable and expensive clothes and already worrying that she
should receive the best possible education as befitted an heir to the
throne.[59] She often came to visit her, either on her own or with
Henry, and wrote regularly to Lady Bryan.

FIGURE 7   The Old Palace at Hatfield in Hertfordshire, which Henry VIII had appropriated by 1533 chiefly for the use of his children, and which he formally acquired in 1538. Elizabeth secured the house for herself in 1549 and it became her main home until her accession.

In March 1534, for instance, she came to see Elizabeth at Hatfield.[60] In April, she and Henry rode the five miles from Greenwich to visit her while she was staying nearby at Eltham, the king's own childhood home that had just been refurbished. As Sir William Kingston, who accompanied the royal party, cheerfully observes, Elizabeth was 'as goodly a child as hath been seen, and her grace is much in the king's favour.'[61] The following October, Anne travelled in the royal barge from Hampton Court to see her daughter at Richmond, attended by the Dukes of Norfolk and Suffolk and several ladies of the Court.[62]

In the early months of 1535, Elizabeth lived at Court for five weeks 'with divers of her servants.'[63] This gave her mother an opportunity for more extended contact. Yet to Anne's dismay, her parental role would be restricted just as Katherine's had been. Convention dictated that her child's upbringing was to be overseen by Henry and the Privy Council, not herself. When, for instance, Lady Bryan sought Cromwell's permission to have the infant weaned at the age of twenty-five months, he forwarded her request to Henry, who instructed Sir William Paulet, comptroller of the royal household, to approve it. In a letter to Cromwell, Paulet tactfully observes that permission had been granted by 'his grace, with the assent of the queen's grace.'[64] But Anne had only been asked to confirm what Henry had already decided.

This issue swiftly evaporated when compared to the problems caused by the king's other daughter, Mary. Suddenly confronted after Elizabeth's birth by a rival for her father's affection and, even worse, excluded from her place in the succession by one of Cromwell's acts of Parliament, she now became as defiant as her mother and just as obstinate as her father.

A family feud was about to begin.

CHAPTER 5

A Family Feud

ARY'S feud with her father and half-sister began even before the herald cried out Elizabeth's title as 'Princess of England' at her baptism. The seeds were sown three weeks earlier when Thomas Cromwell ordered Margaret Pole, still Mary's governess, to surrender the elder princess's jewels and plate to his messenger. Pole indignantly refused, demanding Henry's written orders. Lord Hussey, Mary's chamberlain, who was caught in the middle, exclaimed to Cromwell in frustration, 'Would to God that the king and you did know and see what I have had to do here of late!'[1]

Mary was determined to retain her royal privileges.[2] She had been psychologically stunned when, the moment Elizabeth's birth was announced, the same herald strode in his ceremonial robes to the gatehouse of Greenwich Palace to proclaim that she had been stripped of her royal title. Once this proclamation was made, the livery badges worn by her servants 'were instantly removed and replaced by the king's escutcheon'.[3]

Then living at her father's palace of New Hall in Essex, Mary was sick with worry as to what she should do if Henry called Pole's bluff as she knew he would. 'Speak you few words and meddle nothing' was Katherine's advice.[4] But however hard she tried, Mary found it difficult to follow. Uninvited, she tried to deflect the coming storm by writing to her father, 'saying that she would as long as she lived obey his commands, but that she really could not renounce the titles, rights and privileges which God, Nature and her own parents had given her.'[5]

The response was at first an ominous silence. Then, in October, Henry ordered Mary to move immediately from New Hall, a place she adored, to a 'very wretched' manor house nearby. And in November and December he dismantled her household, dismissing her attendants one by one, beginning with Pole.[6]

Katherine's supporters blamed Anne—it was simply to please her, they murmured, that Mary was to be demoted. It was even said that she would be shut up in a nunnery or forced to marry a nonentity.[7] And when Henry gave New Hall and its park to Anne's brother George and his wife Jane as their new country estate, it seemed that such fears might prove all too true.[8]

◆   ◆   ◆

For Mary, the ensuing years would be harrowing. To teach her a lesson in obedience, her father decided that—at the age of almost 18—she should go and live with Elizabeth in her nursery as an inferior person to her half-sister. Humiliatingly, he created a joint household for his two daughters, with precedence given to Elizabeth.[9]

Sir John Shelton and his wife, Lady Anne, were put in overall charge. Once more, Henry's new queen seemed to be behind the move, since Anne Shelton was her paternal aunt. How far the Sheltons themselves were happy with the decision may be questioned. The joint household would prove to be an awkward and inconvenient structure. Many times would the Sheltons find themselves trapped in the middle of endless rows between Mary, who was meant to be a subordinate but had no governess appointed, and Lady Bryan, Elizabeth's governess, who was expected to exercise authority on behalf of her young charge.[10]

Mary's health soon buckled under the strain. When first sent in disgrace to Hatfield, she kept to her room and wept continually. In retaliation, Henry ordered that no food or drink should be served to her there and that her best clothes should be given away to punish her.[11]

In March 1534, after a more than usually abrasive confrontation with Anne conducted through intermediaries, Mary had a breakdown so disturbing that a seriously worried Henry had to relent as far as sending his own physician, Dr William Butts, to attend her.[12]

Butts's diagnosis was that Mary was suffering a fresh bout of the menstrual problems she had endured at the onset of puberty. A more conspiratorial theory circulating at Henry's Court was that Anne— who had urged the king to 'put down that proud Spanish blood' by beating Mary into submission—had attempted to poison her.[13]

Forced to live like a cuckoo in her half-sister's nest, Mary snubbed her at every opportunity. When Elizabeth began to toddle, Mary would not walk by her side. And whenever they were taken out somewhere, Mary demanded to ride separately, preferably in front. She refused point-blank to share a horse litter with her sibling, and if she was forced to do so by the Sheltons, she vociferously protested.[14] She also always expected to sit in the best seat in the royal barge.[15]

Anne was so incensed with Mary that, one day losing her temper completely, she threatened to kill her if Henry ever went abroad.[16]

♦   ♦   ♦

Towards Fitzroy, Anne's animosity would be less aggressive but equally detrimental, even though he did little or nothing to earn it. Just as Mary had been recalled from Wales, the king's illegitimate son had been recalled from Yorkshire shortly before Wolsey's fall. No longer did Henry consider the marginal improvements in efficiency and reliability achieved by the two regional councils sufficient to justify the prodigious expense of coupling them to his children's households.

And with Fitzroy back at Court where everyone could see him, Anne—fearing him as a potential rival for any child she might have—arranged for her uncle, the Duke of Norfolk, to take over his upbringing. In particular, she asked the duke to begin negotiations for the 10-year-old boy's betrothal to one of the duke's own daughters, so that he would cease to be available for a royal match.[17]

Since Fitzroy was so often at Court, he needed company, and at Anne's instigation, Norfolk made his own eldest son, Henry Howard, Earl of Surrey, the boy's constant companion. Three years older than Fitzroy, the young earl was a brilliant student and linguist as well as a fine horseman trained in the skills and ideals of chivalry. The king considered him to be a perfect role model, and in November 1532, when his son was 13, he sent the pair off to France, ostensibly to improve their French and to attend the marriage of Henry, Duke of Orléans to the pope's niece, Catherine de' Medici.[18]

In reality, Fitzroy was sent to boost his father's ego by showing himself off to the European powers as the living proof of Henry's ability to father a healthy son. Warmly received at the French Court, the youth was quartered in the Dauphin's lodgings and took his meals with the prince.

During the winter months, Fitzroy and Surrey stayed in Paris, but in the spring of 1533 they travelled with Francis I to Fontaine-bleau and on to Lyons, and then to Toulouse and Montpellier. There, in August, they made ready to witness the spectacular entertainments planned to greet Francis and the pope as the prelude to de' Medici's wedding.

But when news reached England that Pope Clement had finally passed judgment in Katherine's suit, declaring Henry's separation from his first wife to be unlawful and threatening him with a decree of excommunication, the two teenagers were recalled in haste.[19]

Anne's hostility towards Fitzroy crystallized after his return: it was said that in a tantrum she threatened to poison him too.[20] Her New Year's gifts to him were paltry and meant to insult him. She constantly badgered Henry to marry him off, until he yielded and obtained the necessary dispensation from the Church. On 26 November 1533, Fitzroy duly exchanged his vows with Mary Howard, Surrey's younger sister and one of Anne's most favoured gentlewomen, who had carried the chrism at Elizabeth's baptism. Both partners were still just 14.[21]

Since the young couple agreed at the outset that their union would not be consummated, it could hardly have been a love match. This was a far cry from the nuptials of de' Medici and the Duke of Orléans, who by coincidence were also both 14 and who, after their wedding feast, were led by Queen Eleanor to a sumptuously decorated bridal chamber, where they enjoyed uninhibited sex watched by Francis, who declared 'each had shown valour in the joust.'[22]

• • •

But Anne would shortly be on the defensive. When, in July 1534, she miscarried, it would take over a year for her to get pregnant again. Henry's eye, meanwhile, started to rove. In October, George Boleyn's wife Jane was rusticated from Court for colluding with Anne to secure the exile of an unidentified woman with whom the king was flirting.[23] Whoever his amour was, Henry had dropped her by February 1535, but that was only because he was trying to seduce a girl known as 'Madge' Shelton. 'Madge' was almost certainly the nickname of Mary Shelton, the youngest daughter of Mary and Elizabeth's joint custodians and Anne's cousin, who took a leading part in the games of courtly love in the queen's privy lodgings and was the muse of several of the 'poets-as-lovers' or 'lovers-as-poets' who offered to serve ladies and win their hearts.[24]

In late October 1535, Anne was at last pregnant, but, as was his old habit, this only seemed to encourage Henry's dalliances. The previous month, he and Anne had stayed for five days with Sir John Seymour and his wife at Wolf Hall in Wiltshire at the end of six weeks of hunting and hawking in the Severn Valley in Gloucestershire. Jane, one of Sir John's daughters who was 26, had served Katherine and then Anne as a gentlewoman. Her two brothers, Edward and Thomas, were ambitious, and in Edward's case outstandingly able. The king did not fall in love with Jane at first sight—but soon he would be thinking constantly and wistfully of her, for unlike Anne, who was increasingly becoming waspish, sweetness was Jane's trademark.[25]

When Katherine died at 2 p.m. on Friday, 7 January 1536, fortune briefly seemed to favour Anne. Henry rejoiced, and for several reasons. He had come to despise Katherine for her intransigence over the divorce, but more significantly her nephew, Charles V, was a pragmatist. Honour forbade him to treat with Henry or recognize Anne while his aunt was alive, but after her death he could—and did. The move coincided with a souring of relations with Francis for his reluctance to follow Henry's lead and break with Rome. All the ships belonging to the English merchants had been seized at Bordeaux and Henry was furious.

At first Henry threatened to ally with Charles simply to pile the pressure on Francis, but gradually Cromwell won him round to the idea of switching sides for good.[26] Charles, for his part, feared an imminent French attack on his position in Italy and so needed Henry as an ally to harry Francis in northern Europe.

Dressed from head to toe in yellow satin and sporting a white feather in his hat, Henry took Elizabeth to mass at Greenwich Palace on the Sunday after Katherine's death, walking beside her in the procession 'with trumpets and other great triumphs'. After dinner he danced with her in his arms, showing her off 'first to one and then to another' of his courtiers.[27]

Cromwell, never seriously in doubt that the Anglo-French alliance benefited only Francis, continued to strive for a *rapprochement* with Charles. With his eye on events in Rome rather than in Paris, he sought to tie the Holy Roman Emperor to Henry in ways that would ensure a papal excommunication of the English king would never be published, nor a Catholic invasion launched against him.[28]

Anne, meanwhile, looked at her most vulnerable. Her cutting remarks and dictatorial methods had breached the limits of conventional gender roles, upsetting Court officials and her own family, notably Norfolk and his wife. Her vehement and outspoken opposition to Cromwell's diplomacy and her proposals to divert the proceeds of the Dissolution of the Monasteries towards education and social reform rather than to cash reserves, which she made known by setting her chaplains to work on a preaching campaign in which Cromwell was pilloried, had turned the king's chief minister into a powerful enemy. If that were not enough, her connections to the evangelical reformers were considered to be heretical.

Now Henry started to share his doubts about his second wife with a trusted Privy Chamber intimate. He had married her, he confided, while 'seduced by witchcraft, and for that reason he considered it null.' 'This', he added, 'was evident because God did not permit them to have any male issue, and that he believed he might take another wife.'[29]

It was essential that Anne had a son—and quickly.

* * *

Instead, on 29 January, she miscarried. The foetus was about three and a half months old, ascertainably male.[30] With another pregnancy failure and his eye on Jane Seymour, Henry's confidence in his second marriage was shattered.

Anne, in desperation, cast the blame on a severe shock she had received five days earlier. While jousting at Greenwich, Henry had been unseated by an opponent, tumbling to the ground while fully armed with his horse on top of him. It was fright, Anne claimed, that had caused her to miscarry.

Except the timing seems wrong. Within two hours of his accident, Henry recovered consciousness. And when his servants had divested him of his armour, he declared that he 'had no hurt'. Certainly there was no brain damage and no serious injury was apparent at the time, although it would only be a year before rumours of trouble with his left leg started to seep out.[31] In the longer term, the consequences of hunting and jousting accidents like this would be severe, but at the time the general verdict was that Anne's miscarriage was entirely due to 'her utter inability to bear male children.'[32]

Of course, if the king were positive for the blood group antigen known as Kell and Anne—like Katherine before her—was negative, everything would fall into place. The couple could at most produce one living child successfully. Thereafter, the foetus would almost certainly be miscarried or stillborn, because of the rare genetic incompatibility between the blood groups of the parents. If so, this was as much Anne's tragedy as Katherine's (see Chapter 1).

Henry, however, had invested all his hopes in Anne's giving him a son. He did not intend to tolerate failure. As the Spanish ambassador excitedly informed Charles, the king had spoken fewer than ten times to his wife in more than three months. When she miscarried, he merely said, 'I see that God will not give me male children.'[33]

Anne hit back, rebuking Henry for his dalliances with other women. 'The love she bore him', she angrily insisted, 'was far greater than that of the late Queen, so that her heart broke when she saw that he loved others.'[34]

Anne was only too well aware of his swiftly developing relationship with Jane Seymour. So far it was chaste, but soon the king would find Jane lodgings in the house of Sir Nicholas Carew, another of his Court intimates, at Beddington in Surrey, where he paid her regular night-time visits.[35] Carew and Jane's elder brother coached her in her lines. She was to insinuate to Henry the invalidity of his marriage with Anne, and to resist his sexual advances until she was betrothed. Cromwell was deeply implicated in this *putsch*. It was simply a case of finding an opportunity to strike.

Cromwell's chance came in late April. On Saturday the 29th, Anne was overheard quarrelling violently with Henry Norris, the chief gentleman of Henry's Privy Chamber. Courtly banter in her apartments had got completely out of hand when Anne teased Norris over his relationship with 'Madge' Shelton, with whom he was having a fling. Since Norris was a widower, why had he not married her, Anne wanted to know? When Norris replied, 'He would tarry a time', the queen had petulantly retorted, 'You look for dead men's shoes, for if ought should come to the king but good, you would look to have me.'[36]

Norris, stunned by the folly of her tactless remark, at once declared that if the thought ever crossed his mind, 'he would his head was off'. He knew that such trivial badinage was extremely dangerous if overheard, since it could be misconstrued as a plot to murder Henry.

And so it was. On Sunday, Henry and Anne had a furious row. The king made up his mind to ditch her during the May Day jousts at Greenwich, allowing Cromwell to orchestrate her trial for conspiring Henry's death, an allegation he spiced up with charges of multiple adultery with Norris and three other courtiers, including a musician Mark Smeaton, and incest with her brother George. By raising such monstrous charges of depravity going back over three years, Henry could renounce his paternity of the miscarried foetus and secure his freedom, while Cromwell could eliminate his enemies in the Privy Chamber as the 'violators' of the queen.[37]

Norris and his fellow courtiers were tried and condemned on the 12th, Anne and George on the 15th. On the 17th, the alleged partners in Anne's sexual crimes, including her brother, went to the block. On the same day, Cranmer pronounced Henry's second marriage invalid. Two days later, Anne herself was executed, killed by a single blow of a sword in the French manner—an executioner was specially brought in from St Omer. Her head fell to the ground with her lips and eyes still moving.

◆　◆　◆

The moment Henry heard that he was free, he was rowed straight to Jane 'whom he had lodged a mile from him, in a house by the river'.[38] On the same day, Cranmer issued a dispensation for their marriage, and on 30 May, in the queen's oratory at the king's new palace of Whitehall, the couple exchanged their vows.[39]

The following month, Parliament was recalled to debate the Second Act of Succession, which abrogated the claims to the succession derived from Henry's earlier marriages and declared both his daughters illegitimate, even though the king would never deny his paternity. Now only Jane's offspring would be able to claim the throne, unless perchance she predeceased Henry without bearing a son and he fathered one by another wife.[40]

Anne's dramatic fall affected Henry's children in radically different ways. Elizabeth was still much too young to appreciate the tragedy that had befallen her mother. At this stage in her upbringing, economy was her greatest enemy. She suddenly lost all the luxuries and fine clothes she had enjoyed with the money slipped by Anne to Lady Bryan. She also lost her royal title and privileges as Mary had before her.

But with Elizabeth degraded, Mary felt vindicated, for she had always regarded Anne as little better than a whore. Now at last, if only by virtue of age, she recovered precedence over her sibling in the joint household, currently settled mainly at Hunsdon in Hertfordshire.

Except her victory was brief. Because the pressure to submit to her own degradation, far from decreasing, was unexpectedly ratcheted up. Not only did her father decide not to restore her title, he also demanded, increasingly vindictively, that she should subscribe to the Acts of Supremacy and Succession and acknowledge that her parents' marriage had been 'by God's law and man's law incestuous and unlawful'.[41]

To this end, Henry sent a high-level delegation of privy councillors to Hunsdon. Led by the Duke of Norfolk, they berated Mary with threats, saying menacingly that 'If she was their daughter, they would beat her and knock her head so violently against the wall that they would make it as soft as baked apples.'[42]

When she refused to budge, Cromwell wrote disparagingly to her, 'I think you the most obstinate woman that ever was, and I dare not open my lips to name you unless…you repent your ingratitude and are ready to do your duty. I have therefore sent you a book of articles to subscribe.'[43]

Once again Mary decided to appeal directly to her father, telling him she would 'submit to him in all things next to God, humbly beseeching your highness to consider that I am but a woman, and your child, who hath committed her soul only to God, and her body to be ordered in this world as it shall stand with your pleasure.'[44] It was a plea of desperation. And predictably it failed.

The heightened psychological pressure added a catalogue of neuralgia, insomnia and toothache to Mary's menstrual complaints, which now included amenorrhoea (absent periods) caused by stress.[45] Soon she could bear the strain no longer. After taking counsel from the Spanish ambassador, who advised her that a concession made under compulsion could never be binding in conscience and that the pope would forgive her, she capitulated on 22 June, signing the articles without even reading them.[46]

◆　　◆　　◆

Fitzroy, by comparison, quietly prospered after Anne's execution, securing a grant of her luxurious riverside property, Baynard's Castle, off Thames Street, as his London home, together with such lucrative sinecures as the posts of Warden of the Cinque Ports and Constable of Dover Castle.[47]

Then tragedy struck him down too. On or about 8 July, he was diagnosed with an illness strongly resembling severe bronchial pneumonia, leading to pleural empyema.[48] Within a few days, he would have gone down with a recurring fever and chest pains, before regularly coughing up sputum that had a foul smell, quickly suffering the fatal infection of the lungs and other organs, such as the kidneys, accompanied by severe weight loss.

The verdict of his physicians was that he still had a few weeks to live.[49] That proved highly optimistic, since on the 23rd, the teenager died in his privy apartments at St James's Palace. Since he weakened so rapidly, some said he had been poisoned. More likely, his lungs or kidneys failed.[50]

Henry's reaction is open to question, but the Duke of Norfolk, who was given the responsibility of arranging the funeral but was afterwards rebuked by the king for giving his son a dishonourable burial, was quite clear. His instructions had been to take care that the body was secretly interred at some distance from the capital.

As the duke confided to Cromwell, 'The king's pleasure was that his body should be conveyed secretly in a close[d] cart unto Thetford [in Norfolk]... and there so buried.'[51]

Henry, it appears, had at first not wanted it generally known that he seemed unable to father a living son. Later, when second thoughts prevailed, Norfolk was the casualty of the king's indecision. It was said he was to be sent to the Tower for allowing Fitzroy's body to be wrapped in cloth rather than sealed in a lead coffin. At this, the duke was incredulous, exclaiming, 'When I shall deserve to be there, Tottenham shall turn French!'[52]

FIGURE 8   The tomb of Henry Fitzroy, originally at Thetford Priory in Norfolk, and moved after the priory's dissolution to the Church of St Michael, Framlingham, Suffolk.

But Henry, despite his rumblings of dissatisfaction, made no redress to his son. Provision of a suitable tomb was again left entirely to Norfolk, who constructed a remarkable and costly monument at Thetford Priory, replete with Italian classical motifs, that was clumsily moved after the dissolution of the priory to Framlingham Church, some forty miles away (see Figure 8).[53]

◆   ◆   ◆

Mary's reconciliation with her father became complete when she wrote ecstatically (if optimistically) to him, 'I will never vary from that confession and submission I made to your highness.' And she prayed God that he and Jane would shortly be blessed with a son.[54] As her own gesture of conciliation, Jane had already taken the prudent step of writing affectionately to her stepdaughter. Mary thanked her warmly for a letter she found 'no less full of motherly joy for my towardness of reconciliation than of most prudent counsel for my further proceeding therein.'[55]

On 6 July, Henry and Jane visited Hunsdon, staying there for three full days. Her father treated Mary with much of his old affection, 'continually talking with her'. Jane presented her with a diamond, and Henry threw in a bag of gold and silver coins, 'telling her to have no anxiety about money, for she should have as much as she could wish.'[56] This was the prelude to the reorganization of the joint household, which was now restructured so as to have two separate 'sides'—one each for the two half-sisters, and each with its own separate staff.

Mary's side, as befitted her seniority, was the larger and more lavishly equipped. Some forty-two servants were appointed, including four gentlewomen, four gentlemen, two chamberers, a physician and a chaplain. Among these gentlewomen were two who would come to rank among Mary's closest friends and remain with her for the rest of her life: Susan Tonge (Mrs Clarencius), a young widow, and Frances Baynham, who married Sir Henry Jerningham.[57] While not on the scale of the princely household that the king's elder daughter had been allocated by Wolsey in 1525, it dwarfed Elizabeth's establishment, which was cut back to as little as seventeen servants.[58]

The disparity inevitably provoked more friction. Lady Bryan, Elizabeth's governess, began quarrelling with Sir John Shelton over how the household's meagre budget of £4,000 a year should be redistributed. A redoubtable woman, she wrote very forcefully to Cromwell in August to make quite sure that she had understood the new arrangements correctly and to air her grievances.[59]

Bryan was especially indignant at the fresh economies she was expected to make. She protested that, with Elizabeth growing fast, no suitable garments were available that would fit a 3-year-old, and there was no one to turn to. Sir John, she complained, was throwing his weight about, calling himself 'master of this house'. 'What fashion that shall be', she fumed, 'I cannot tell, for I have not seen it before'.

Shelton had objected to Elizabeth eating apart from the main household on grounds of cost, insisting that she leave her chamber at mealtimes and dine in the great hall at the 'board of estate'. Bryan deemed it inappropriate for a child still so young to eat there. Dietary concerns apart, it would be impossible to stop her snatching 'divers meats, fruits and wine' that would be readily at hand, 'which would be hard for me to refrain her grace from'. Elizabeth was 'too young to correct [i.e. chastise] greatly', not least because she was teething. Her sore mouth meant that Bryan felt obliged to allow her to have her own way more often than she usually did.[60]

Cromwell knew a determined woman when he saw one. Bryan was victorious, after which comparative harmony prevailed for over a year.[61] This, not least, was because Mary, for several months at a time, now left the cloistered environment of Hunsdon and Hatfield to rejoin her father and stepmother at Court. Jane purposely went out of her way to be kind to her, inviting her to spend Christmas at Greenwich Palace with them, and in 1537 to accompany them on their summer progress, when they slowly wound their way from Hampton Court to Woking and Guildford, and from there to Easthampsted in Berkshire, before returning to Windsor Castle.[62]

With much of her old relationship with her father rebuilt, Mary visibly mellowed. To Jane she sent cucumbers, knowing how much she adored them. She even found it within herself to be kinder to Elizabeth, praising her in a letter to her father as 'such a child toward, as I doubt not, but your highness shall have cause to rejoice of in time coming, as knoweth Almighty God.'[63]

By the time the Court reached Windsor, Jane was seven months pregnant. On Friday, 12 October 1537, she gave birth to a son at Hampton Court, who was named Edward after Henry's distant ancestor, Edward III, through the Beaufort line. At the christening on the 15th in the newly redecorated Chapel Royal, Mary was godmother and the 4-year-old Elizabeth, carried in the procession by her step-uncle, Edward Seymour, bore the chrism.[64]

But on 23 October, the queen, who so far had shown no sign of postnatal complications, became ill from heavy bleeding. As the day passed, she rapidly worsened.[65] At 8 p.m. on the 24th, after she was given the last rites, the Duke of Norfolk scribbled a note to

Cromwell, summoning him to Hampton Court. 'I pray you to be here tomorrow early to comfort our good master, for as for our mistress, there is no likelihood of her life, the more pity.'[66]

Jane died during the night and was buried in state at Windsor.[67] But the infant flourished, and with Henry's legitimate male heir safely in the nursery, the spotlight was off his daughters.

◆　◆　◆

The Court spent Christmas in mourning for the queen, but its normal routine was restored by the spring, when the joint household of Mary and Elizabeth was further reorganized. The Sheltons were replaced by Lady Kingston, wife of Sir William Kingston, who had carried Mary's train at Edward's baptism and was one of her favourites.[68] But the arrangement was temporary, since a year later Kingston was supplanted by Sir Edward and Lady Baynton.[69]

For Elizabeth, the major change was Lady Bryan's transfer to serve as Edward's governess in an independent princely household, up and running at Hampton Court in March 1538.[70] In addition, senior male officers were appointed from the very outset, such was the child's dynastic importance. Sir William Sidney was made chamberlain, Richard Cox (soon to be the boy's almoner and later Dean of Christ Church, Oxford) was the tutor and Sir John Cornwallis was the steward.[71]

Elizabeth's replacement governess was Blanche Herbert, Lady Troy, widow of Sir William Herbert of Troy Parva, who had once welcomed Henry VII to his house.[72] To assist Troy, Cromwell appointed four gentlewomen, three gentlemen, two chamberers and a chaplain.[73] One of these gentlewomen was Katherine Champernowne, nicknamed 'Kat', who in or about 1545 would marry

John Ashley, Elizabeth's second cousin* and a gentleman waiter in Prince Edward's household, who would teach the boy to play the virginals when he was older. Another was Blanche Parry, whom her aunt, Lady Troy, had nominated.[74] Both Kat and Blanche would stay with Elizabeth for the rest of their lives and each, in turn, would become her principal gentlewoman after her accession to the throne.

After Jane Seymour's death, the relationship between the Court, the prince's household and the joint household was relatively porous.[75] Mary was sometimes with Elizabeth in Hertfordshire, but more often at Court or visiting her brother at his nursery in her capacity as godmother, spoiling him with presents. Elizabeth spent most of her time in Hertfordshire, but made a number of visits to Hampton Court, Greenwich and Richmond.[76] As New Year's gifts to their half-brother in 1539, Mary sent 'a coat of crimson satin embroidered' and Elizabeth 'a shirt of cambric [i.e. fine linen] of her own working'.[77]

❖　❖　❖

At Court, the following year, there were further momentous changes. To win European allies against the pope, Henry married Anne of Cleves in January 1540, but was a distinctly reluctant bridegroom. Anne, as Cromwell—the architect of the Cleves alliance—had been keen to reassure him, possessed a 'queenly manner', but that was not what Henry was looking for. 'Alas, whom should men trust?' the king complained. 'I promise you, I see no such thing in her as hath been showed unto me of her,

---

* Ashley's aunt, Lady Elizabeth Boleyn (née Wood), was also Anne Boleyn's aunt.

and am ashamed that men hath praised her as they have done, and I like her not.'[78]

After carefully feeling Anne's 'belly and breasts' on his wedding night, Henry decided that 'she was no maid'. He claimed he was 'struck to the heart, and left her as good a maid as he found her.'[79] He admitted to having a couple of shots at consummation over the ensuing weeks, but when he failed ignominiously, Cranmer annulled the match. And when the Duke of Norfolk triumphantly produced irrefutable evidence that Cromwell was a closet Lutheran who had encouraged iconoclasm and sheltered a secret cell of radical Protestants at Calais, Henry had his second chief minister convicted of high treason and heresy by Parliament, then executed.

The king then married the duke's niece, Katherine Howard, a girl barely out of her teens, but after eighteen months of ecstasy, he caught her out enjoying secret assignations with an old flame. In February 1542, she was executed for adultery, after which Henry chose Katherine Parr, widow of John Neville, Lord Latimer, as his sixth and final queen.

The wedding took place in the queen's oratory at Hampton Court on 12 July 1543 with Mary and Elizabeth prominent among the guests.[80] Mary was now 27, and within a month, her father decided that she should be 'retained with the queen, who shows her all affection'.[81] With Henry's marriage to Katherine Parr, his elder daughter thus finally managed to escape from the humiliating constraints placed upon her by Anne Boleyn and was allowed to live permanently at Court.

Elizabeth, already 9, was sent to join Edward's household along with Lady Troy, Kat Champernowne and Blanche Parry.[82] She was still provided with a separate 'side' and kept her chamber servants, but her establishment was redesigned largely to function as a satellite of Edward's. Or at least it was in theory. For the two 'sides' were often physically apart. After Henry's wedding to Katherine Parr, Edward spent several months at Ampthill in Bedfordshire or Ashridge on the Hertfordshire–Buckinghamshire border, while Elizabeth lodged at Hatfield or Enfield.[83] Generally the two 'sides' moved about the country more or less in tandem, but they were not always in the same place.

Then, in July 1544, Edward was summoned to Hampton Court to attend on Katherine, who was made regent while Henry led his armies in a full-scale invasion of France in a fresh alliance with Charles V.[84] It signalled the start of a new phase in all three children's lives.

CHAPTER 6

Ruling from the Grave

W HEN Henry married Katherine Parr, he was 52 and beginning to deteriorate physically. Overweight and sometimes walking with a staff, his chest had ballooned to fifty-two inches and his waist to forty-nine.[1] An ulcer on his left leg (eventually on both legs)—possibly the result of varicose veins, more likely of chronic osteomyelitis, a septic infection of the bone caused by the injuries he had sustained from hunting or jousting—gave him regular pain. He could be laid up in agony for up to twelve days, black in the face and barely able to speak, if the passageway in the skin through which the pus escaped closed up, obliging his physicians to cut open, cauterize and freshly bandage it.[2]

Contrary to legend, Henry never suffered from syphilis. His apothecary's accounts prove that the drugs administered to him did not include mercury, the basis of the standard treatment for venereal disease in his lifetime.[3] Rather it was gluttony, bad diet, and lack of exercise after he gave up jousting following his accident in 1536 that transformed Henry from an ebullient, statuesque athlete into a semi-mobile hulk.

His decrepitude has helped to fuel an image of his last queen as a middle-aged bluestocking. The Spanish ambassador described her as barren and less beautiful even than Anne of Cleves, but this was pure spite.[4]

No more than 31 when she married Henry, Katherine was vivacious and pretty, of middling height and with auburn hair and grey eyes. Had she not been sexually attractive, she would never have caught Henry's attention. And it is improbable that he would have married her if he had not believed her fecund, as he yearned for more sons.[5]

She already had a suitor—she was in love with Thomas Seymour, Queen Jane's younger brother, and he with her. As she would reassure him after Henry's death, 'As truly as God is God, my mind was fully bent, the other time I was at liberty, to marry you before any man I knew'.[6] But she realized at once that she must choose Henry when he made his move.

Katherine was not simply politic; she also had a mission: she was a convert to the evangelical reform movement and may have been one for a decade or more.[7] Well educated by her mother along the lines pioneered by Thomas More for his own daughters, she was familiar with a wide range of the writings of the continental religious reformers, which (like Anne Boleyn) she probably read in French.[8]

The trouble was that Henry—despite resoundingly rejecting the pope and having reservations about auricular confession and the priesthood—was himself still very much a Catholic in theology. In 1539, he had persuaded Parliament to pass an Act of Six Articles reasserting the primacy of the Catholic sacraments. More recently he had severely restricted who was allowed to read the English Bible.

Katherine therefore knew she would need to dissimulate. Unlike Anne Boleyn, she never lectured the king or spoke out of turn, skilfully cultivating the impression that all her opinions were subject to her husband's guidance. Although publishing some of her translations and writings while he was alive, she waited until after his death before allowing her friends to publish a penitential meditation, largely drawn from the Epistles of St Paul, that echoed the Lutheran doctrine of justification by faith alone, attacked the cult of saints and rejected as superstition beliefs or ceremonies not found in the Bible. Given the title *The Lamentation of a Sinner* when it finally appeared in print, the book was politically explosive, since one of its aims was to persuade Parliament to lift the restrictions Henry had imposed upon reading the vernacular Bible.[9]

But for all her caution not to cross the line, Katherine would come within a cat's whisker of being the victim of a Court conspiracy. Only a hastily snatched word of warning from one of Henry's physicians, followed by her own nimble footwork, saved her from the fate suffered by Anne Askew, an evangelical member of the queen's own circle, who was burned at the stake for heresy.[10]

And yet, Katherine was never narrow-minded or a killjoy. She adored shoes, ordering 250 pairs in less than two years in a range of colours including black, crimson, white and blue, many of them trimmed with gold. Mary bonded well with her despite their differences over religion. With a four-year age gap only between them, it was as if Katherine was the elder sister Mary never had. The two women shared an addiction to jewels and fine clothes, which they ordered liberally and in many cases from the same suppliers. French gowns were their favourites, especially when made from cloth of gold or silver, cloth of tissue, or pink, purple and crimson satin, preferably with flamboyant embroidered sleeves and square open necks filled in with high-collared silk partlets.[11]

Black was another favourite colour, and as long as Katherine dictated fashion, blackwork designs using naturalistic motifs, including trailing plants and flower patterns, were in vogue.[12] But rarely were these flashy enough for Mary. She wanted her black satin or velvet gowns to be embroidered with diamonds and pearls and the most delicate passementerie of gold and silver thread. Her dresses must literally sparkle. She notably hoarded pairs of Spanish leather gloves, which were imported by the dozen.[13]

A patron of up to half a dozen artists and miniaturists, Katherine posed for a full-length portrait of herself from 'Master John' in which she wore a sensational French gown trimmed with the fur of sables and lynxes and in which she showed off a spectacular crowned brooch with three pendant pearls (see Plate 2). And where she led, Mary followed, ordering a three-quarter-length portrait of herself from the same artist in which she wore cloth of gold.

◆　　◆　　◆

Before Henry left for the war in France on 12 July 1544, he got Parliament to enact a new succession settlement. The Third Act of Succession, passed in March, reinstated Mary and Elizabeth in the line of succession, although neither was formally legitimized. The Act determined that the succession would fall in turn, assuming the king had no more children, to Edward and his lawful heirs, Mary and her lawful heirs, and then Elizabeth, with the proviso that Henry might devise specific conditions for the succession of both his daughters by letters patent or in his last will and testament. Should either ignore the conditions relating to the terms under which she would be permitted to marry, she would forfeit her claim to the throne.[14]

To memorialize his daughters' restoration to the line of succession, Henry commissioned an unknown artist to make a family group portrait to hang at Hampton Court. The original idea could well have been Katherine's. If so, it was a brilliant one, an echo on a much smaller, more intimate scale of a massive dynastic fresco that Henry had himself commissioned in 1537 from Hans Holbein the Younger for his Privy Chamber at Whitehall, but this time including the king's children whom the earlier mural had omitted.

Besides a sophisticated understanding of the power of art, however, Katherine also had the wisdom to realize that in Henry's eyes it would always be Edward's mother, Queen Jane, rather than herself, whom he would regard as the matriarch of the dynasty. It was not simply from a cultural debt to Holbein's fresco that the new painting showed the king seated in majesty on his throne with his right arm on Edward's shoulder, with Mary and Elizabeth standing, one on each side, at an appropriate distance, but with Jane Seymour instead of Katherine sitting by his side.

No longer was Elizabeth tainted by the catastrophic events that had destroyed her mother. Some historians have tried to argue the opposite—that, far from being rehabilitated, she had been 'exiled' by her father, or at the very least forgotten.[15] The point turns on a letter to Katherine written on 31 July 1544 in which the 10-year-old Elizabeth appears to complain that she has neither seen her stepmother since the day of her father's wedding nor has she 'dared' to write to Henry, 'for which at present I humbly entreat your most excellent highness that in writing to His Majesty, you will deign to recommend me to him.' 'In this my exile', she continues, 'I surely know that your highness's clemency has had as much care and solicitude for my health as the King's Majesty would have done.'[16]

But the letter was not sent from Hertfordshire where a Cinderella figure might plausibly have been quarantined, but from St James's Palace.[17] Elizabeth was there because Henry had invited all three of his children to a dinner at Whitehall on the eve of his departure for France.[18] Spacious as the king's principal palace was, there was not room to house everyone and their servants within its precincts, but St James's was less than a mile away across the park. The queen herself lodged there sometimes.[19] In any case, Katherine must have been in contact with Elizabeth by messenger a week before the so-called 'exile' letter was written, since she reassured Henry on 25 July that all his children were in good health.[20]

Elizabeth's letter said that she looked forward to being with her 'illustrious' stepmother soon.[21] This was not backhanded. All three siblings would shortly rendezvous with Katherine at Hampton Court. Edward was sent there first with his independent 'side', occupying a newly refurbished Prince's Lodging in a different wing of the palace to Katherine's own, but one which was connected to the royal apartments by a long gallery.[22] Katherine and Mary came next by barge.[23] Finally, Elizabeth was brought from St James's.

Again in September, Katherine was accompanied by all three children when she took the Court on a miniature royal progress through the forests of Surrey to avoid the plague in and around the capital. And on 3 October, everyone was together at Leeds Castle in Kent to greet the king on his return from France, triumphant after the capture of Boulogne.[24]

•   •   •

Further changes were made in Edward's household during 1544. With the prince approaching 7—the age at which protocol dictated that he should be treated as a young adult—Lady Bryan and her female assistants were discharged. Richard Page, who had invaluable experience as Fitzroy's former vice-chamberlain, was brought in to replace Sir William Sidney as head of the enlarged establishment, while Sidney took over as steward.[25]

So far, the prince had been taught to read and write in English by Richard Cox. As part of the latest reorganization, John Cheke, an inspirational teacher from St John's College, Cambridge, was put in overall charge of the prince's studies. Cox was given the post of almoner, but retained chiefly as the prince's grammar coach. A year or so later, a Frenchman, John Belmain, a Calvinist refugee and Cheke's nephew by marriage, was brought in to teach the boy French.[26] Now Edward's education could commence in earnest.

On the principles recommended earlier by Vives, companions of roughly the prince's own age were recruited to join him in the schoolroom. They included Henry Brandon, the eldest son of Charles Brandon, duke of Suffolk, by his fourth marriage to the 14-year-old Katherine Willoughby. Two years older than Edward, Brandon was the same age as Barnaby Fitzpatrick, heir to the barony of Upper Ossory in Ireland, another of the recruits. Sent to live at Henry's Court as proof of his father's loyalty to the king, Fitzpatrick would soon become Edward's closest friend.[27]

One of the great myths about Fitzpatrick is that he was the prince's 'whipping boy', the unlucky recipient of the corporal punishment Edward would otherwise have received when he refused to do his lessons had he not been the heir to the throne.[28] The story is romantic fiction, since Cox shared none of the timidity of Fitzroy's schoolmasters. When in December 1544, the frustrated tutor found his pupil bored, sulking and intractable, he gave him a final warning, and then, 'I took my morris pike [i.e. staff used for morris dancing] and at will I went and gave him such a wound that he wist [knew] not what to do....Me thought it [was] the luckiest day that ever I had in battle.'[29]

Over the next two years, Edward settled down to reading Cato's *Moral Precepts* and Aesop's *Fables*, using the Latin editions rather than Caxton's translations. Guided by Cheke, he turned next to Erasmus's *Colloquies*, intermingled with a variety of biblical texts and the writings of Vives. By Christmas 1546, he was poised to embark on more advanced authors such as Cicero, Livy, Pliny the Younger and the Latin translations of dialogues from Lucian. He did not begin Greek yet—his first serious foray into that language was not until 1548, when he was reading the second oration of Isocrates to Nicocles.[30] But he made progress in written French.[31] Spoken French he found more challenging. When introduced to the French ambassador in February 1547, he spoke in Latin, 'because he does not yet understand French very well and has only just begun to learn it.'[32]

◆　◆　◆

Elizabeth was 11 before her father woke up to the need to equip her with a schoolmaster. Until then, Kat Champernowne had taught her, doing it so successfully that when, in late 1539, Cromwell's secretary and man of business Thomas Wriothesley had visited her at Hertford Castle, he found she could converse 'with as great gravity as [if] she had been forty years old'.[33]

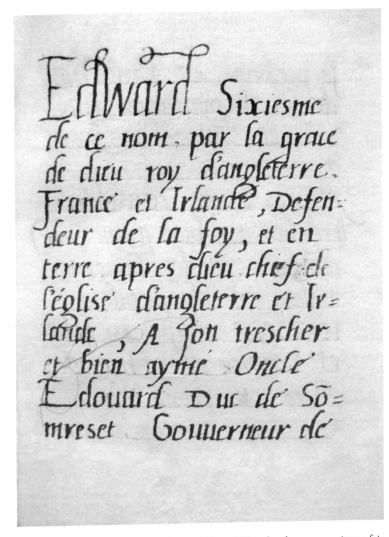

FIGURE 9 The opening page of one of Edward VI's schoolroom exercises, a fair copy of a treatise in French against the papal supremacy, written in a fashionably bold, if somewhat clumsy, italic script, and done chiefly during the winter of 1548–9. The young king addresses the work to his elder uncle, Edward Seymour, Protector Somerset.

But someone else must have been teaching her unofficially, since she could manage an italic hand by the time she wrote the so-called 'exile' letter to her stepmother. Kat, although an educated woman, wrote all her life using an old-fashioned, cursive style of penmanship.

The explanation lies with Kat's brother-in-law, Sir Anthony Denny, one of the king's Privy Chamber intimates. It was Denny who had recommended John Cheke to Henry as Edward's principal schoolmaster, and he had almost certainly sent John Picton to help Kat with Elizabeth. Besides an italic hand, 'Master' Picton must also have begun teaching the young girl Italian, because her 'exile' letter was written in that language throughout. This also fits, since several of Denny's closest friends, notably Philip Hoby and his brother Thomas, were fluent Italianists.

Denny, who would shortly rise to the position of chief gentleman of the Privy Chamber, was the keeper of Hatfield manor and had a house in the grounds as well as at Cheshunt nearby. He stood at the hub of a network of evangelical friends who were fervently committed to the idea of moderate religious reform along Protestant lines. They included Henry's chief physician, William Butts, another of the king's doctors Thomas Wendy, Thomas Cawarden and Richard Moryson. Both Cawarden and Moryson were gentlemen of the Privy Chamber planted there by Cromwell shortly before his fall. Their patronage links ran deep into the universities, chiefly Cambridge. As with Katherine Parr, discretion was their watchword, for if Henry had appreciated the full extent of their susceptibility to Protestantism, he would have savagely reined them in.

Born into a Hertfordshire gentry family in 1501, Denny had first studied under a legendary grammarian, William Lily, at St Paul's

School before progressing to St John's College. Butts was a Norfolk man who had attended Gonville and Caius College, barely a hundred yards from St John's, where he had stayed until he married a gentlewoman in Mary's household and was summoned to Court as a royal physician. For twenty years he had been a patron of preachers and scholars with links to Cromwell and Cranmer, acclaimed by his admirers as 'Maecenas' and 'master'.[34]

A Fellow of Denny's college and a client of Butts, John Cheke had made his name at Cambridge as another leading champion of the Renaissance and its values by devising a new system for pronouncing classical Greek that for the first time made it fully intelligible. The trail does not end there, because Cheke was Roger Ascham's tutor, a rising star among the new intellectual elite whom Thomas More's eldest daughter, Margaret, had attempted in vain to recruit as a tutor for her own children.[35]

Before long, Ascham would be lobbying to secure an appointment for himself as Elizabeth's schoolmaster, which he believed would guarantee his position in the pantheon of scholars. But at first, Cheke selected a younger man, one of Ascham's own pupils, William Grindal, whose appointment Henry confirmed in October 1544.[36]

By then, the king had returned from France. On his homecoming, his two younger children's households were once more detached from Katherine Parr's and sent back to Hertfordshire. Circling in an orbit based on Ashridge, Hatfield, Hertford and Hunsdon, Elizabeth's establishment became a satellite of her half-brother's in reality rather than just in theory, and would remain so until Henry's death.[37] It was Mary, now almost thirty, who stayed largely at Court, where she and the queen continued to draw down prodigious quantities of fabric from the Whitehall silk store.[38]

Edward did his best to keep in touch with his elder sister, writing her letters and regularly exchanging gifts and other small tokens of affection.[39] But although Mary regularly returned gifts, including a clock, she rarely wrote him letters. To Elizabeth she did not write at all.

Under Grindal's direction, Elizabeth advanced by leaps and bounds, getting to grips with Latin and starting on Greek.[40] She also became fluent in French, taught by Belmain—a teacher she shared with Edward—and was continuing her Italian, most likely now as a pupil of Giovanni Battista Castiglione, who had fought with Henry's troops in France in 1544 and returned with them to England.[41]

But Henry never allowed his youngest daughter to stray far from the limits Vives had set for her half-sister when he had urged that she should hear and speak only 'what pertains to the fear of God'. The purpose of educating a woman, the king still believed, was to increase her feminine virtue, not to equip her to rule, which was to be her brother's work. This explains why the tasks her tutors set for her—rather than original compositions or extempore speeches—were translations of texts to be given as New Year's gifts to her father, stepmother, and half-brother.

Of these translations, the most proficient is of a mystical religious poem, *The Mirror or Glass of the Sinful Soul* by Margaret of Angoulême, the devoutly evangelical sister of Francis I. Elizabeth turned the poem, a meditation by a tormented sinner on the nature of God's redemptive love, into English prose for her stepmother as a New Year's gift for 1545, sending it with a letter and an elaborate needlework cover embroidered by herself.[42]

Since the original poem includes metaphors of love, spiritual and physical, that to modern ears can appear to border on the incestuous, it is sometimes said that Elizabeth's choice of copy text reflects a congenital distaste for matrimony on her part. In reality, little was unusual about her selection. Her great-grandmother, Margaret Beaufort, had translated an equally disturbing text on the filthiness and misery of human beings and the joys of Paradise entitled *The Mirror of Gold for the Sinful Soul*.[43] The aim was to combine training in translation with a religious exercise on a penitential theme. Texts of this nature were routinely given as exercises to young aristocratic women. Elizabeth's choice does not necessarily imply anything about her personal opinions.

◆   ◆   ◆

Henry died in the early hours of Friday, 28 January 1547, leaving a will that reaffirmed the terms of the Third Act of Succession and made the inheritance of Mary and Elizabeth strictly conditional. Each would be excluded from the throne if she married without the 'assent and consent' of those privy councillors he had now named, or as many of them as were still living.[44]

The dying king had never shaken off his conviction that females in the succession were a dangerous risk.[45] He spelled out what was to happen if either of his daughters married without permission— she would lose her place. And if both were disqualified, then the throne would pass, in turn, to the heirs of his nieces, the Ladies Frances and Eleanor Brandon, the daughters of his younger sister, Mary, who had been Charles Brandon, Duke of Suffolk's third wife.[46]

Henry appointed sixteen privy councillors to govern in his son's name until he was 18. Twelve other individuals were to assist and be 'of counsel' to them. The copious amount of small print explaining precisely how this arrangement was meant to work, ensuring stability and a political consensus during the years of Edward's minority, shows just how far Henry was attempting to rule from beyond the grave.

The will made no provision for the appointment of a single person to act as a Lord Protector, quite the opposite. Since, however, Henry entrusted his will to the safekeeping of his erstwhile brother-in-law, Edward Seymour, he was clearly someone whom the old king expected to exercise leadership in the new reign.[47]

Many of Henry's wishes would quickly be set aside. Edward Seymour, although created Duke of Somerset and given a generous grant of lands, was dissatisfied. On 12 March, he broke the will after a series of backstairs manoeuvres masterminded by his ally Sir William Paget. By a menacing combination of inducements and threats, a majority of Edward's new councillors were inveigled into making Somerset Lord Protector and Governor of the King's Person. A grant of letters patent gave the duke near-sovereign powers as regent until Edward was 18.[48]

◆　　◆　　◆

Over the next two years, Somerset would succeed in alienating the very same men whom Henry had tried to shape into a consensus.[49] His fellow privy councillors envisaged that, as Protector, the duke would consult them about key policy decisions and not attempt to govern as if he were himself the king. Instead, he made critical decisions about entering into wars with Scotland and France, about domestic security and the economy in England and Ireland, and about the advance of the Protestant Reformation in ways that his fellow councillors considered to be arbitrary and ill-informed.

But Somerset's nemesis was his younger brother, Thomas Seymour, who jealously coveted the post of Governor of the

King's Person.[50] Although made Lord Admiral and given a barony as Lord Seymour of Sudeley, Seymour was not so easily bought off. Handsome, dashing and reckless, his consuming ambition made him a highly disruptive force.[51]

Aiming at nothing less than to control the king and bind himself into the royal family, Seymour sought first to persuade his brother to allow him to marry Mary.[52] When he was rebuffed, he began to milk his Court connections ruthlessly. A gentleman of the king's Privy Chamber and on familiar terms with John Cheke and several of Edward's body servants, he had the potential to cause dissension from the outset. He even had a duplicate key to every door in the palace of Whitehall.[53]

Seymour set about suborning the young king, telling him that 'Ye are a beggarly king, ye have no money to play or to give' and sending him tidy sums with which to supplement the meagre allocations to his privy purse.[54] This clearly struck a chord with Edward. As he ruefully reflected, 'My uncle of Somerset dealeth very hardly with me and keepeth me so straight that I cannot have money at my will, but my Lord Admiral both sends me money and gives me money.'[55]

Seymour's ace of trumps was his relationship with Katherine Parr. With unseemly haste, he paid court to the Dowager Queen, who was soon admitting him to her Presence Chamber every morning at 7 a.m. at her dower houses at Chelsea and Hanworth in Middlesex. He also put out feelers to Edward and Mary, seeking their goodwill towards the marriage.

Mary was no longer at Court. She had been granted lands in Norfolk, Suffolk and Essex worth £3,000 a year together with the royal manors of Hunsdon and New Hall as part of the settlement of her father's will and was living mainly at New Hall.[56] Her reaction to what she disparagingly called Seymour's 'strange news' was cold. It was surely up to Katherine to decide, she replied. Her own opinion hardly mattered. But 'if the remembrance of the King's Majesty my father (whose soul God pardon) will not suffer her to grant your suit, I am nothing able to persuade her to forget the loss of him, who is as yet very ripe in my own remembrance.'[57]

Edward did write a letter of encouragement to Katherine, which, if read at face value, makes it appear that he had personally instigated the proposed marriage. Except it turns out that the letter had all along been dictated by Seymour.[58]

Besides, by the time Edward's letter was sent out on 25 June 1547, the wedding had already taken place. Katherine was pregnant early in 1548, and it would not be long before Seymour would be chortling with delight at the news that 'my little man'—he, like the old king, was wholly confident of a son—had been felt 'shaking his head' in her womb.[59]

•   •   •

The true extent of Seymour's ambition was now revealed. A week before Somerset was sworn in as Lord Protector, Katherine had been granted custody of Elizabeth, who was brought by Kat Ashley—as she was known since her marriage—from Hatfield to Chelsea in the middle of March.[60] Despite the fact that Lady Troy was still technically in charge of Elizabeth's establishment,[61] Kat had somehow contrived to replace her as Elizabeth's governess shortly before the old king died.[62]

Katherine, Seymour and Kat were in cahoots, making it easy for Seymour to merge the two households, their staffs and budgets. It would not be much more than another year before Lady Troy, who thus far had been accustomed to sleep on a pallet in Elizabeth's bedchamber, was displaced and pensioned off, ostensibly on the grounds that the bedchamber at Chelsea was too small.[63] Blanche Parry briefly replaced her on the pallet, but was soon ousted from it by Kat, who 'could not abide to have nobody [sic] lie there, but only herself'.[64]

Not content with this, Seymour purchased the guardianship of Lady Jane Grey, the eldest surviving child of Frances Brandon and so the first residuary legatee to the throne by the terms of Henry's will. Jane's father, Henry Grey, Marquis of Dorset, agreed to the unusual bargain after Seymour promised him in almost as many words that the 10-year-old girl would one day marry Edward.[65]

But when Seymour moved in at Chelsea, he began flirting with Elizabeth, who was nearly 14 and sexually aware. This had not been part of the plan. As Kat later confessed under interrogation, with Lady Troy gone from the pallet, he would visit Elizabeth in her bedchamber early in the mornings, sometimes before she had risen or was dressed. 'And if she were up, he would bid her good morrow and ask how she did, and strike her upon the back or on the buttocks familiarly, and so go forth through his lodgings.... And if she were in her bed, he would open the curtains and bid her good morrow, and make as though he would come at her. And she would go further in the bed, so that he could not come at her.'[66]

When one morning he tried to kiss Elizabeth, Kat spotted him, and 'bade him go away for shame.' Katherine at first seemed to condone her husband's actions, perhaps considering them harmless or perhaps in a naive attempt to control them, since at Hanworth she twice came with him into the chamber early in the morning and they tickled Elizabeth in bed together. A notorious incident took place in the garden at Hanworth, when Katherine and Seymour frolicked with Elizabeth and 'cut her gown in[to] a hundred pieces, being black cloth'. Kat severely rebuked Elizabeth for this unseemly behaviour, but she answered, 'I could not do withal, for the queen held me while the Lord Admiral cut it.'[67]

Worse, the Dowager Queen later told Kat one day at Hanworth that Seymour had chanced to look in at a gallery window and seen Elizabeth with her arms around another man's neck. Kat was shocked. But who could this man be?[68]

Kat confronted Elizabeth, 'who denied it weeping'. Kat realized she was telling the truth, 'for there came no man, but Grindal.' The mention of Elizabeth's schoolmaster dates the episode to before the end of January 1548, when he died of the plague. Kat thought the incident proved that Katherine had become 'jealous' of the friendship between her husband and stepdaughter. She had 'feigned' the story, Kat surmised, to make sure that a closer watch was kept on Elizabeth.[69]

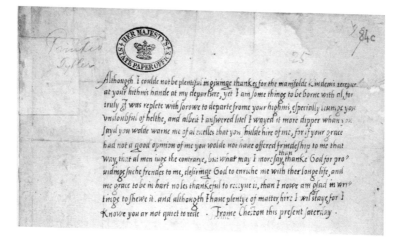

FIGURE 10   Elizabeth wrote this letter in her finest italic script to her stepmother, Katherine Parr, as soon as she arrived at Sir Anthony Denny's house at Cheshunt in May 1548, where she was sent to escape the scandal caused by rumours of her relationship with Sir Thomas Seymour.

Finally, Katherine, realizing the situation was fast slipping out of her control, sent Elizabeth away. The date has often been disputed, but Kat remembered it was in 'the week after Whitsuntide', i.e. the week beginning 20 May 1548.[70] The teenager was taken back to Hertfordshire under a cloud, not at first to Hatfield, but to Cheshunt where the Dennys lived. Arriving on a Saturday, Elizabeth wrote a letter to her stepmother in her finest italic hand (see Figure 10). At their parting, Katherine had warned her of the danger to her reputation. 'Truly I was replete with sorrow to depart from your highness', Elizabeth responded. 'And albeit I answered little, I weighed it more deeper when you said you would warn me of all evils that you should hear of me.'[71]

Katherine clearly feared a sex scandal could have lethal consequences. It had not helped that Seymour had insisted on riding with Elizabeth on the first stage of her journey from Chelsea in full public gaze.[72]

Whether Elizabeth had a teenage crush on Seymour is a secret she took with her to the grave. John Ashley warned his wife that 'the Lady Elizabeth did bear some affection to my Lord Admiral. For he did mark that when anybody did talk well of my Lord Admiral, she seemed to be well pleased therewith, and sometime she would blush when he were spoken of.'[73]

A month or so after Elizabeth's departure, Katherine herself left Chelsea, attended by Jane Grey, for her husband's castle of Sudeley in Gloucestershire. With the risk of plague still present, she wished to have her baby in the safety of the countryside. She gave birth to a healthy daughter on 30 August, but died of puerperal fever six days later despite her physician's strenuous efforts to save her life. The chief mourner at her funeral, the first Protestant royal funeral in English history, was Jane.

Now Seymour's ambition would be his undoing. He approached Thomas Parry, Elizabeth's cofferer (i.e. chief accountant), a broadfaced Welshman who had first been employed by Thomas Cromwell during the Dissolution of the Monasteries, with a view to finding out the extent of her wealth. Utterly unscrupulous, Seymour was also attempting to marry Mary even as he pitched his suit to marry Elizabeth.[74] As his Court agent, William Wightman, confided to one of Katherine Parr's cousins at Sudeley, his 'desire of a kingdom knoweth no kindred.'[75]

At 8 p.m. on Thursday, 17 January 1549, Seymour was arrested and the interrogations swiftly followed. Somerset sent two of Katherine Parr's most senior officials, Sir Robert Tyrwhit, her comptroller, and Sir Walter Buckler, her secretary, to take immediate control of Elizabeth's household. And he ordered Sir Robert, whose wife, one of Katherine's long-standing attendants, had firsthand knowledge of many of the incidents at Chelsea and Hanworth, to get to the truth.

Tyrwhit, however, despite repeated attempts to secure a confession, could not browbeat Elizabeth. She barracked him so successfully, he was forced to admire her pluck. 'I do assure your grace', he reported back to the Protector, 'she hath a very good wit, and nothing is gotten of her, but by great policy.'[76]

Kat Ashley and Parry were sent to the Tower, where they quickly babbled what they knew—or most of it. The crux was whether Elizabeth, advised by Kat, had entertained Seymour's suit. Tyrwhit was incensed by the answers he got to this question.[77] Elizabeth adamantly insisted that Kat had never urged her to marry Seymour after Katherine Parr's death—other, that is, than with the Council's consent. Tyrwhit knew that this was almost certainly a lie. But no one could be broken on the point. In her own interrogation,

Kat confessed that she had asked Elizabeth if she would marry Seymour now that he was free again. When she had replied 'Nay', Kat claimed to have gone on to say, 'I know you would not refuse him *if the Council would be content therein.*'[78] But all Elizabeth's servants used almost exactly the same phrase, chanting it like a mantra.[79] It seemed quite incredible that they were all experts on the precise wording of Henry's will.

Elizabeth survived along with her servants, including Kat, but she was a changed woman. It had been a searing experience, the moment she was thrust into adulthood. She was shocked by rumours that she was pregnant by Seymour and complained indignantly to Somerset. Such 'shameful slanders', she fumed, be 'greatly both against my honour and honesty, which above all other things I esteem.'[80]

Seymour was charged with plotting to seize Edward and take him 'into [his] own hands and custody' and with attempting to marry Elizabeth.[81] On 25 February, a bill of attainder was introduced into Parliament in which his offences were declared to be high treason. On 5 March, the bill passed and Seymour was executed on Tower Hill on the 20th.

What few had predicted was that Seymour's fall would become the prelude to the dismantling of the Protectorate itself. Increasingly loathed by his colleagues in the Privy Council for his autocratic methods, Somerset was unable to react quickly enough when confronted by a threatening run of popular 'stirs' and uprisings across the southern and eastern counties of England in the spring and summer of 1549. His dithering led to a coup. Articles of impeachment accused him of governing ineffectively and of failing to consult his colleagues, or else of summoning them only occasionally and 'for the name's sake' to rubber stamp decisions he had taken already.[82]

On 14 October he was sent to the Tower and the Protectorate was dissolved. Henry's attempt to build a consensus government for his young son from the grave had been a failure. His will had been subverted, but the Protectorate had failed largely because the ambition of Thomas Seymour had thrown the political system into crisis. Now the architects of the coup claimed that they would govern through the agreement of the Privy Council and with the support of the wider governing elite.

The wheel had turned full circle.

CHAPTER 7

Faith and Exclusion

THE cool intelligence behind the coup against Protector Somerset belonged to John Dudley, Earl of Warwick. A pragmatic realist who had risen to a dominant position in the Privy Council as a naval commander in Henry VIII's last wars, he wisely shunned the title of Protector, taking instead that of Lord President of the Council. His ally Thomas Wriothesley, once Thomas Cromwell's secretary and who had dipped a toe into the evangelical reform movement in the 1530s, led a faction of traditionalists staunchly opposed to the Protestants. But Wriothesley's appetite for intrigue made him dangerously unstable—Warwick did not trust him an inch. Nor did Mary, since when the conspirators against Somerset attempted to win her support by offering her the regency in his place, she brushed them aside, saying that she 'was sad to see the realm going to perdition so fast' and that 'no good will come of this move'.[1]

The thirty or so months after Somerset was sent to the Tower in October 1549 were among the most fraught and fragile since

Henry VII had won the crown at the battle of Bosworth. Warwick's own faith and interest firmly aligned him with the religious reformers, and early in February 1550 he was forced to purge Wriothesley from the Privy Council and banish him from Court for plotting against him.[2] His dilemma was that to do so, he had to free Somerset and allow him to return to the Council under stringent conditions, because if he was to marginalize and exclude Wriothesley's faction, he needed Somerset back on his side.

Wasting no time, Warwick made a largely successful effort to reverse the destabilization permitted, or left unchecked, by Somerset. He suppressed the 'stirs' and revolts of 1549 using a cohort of crack troops assisted by Italian and German mercenaries. Above all, he speedily began peace negotiations with France and Scotland to end Somerset's disastrous wars and put England's finances back on the slow road to recovery.

Warwick's fixer in conjuring a political consensus was Cranmer, Edward's godfather. As the man closest to the young king apart from John Cheke, the archbishop was in a position where he could pack the boy's Privy Chamber with Warwick's nominees. Cranmer's beliefs had by now moved well beyond Lutheranism and come closer to those of the mainstream of the Swiss reformers. And it was to this more radical version of the Reformation that Cranmer meant to convert the king.

Just as Henry VIII had been said to be a second King David or King Solomon or a second Emperor Constantine or Justinian, Edward was to be a second King Josiah. No more than a child of eight when he had succeeded to the throne, the Old Testament Josiah had purged Judah and Jerusalem of the 'carved images, and the molten images. And they brake down the altars of Baal in his presence' (2 Kings 22–23). It was in his reign that 'the book of the

FIGURE 11 A woodcut specially designed in 1570 for an enlarged edition of
John Foxe's *Acts and Monuments* (or 'Book of Martyrs') to illustrate the swing to
Protestantism in the reign of Edward VI, whom the Protestants hailed as a second
'King Josiah'.

law' had been rediscovered by the high priest of the temple at Jerusalem. But significantly, Josiah's attack on idolatry had been less
the work of the boy himself than of his 'godly councillors' acting in
his name. This was a lesson that Warwick and Cranmer would set
out to replicate, casting themselves and their fellow privy councillors in the role.

◆   ◆   ◆

Warwick and Cranmer did not begin entirely from scratch. Somerset in 1547–8 had already revived Cromwell's iconoclasm, authorizing the stripping of rood lofts and related statuary from the parish churches and repealing Henry VIII's Act of Six Articles. To Protestant acclaim, he also abolished the restrictions on who was allowed to read the English Bible. But his attempt in 1549 to impose, with Parliament's assent, 'one convenient and meet order, rite and fashion of Common Prayer' in the English language to replace the Latin mass was botched and proved extraordinarily divisive.

Lacking an officially defined theology of the Eucharist, Somerset's new liturgy was ambiguously traditional and failed to satisfy anyone. Its single achievement from the reformist perspective was to allow communion in both the bread and the wine. The Protector claimed that his approach was bipartisan, but in reality he sought to appease Mary's cousin, Charles V, whose neutrality towards England he wished to guarantee whilst the country was at war with Scotland and France.[3]

When, early in 1550, Wriothesley had begun plotting against Warwick, he aimed to reverse the Reformation if he could. After that brush with danger, Warwick meant to exclude the traditionalists from power by placing as many Protestants as possible in influential positions. Soon he would even risk antagonizing Cranmer by appointing the aggressively advanced reformer John Hooper to the bishopric of Gloucester and the fiery Scottish preacher John Knox to be one of Edward's chaplains. Both attacked what they believed to be Cranmer's timidity and moderation, especially over reforming the ceremonies of the Church and the dress of the clergy.

Warwick, meanwhile, unleashed Cranmer to overhaul the liturgy that Somerset had botched. A large number of Protestant refugees were arriving in London during Edward's reign after Charles's victory over the forces of the Schmalkaldic League at the battle of Mühlberg in 1547. For the very first time, England was regarded as a safe haven for the reformers, several of whom such as Peter Martyr Vermigli and Martin Bucer were Cranmer's friends and to whom he gave important preaching or teaching positions in the Church and universities.[4]

In this volatile, intoxicating atmosphere, Cranmer and his continental friends in 1551 began discussing a template for a fully reformed theology of the Eucharist. The debate, rooted in a theological compromise reached in 1549 between the church leaders of

FIGURE 12   A woodcut illustrating a government-sponsored Protestant sermon delivered by Hugh Latimer from the 'preaching place' at Whitehall Palace. The young king and his councillors can be seen listening through open windows on the upper left-hand side of the image.

Zürich and Geneva known as the *Consensus Tigurinus*, broadened out to include reformist courtiers and their opponents. In October and November 1551, they thrashed out their differences at the London houses of William Cecil and Richard Moryson, leading in 1552 to a second Book of Common Prayer. Cutting to the quick of the theological debates, this version affirmed Christ's spiritual presence in the Eucharist only to the elect believer, so was unambiguously Protestant. Despite some inevitable qualms and hesitations, Parliament then declared this revision to be the only permissible liturgy in the realm.[5]

◆ ◆ ◆

Mary put up a barrage of resistance to these religions innovations, holding multiple masses daily in her household and saying she would rather give up her life than her Catholic faith.[6] Acting in ways seen as deliberately subversive, she repeatedly challenged the Privy Council's authority, seeking advice from Charles V's ambassador and writing to entreat her cousin to help her to flee abroad or at the very least to intervene on her behalf so that she could continue to 'live in the ancient faith and in peace with my conscience.'[7]

Even before Warwick's coup against Somerset, Mary was holding up to four masses daily in her household to make her point and allowing passers-by to attend.[8] The Privy Council, divided over how to react, offered her a licence to hear mass daily without interference, provided it was done unobtrusively with only a few servants present. But she kept on insisting that the licence be put in writing, which the councillors refused.[9]

After the coup, Mary increased the number of chaplains she employed to six.[10] She was determined to flaunt her nonconformity.

Now she celebrated her masses with 'greater show' than before and provocatively invited as many visitors as wished to attend, even when she was not at home.[11]

Challenged by the Privy Council, Mary appealed to her conscience, including arguments similar to those she had tried before when her father demanded that she recognize his marriage to Anne Boleyn and the Acts of Supremacy and Succession. It was 'no small grief' to her, one of her more defiant letters to the Council began, to see how men whom her father had raised up from nothing 'and at his last end put in trust to see his will performed' had so casually broken it. She was, she said, most heinously affronted by the 'usurped power' these councillors had arrogated to themselves 'in making (as they call it) laws both clean contrary to his [Henry's] proceedings and will, and also against the custom of all Christendom and (in my conscience) against the law of God and his Church.'

Faced by such flagrant apostasy, she would, she said, remain 'an obedient child' to her father and his laws, at least until her brother was old enough 'to be a judge in these matters himself.'

'I do not a little marvel', she concluded, 'that you can find fault with me for observing of that law which was allowed by him that was a king not only of power, but also of knowledge how to order his power.'[12]

In a futile effort to intimidate her, the Council summoned the head officers of her household, demanding that she should be compelled to conform.[13] She indignantly protested, retorting that she was 'mistress in her own house'. No longer a child under a governess, she was a grown-up woman with a substantial landed estate in her own right. The councillors were 'not to meddle with religion or her conscience'.[14]

Already Warwick had misgivings about the lands Somerset had given her in May 1548 on discovering that the £3,000 a year she had been left in her father's will was unaffordable in cash. Warwick feared that Mary was using her estates to build up an East Anglian power base that drew its strength from regional and family connections and was united by its Catholic allegiance. He was convinced that she meant to create a bastion of resistance to Protestantism.[15]

Keeping a close watch on these events, Mary's cousin Charles feared the consequences if she decided to launch a one-woman crusade against the regime. In a confidential memo dictated at Augsburg in Bavaria and dated 17 March 1551, he urged his English ambassador to tell her straight that if the Council allowed her to 'hear mass privately in her own house, without admitting any strangers', she should 'be satisfied with that'. Charles saw the danger of a spectacular collision with a ruthless regime determined to stay in power. For that reason, Mary should avoid hectoring language 'and not push her arguments.' She should know when to speak, and when to keep silent.[16]

Charles, a ruler possessed of a wealth of experience in the ways of the world, foresaw that before long Warwick would succeed in drawing Mary into a showdown with her half-brother that would be staged to make it appear that she was set on defying the king and so was a traitor, a move that would turn her rhetoric of 'obedience' to her father's will on its head.

An attempt to do exactly that the previous January had misfired. While putting her case for her right to hear mass to Edward, Mary had burst into tears, causing him to do the same. Then, when their tears were dry, Edward (as Mary reported) said 'he thought no harm of me'. On hearing this, one of Warwick's henchmen had brought the conversation to an abrupt close. The carefully scripted lines that Edward had been coached in beforehand had to be sent to Mary afterwards in a letter.[17]

At a second interview at Whitehall on 17 March, as chance would have it even as Charles was dictating his memo, Warwick was better prepared. Mary, for her part, set out to be as combative as possible. Riding into London on the 15th in readiness for the meeting, she clattered through the streets with a retinue of fifty knights and gentlemen wearing velvet coats and gold livery chains, followed by eighty gentlemen and ladies, every one of whom sported a black rosary as they rode down Cheapside and past Smithfield on their way to lodge at Mary's London home in Clerkenwell.[18]

When the interview began, Edward—according to Mary's version—delivered a halting speech reminding her of the Council's instructions, to which she responded by acknowledging that she had defied them. At this, an unnamed councillor stepped forward. The king's will, he informed her, was that she should no longer practise the old religion. The argument went furiously to and fro, until Mary suddenly snapped and turned to Edward, saying 'Riper age and experience will teach you much more yet.'

He sharply rejoined, 'You also might have something to learn, for no one is too old for that.'

When the councillors ordered Mary to cease her defiance, she icily replied that she had carefully read her father's will and was bound to obedience only on the issue of her marriage on which she had not been disobedient. Once more the debate raged over the terms of the will and the duties of her father's executors and councillors, until Warwick, puce in the face, said, 'How now, my lady, it seems that your grace is trying to show us in a hateful light to the king, our master, without any cause whatsoever.'

The stand-off ended with a direct appeal from Mary to her half-brother, once again echoing what she had said to their father at the height of their quarrel in 1536. 'There are only two things, body and soul. My soul I offer to God, and my body to Your Majesty's service, and may it please you to take away my life rather than the old religion, in which I desire to live and die.'[19]

Edward gave his own, less melodramatic version of the confrontation in his journal. 'The lady Mary my sister', he wrote, 'came to me at Westminster, where after salutations she was called with my Council into a chamber, where was declared how long I had suffered her mass.' At first, he had written, 'how long I had suffered her mass *against my will*', but then crossed out the last three words. 'She answered', he resumed, 'that her soul was God's and her faith she would not change, nor dissemble her opinion with contrary doings. It was said [by the councillors] I constrained not her faith, but willed her not as a king to rule, but as a subject to obey. And that her example might breed too much inconvenience.'[20]

If Mary's account is a true record, she had put on a theatrical performance worthy of her mother. If Edward's is accurate, Warwick and Cranmer still had some way to go in converting the young Josiah to their way of proceeding, because his relationship with Mary was too strong. She was, for all their differences over religion, still his own flesh and blood.[21]

* * *

For Elizabeth and Kat Ashley, now settled mainly at Hatfield but with regular stays at Enfield and Ashridge, Warwick's coup in 1549 brought welcome relief from the imposition by Somerset of Sir Robert Tyrwhit, his wife and fellow officials on their household.

The exact moment when the Tyrwhits left is clouded by a miasma. There is little direct evidence of Sir Robert directing and controlling Elizabeth's affairs after February 1549, but both he and Sir Walter Buckler were still being addressed as 'councillors to the most excellent princess the Lady Elizabeth her grace' until the spring of 1552 and Buckler was countersigning all of Elizabeth's household accounts until the end of September that year.[22] But the end of the Protectorate broadly marked the moment that the 16-year-old Elizabeth became the head of her own large household, with around twenty-five people at its core and another hundred or so officials and servants over whom Kat and Thomas Parry exercised everyday control.[23]

To score off Mary, Warwick also gave Elizabeth the whole of the £3,000 a year her father had left her in his will in the form of a landed estate. As long as Somerset was in power, her income had been paid irregularly, and rarely in full.[24] Many of the lands she now received had been in her hands informally by the time Thomas Seymour made his suit to marry her, but Somerset would never grant them to her officially.[25] On 17 February 1550, Warwick ordered that she should have 'the supplement of the lands assigned to her', and a month later an estate worth £3,106 a year was granted to her, concentrated in Buckinghamshire, Hertfordshire, Huntingdonshire, Northamptonshire, Lincolnshire and Berkshire.[26]

What clearly made the difference was Elizabeth's willingness to conform to Cranmer's religious innovations. When she arrived at Court shortly after Warwick's coup, she was greeted 'with great pomp and triumph' and spent several days closeted with Edward.[27] Of the three siblings, it was always Edward and Elizabeth who felt the strongest ties for one another.

Some four months after their next lengthy reunion at Epiphany 1551, when they dined with the French ambassador and attended a bear-baiting together, Elizabeth sent her half-brother her portrait, painted by William Scrots (see Plate 6), a Flemish artist first introduced to the Court by Katherine Parr.[28] With the portrait, in which she wore a gown of crimson cloth of gold, came a letter in which Elizabeth wrote affectionately, 'I shall most humbly beseech Your Majesty that when you shall look on my picture you will vouchsafe to think that as you have but the outward shadow of the body before you, so my inward mind wisheth that the body itself were oftener in your presence.'[29]

Elizabeth's star rose higher still in and after October 1551, when Warwick gained enough support in the Privy Council to destroy Somerset. On the 16th, the former Protector was rearrested and tried on 1 December on charges of conspiracy to 'seize' and 'rule' Edward, to which ends it was said he had attempted to obtain the great seal and capture the Tower with its munitions and treasure. A jury of his peers acquitted him of high treason, but found him guilty on a secondary charge of felony. He was beheaded at sunrise on 22 January 1552 on Tower Hill.[30]

Warwick, who created himself Duke of Northumberland a week before Somerset was sent to the Tower, now gave Elizabeth the freedom to come and go from the Court as she pleased. In March 1552, during a visit to Whitehall, she was allowed to lodge with Kat at St James's Palace for the first time since her father's death, and at government expense.[31] And like Mary when she choreographed her retinue to carry their rosaries, Elizabeth meant to turn it into a spectacle. According to an eyewitness, as she rode through the streets of London, she was preceded by 'a great company of lords and knights and gentlemen, and after her a great number of ladies and gentlewomen to the number of 200 on horseback.'[32]

Enjoying something of a political comeback, Elizabeth set about consolidating her influence. To do so, she began systematically recruiting advisers whom she felt she could trust and whom one day she could mould into a group of loyal councillors, for she would need them to help her manage her estates if nothing more.

In fact, she had been recruiting advisers less systematically for some time. Those she had so far identified had links to Thomas Parry, her devoted cofferer, and the circle of evangelical reformers around Sir Anthony Denny, a network that already included John Cheke, Roger Ascham and Thomas Cawarden, now promoted Edward's Master of the Revels. After Denny died in September 1549, Cawarden, his close ally in the Privy Chamber, stepped forward as one of Elizabeth's backstairs contacts at Court. Around 1552, she signed a letter to him, asking him to do her service, styling herself 'Your loving friend' and on her accession as queen in 1558, she would appoint him to the key position of lieutenant of the Tower.[33]

The linchpin of this evolving affinity was William Cecil. Educated at St John's College, Cambridge, he was a long-standing friend of Cheke and Ascham and a secretary, in turn, to both Somerset and Northumberland. Blanche Parry, Elizabeth's gentlewoman, was his cousin and Thomas Parry a more distant kinsman.[34] His first wife was Cheke's sister, Mary, who had died in childbirth in 1544.

As early as September 1549, Elizabeth had sent Cecil a message that shows he was already acting as her principal agent at Court. 'I am well assured', she ordered Parry the cofferer to say to him, 'though I send not daily to him, that he doth not, for all that, daily forget me. Say indeed I assure myself thereof.'[35]

Elizabeth sealed the tie when she made Cecil surveyor of her estates in 1550. His father, Richard Cecil, was already joint keeper of several of her properties and the Cecil family's own estate at Stamford in Lincolnshire was very close to one of Elizabeth's own plum properties at Collyweston.[36]

The *raison d'être* of this evolving affinity, however, was a shared commitment to the reformers. Cawarden and his wife had narrowly escaped a charge of heresy in 1543. And when, in an undated letter of about 1548, Kat had urged Cecil to intervene with Somerset to negotiate the exchange of an English prisoner in Scotland, she reminded him that the bond between him and her mistress was rooted in their shared view of religion. Elizabeth was approaching him, she said, 'being so much assured of your willing mind to set forth her causes to my Lord Protector's grace, especially the matter being so godly'. Elizabeth then added a postscript in her own hand: 'I pray you further this good man's suit. Your friend, Elizabeth.'[37]

Shortly afterwards, Elizabeth wrote entirely in her own hand to ask Cecil to secure a preaching licence for one of her former chaplains, Hugh Goodacre. He was, she said, a man 'long time known unto us to be as well of honest conversation and sober living as of sufficient learning and judgment in the Scriptures to preach the Word of God, the advancement whereof we so desire'.[38]

Her new chaplain, Edmund Allen, had much to do with shaping Elizabeth's personal beliefs. Another Cambridge man, he had fled into exile in Germany to escape the Act of Six Articles, returning on Henry VIII's death. Possibly Matthew Parker, the Vice-Chancellor of Cambridge, had recommended him, since a few days before her execution, Anne Boleyn, who had made Parker one of her own chaplains, committed her daughter's spiritual care to him. Or perhaps Elizabeth had discovered Allen in Katherine Parr's household, where he was one of a group of scholars the Dowager Queen had commissioned to translate Erasmus's *Paraphrases*.[39]

Allen was with Elizabeth before the end of 1547, because the following February he was granted the benefice of Welford in Berkshire by Thomas Seymour at her request. In 1548, he wrote a catechism which, although decidedly evangelical in tone, contradicted the Swiss reformers' more radical interpretation of the Eucharist, which fits very well with Elizabeth's hostility to the Catholic doctrine of transubstantiation on the one hand, and her beliefs, later expressed, that 'God was in the sacrament of the Eucharist' on the other.[40] Although reformist, Elizabeth's beliefs retained many traditional elements. Like Katherine Parr, she venerated the symbol of the cross, and after her accession, she would set up a crucifix in the Chapel Royal to the disgust of the more radical Protestants and veto all attempts to have it removed.[41]

Another likely influence was Roger Ascham, who in 1548 succeeded William Grindal as Elizabeth's schoolmaster for two years until he was sent away in disgrace for flirting with her gentlewomen.[42] Kat had recommended him for the post. As he wrote afterwards to her, 'Your favour to Mr Grindal and gentleness towards me are matters sufficient to deserve more goodwill than my little power is able to requite'.[43]

Ascham had cultivated Elizabeth in a variety of ways, sending her a pen, an Italian book and a book of prayers, and he offered to have a broken pen mended. With his eye to the main chance, he also charmed his way into Edward's circle. 'Many times by mine especially good master Mr Cheke's means', he wrote to Cecil, 'I have been called to teach the king to write in his Privy Chamber.'[44]

Under Ascham's guidance, Elizabeth continued to read Latin and Greek together with the Bible, but the slant was evangelical, since he records that the religious authors she studied with him were only those 'from whom she can drink in purity of doctrine along with elegance of speech'.[45] He exaggerated when he boasted to his friend Johann Sturm that 'she speaks French and Italian as well as she speaks English; her Latin is smooth, correct and thoughtful; frequently and voluntarily she has even spoken with me in Greek tolerably well.'[46] Modern experts believe that her French was fluent, her spoken Italian more hesitant, her Latin translations competent but no more, and her Greek rudimentary.[47]

Ascham inflated his claims to float the idea that he was single-handedly transforming Elizabeth into an 'exceptional' woman, meaning a Christian woman of 'exemplary' virtue, one who—as a Protestant and the king's sister—God had destined for higher things. It was, said Ascham, as much her energetic 'study of the true faith' as her other qualities that enabled her to realize her full potential 'without a woman's weakness.'[48]

By 1550, Ascham had introduced Elizabeth to the writings of some of the easier exponents of classical oratory, chiefly Cicero, Livy, Sophocles and Isocrates.[49] These were among the authors that Vives had reserved for men—Edward had already started on Isocrates, despite using a crib in French—but the boundaries were becoming porous.[50] Elizabeth, the Protestant John Bale reports, read the first and third orations of Isocrates to Nicocles, the young king of Cyprus.[51] And at least one passage on the duties of rulers from the first oration stuck with her, to be quoted at critical moments in her life: 'Throughout all your life show that you value truth so highly that a king's word is more to be trusted than other men's oaths.'[52]

She had quoted another maxim from this author when she sent her portrait to her half-brother. 'I think that statues of bodies are fine memorials', Isocrates had advised Nicocles, 'but images of deeds and of character are worth much more.'[53] In the letter accompanying the portrait, Elizabeth wrote, 'For the face, I grant, I might well blush to offer, but the mind I shall never be ashamed to present. For though from the grace of the picture the colours may fade by time ... yet the other nor time with her swift wings shall overtake, nor the misty clouds with their lowerings [i.e. scowling] may darken.'[54]

◆   ◆   ◆

On 13 June 1552, while Edward was at Greenwich preparing for an extended summer progress, Mary paid him another visit.[55] It lasted barely six hours and must have passed off without incident, as the young king fails to mention it in his journal. But it came a month or so after he had recovered from a severe attack of measles and marked the day after he completed his formal education.

'Thank God', he wrote with feeling as he ended what was probably his last Greek exercise after eight hard years at his Latin and Greek.[56] When he returned to Whitehall in October at the end of the progress, he would be 15. Although not officially 'of age' by the terms of his father's will, he already considered himself to be a man.[57] As Cheke advised him, 'You are now coming to a government of yourself, in which estate I pray God you may always be served with them that will faithfully, truly and plainly give you counsel.' To this end, Cheke recruited William Thomas, one of the clerks of the Privy Council, to introduce Edward to political essays on issues of state and assist him in drafting model state papers and agendas shadowing items of current business in which he could learn the techniques of kingship.[58]

And yet it was Edward's determination to hunt, joust and excel in war like his father that most visibly marked his near-coming of age. For almost a year, Northumberland had allowed him to 'shoot and run at [the] ring' with his companions. 'Running at the ring' while mounted and wearing full armour was the way to learn how to joust. Participants took turns to ride along the barrier in the tilt-yard that divided the contestants in a real-life tournament, before taking aim with their lance at a ring suspended from a post that replaced the opponent in a genuine contest. The winner would be whoever speared the ring with his lance the most times after a set number of courses.[59]

On his long summer progress in 1552, Edward spent whole days hunting like his father.[60] On the outward part of his journey after leaving Hampton Court, he hunted 'in the bear wood in the forest of Windsor and there did his grace kill a great buck.'[61] And after inspecting the fortifications at Southampton and Portsmouth in August, he wrote excitedly to Barnaby Fitzpatrick to inform him that he had 'devised' two strong castles on either side of the mouth of Portsmouth Haven, since the existing defences were 'ill flanked, and set in unmeet places, the town weak in comparison of that it ought to be.'[62]

Like his father, Edward became increasingly acquisitive, collecting and encouraging gifts of fine jewels, gold and silver plate, books and manuscripts, hawks, falcons, greyhounds, horses and mules.[63] He wore the finest linen shirts. His satin doublets were worked with gold and studded with tiny gemstones. And he insisted on having matching hose. As to his gowns, he preferred highly decorated black or coloured examples, in silk for summer and velvet for winter, all embroidered and fringed with gold. On state occasions he wore a coat of purple or crimson cloth of gold, trimmed with silver and gold cord, or else a mantle of cloth of gold. Around his neck he wore a collar of rubies.

As in his father's reign, he continued to wear a cap, usually of black velvet, sparkling with gold or jewels, and with a white Prince of Wales feather falling to the left in front (see Plate 5).[64]

If a story told at Blois by one of Charles V's ambassadors is true, Edward also shared his father's cruelty. Angry at the way Northumberland and his allies kept him on a string, he was said to have taken his prize falcon, which he kept in his Privy Chamber, and plucked it alive, tearing it into four pieces and saying as he did so that he likened himself to the falcon, whom everyone plucked, 'but I will pluck them too hereafter and tear them in four parts.'[65]

Then, in February 1553, the teenager caught a feverish cold. With his immune system already weakened by measles, he succumbed around mid March possibly to tuberculosis, more likely to all the known symptoms of bronchopneumonia leading to pleural empyema, the same illness that had killed Fitzroy. His physicians, who specifically remarked on the fatal coincidence, advised that he be confined to his room, watched night and day. Northumberland informed Mary and began doing all he could to court her favour. But his shady manoeuvres during the coup against Somerset rankled with her and he soon realized that he would need to protect himself should Edward die.[66]

Edward, meanwhile, convinced himself (or was convinced by others) that his half-sisters should be excluded from the succession. Both women had been declared illegitimate by his father's Parliaments, something he believed took precedence over his

PLATE I Henry VIII as he approached the age of 55. A posthumous image by Cornelis Metsys, engraved at Antwerp in *c*.1548. The artist had fled to England after being exiled from Brabant in 1544.

PLATE 2 Katherine Parr, Henry VIII's sixth and last queen, aged about 33. By the artist known as 'Master John', c.1545.

PLATE 3 Henry Fitzroy, Duke of Richmond and Somerset, Henry VIII's illegitimate son, aged about 15. By Lucas Horenboute, *c.*1534.

PLATE 4 An unknown man, said to be Sir Thomas Seymour, aged about 35. Attributed to Hans Holbein the Younger, *c.*1543. In Edward VI's reign, Seymour first scandalously flirted with Elizabeth, and then attempted to marry her.

PLATE 5 Edward VI shortly after he became king in 1547, holding a leather purse in one hand and a red rose in the other. To the left of the painting among the roses and violets is a sunflower (the colour now faded), that instead of turning to the sun as heliotropic plants do, turns to the young king, who is eulogized in Italian and Latin texts below. Attributed to William Scrots.

PLATE 6 Elizabeth, aged 17, commissioned this portrait of herself from William Scrots as a gift for Edward in 1551, sending it with an affectionate letter dated 'from Hatfield, this 15 day of May'. The only year in Edward's reign that Elizabeth was at Hatfield on 15 May was 1551.

PLATE 7 An unknown woman, said to be Lady Jane Grey shortly after her marriage to Guildford Dudley in May 1553, attributed to Levina Teerlinc. The 'ANO XVIII' (i.e. 'anno aetatis xviii') inscription presents a difficulty in that Jane was not quite 17 when she was executed; however, such inscriptions are not always reliable.

PLATE 8 Philip and Mary as king and queen of England, by Hans Eworth. Although dated 1558 and apparently set at the palace of Whitehall, the date cannot be correct since Philip left England in July 1557, never to return. The view through the open window of the opposite bank of the Thames also appears to be fictional.

PLATE 9

This rare image shows Elizabeth I at the beginning of her reign and as she really looked. In the background is the 'cloth of estate' (its crimson now faded), which sets this portrait apart from all the other known early images of the queen. By an unknown artist.

PLATE 10

Elizabeth's most glittering favourite, Sir Robert Dudley, painted around the time she created him Earl of Leicester in 1564. Dudley was the one man Elizabeth would almost certainly have married as queen had the circumstances been right. By Steven van der Meulen.

PLATE II
An Allegory of the Tudor Succession, a copy of another version that Elizabeth sent as a gift to Sir Francis Walsingham in 1572. A reinterpretation of an earlier family group portrait, commissioned by Henry VIII in 1544, the image depicts Elizabeth as a champion of peace and plenty and Philip and Mary as champions of war. By an unknown artist.

father's will.[67] And where religion was concerned, he came to think that not even Elizabeth could be trusted with his new Protestant settlement.

At the outset, Edward was as determined as his father not to be succeeded by a woman. When he first began to follow in his father's footsteps and jot down his ideas for his own succession settlement in early April, his illness was briefly in remission. He still envisaged that, before his death, Lady Frances Brandon, whose husband Henry Grey had been created Duke of Suffolk in 1551 and whose children were the first residuary legatees to the throne by the terms of Henry VIII's will, might have a son or that her eldest daughter, Lady Jane Grey, would marry and give birth to a son.

Since, however, Frances would shortly be approaching the menopause, it was more likely that Jane would marry and that her son (in Edward's eyes) would be the rightful successor. To this end, Northumberland married his 19-year-old son Guildford to the 16-year-old Jane on 25 May, while on the same day her younger sister Katherine, who was just old enough to be legally wed, married Henry Herbert, son of the duke's ally, the Earl of Pembroke.

Jane's marriage greatly strengthened Northumberland's hold on the dynasty, because Edward had the highest regard for Guildford, intriguingly describing him some time after the wedding to the councillors standing around his sickbed as 'one of the sons of our guardian, the duke of Northumberland, and a man, unless I am mistaken, born to achieve celebrity; from him you may expect great things.'[68]

By the end of May, Edward knew he was dying. As his physicians reported, he had 'a harsh, continuous cough, his body is dry and burning, his belly is swollen, he has a slow fever upon him that never leaves him.' His sputum was 'livid, black, fetid and

FIGURE 13 'My devise for the succession': the original draft, also incorporating its first revision, of Edward VI's proposed resettlement of the crown, which he altered to allow the direct succession of Lady Jane Grey.

gouuernres after as is aforsaid, til same
heire maste be borne, and then the
mother of that child to be gouuernres.
6 And if the during the rule: of the
gouuernres ther die 4 of the counsel
then shal she by her leters cal an asse-
ble of the counsel thre on month folowing
and chose 4 more, wherin she shal
haue thre voices. But after her death
the 16 shal chese emong themselues
til there come to 14 yeare olde,
and then he by her aduise shal
chose the.

full of carbon; it smells beyond measure....His feet are swollen all over.'[69]

With insufficient time to summon Parliament, Edward altered his earlier jottings. At first, he had 'devised' the crown 'To the L[ady] Fraunceses heires masles' and then 'For lakke of such issu to the L[ady] Jane's heires masles'. Now, he left it 'To the L[ady] Fraunceses heires masles, *if she have any such issu befor my death*' and then '*To the L[ady] Jane and* her heires masles', followed—this in a subsequent revision (not illustrated)—by Jane's sisters, Katherine and Mary, and their heirs male, and finally by the eldest son of their cousin, Margaret Clifford, daughter of Lady Eleanor Brandon by her marriage to Henry Clifford Earl of Cumberland, if all three Grey sisters died without heirs.[70] How far the young king was Northumberland's puppet in making his 'Device for the Succession' (as it is known) is hotly contested, but the original draft and its first revision are in Edward's own handwriting throughout (see Figure 13).[71]

On 24 June, the bulletin from the sickroom was that Edward 'has not the strength to stir and can hardly breathe. His body no longer performs its functions, his nails and hair are dropping off, and all his person is scabby.'[72] He died on 6 July, by which time letters patent confirming his 'Device' had been signed by Cranmer, the Privy Council, the judges, the Lord Mayor and aldermen of London, and as many other notables as could be convened in a hurry.[73]

Before allowing news of Edward's death to leak, Northumberland sent his allies to take control of the Tower and the royal treasury and to swear the head officers of the royal household and the guard to an oath of loyalty to Queen Jane.[74]

On the 10th, Jane was proclaimed queen amid rumours that Edward had been poisoned.[75] When told she had been chosen, she wept, but prayed to God for 'such grace as to enable me to govern this kingdom with his approbation and to his glory.'[76] A confident and assertive young woman whom Roger Ascham in a moment of indiscretion had hinted was a better scholar than Elizabeth, she saw herself as called by God to lead the Protestant cause.[77] In his will, Edward insisted that his executors should 'not suffer any piece of religion to be altered.'[78] He would have known that he could trust Jane and Guildford on that score.

Northumberland, however, had allowed Mary to escape. On 3 July, while riding to visit Edward at Greenwich, she was secretly informed of his lapse into unconsciousness and of Northumberland's plans to capture her.[79] Considering herself to be the rightful heir under her father's will, she fled to the heartland of her estates in Norfolk. On the 9th she began mobilizing her forces, which she mustered at one of her fortified houses, Framlingham Castle in Suffolk. Northumberland was sent with an army to defeat her, but when a naval squadron off the Norfolk coast defected and handed over its artillery to her, his troops melted away.

As late as the 18th, Jane was still sending out letters signed 'Jane the Quene' to sheriffs and magistrates, insisting that her rule was founded on 'consent' to Edward's 'Device' and that she was queen 'through God's providence to the preservation of our common weal and policy'. It was she alone, not Mary, as one of these letters claimed, who could preserve the English crown 'in the whole undefiled English blood.'[80]

Chaos, however, ruled in the localities. In Northampton, Jane and Mary were both proclaimed queen, causing a 'great stir' in the shire. In Sussex, Jane was rejected as 'a queen of a new and pretty invention'. Northumberland found it difficult to win and hold gentry support and soon many of the southern counties were declaring themselves for Mary.[81]

Between 5 p.m. and 6 p.m. on the evening of 19 July after the Privy Council split into two rival camps, Mary was proclaimed queen in London. Northumberland and his allies were sent to the Tower. Jane, stripped of the crown jewels and her canopy of state, was led from the royal apartments and put under house arrest at the home of William Partridge, an officer in the royal ordnance within the Tower.

To celebrate, *Te Deum* was sung at St Paul's, bells were rung and bonfires lit.[82] Ten days later, Elizabeth entered the city with a heavily armed retinue dressed in the Tudor livery colours of white and green.[83] Mary herself arrived on 3 August, riding side-saddle on her palfrey and wearing a magnificent French gown of purple velvet that was thick with gemstones, and entering the city to the sounds of trumpets and cheering crowds. Elizabeth had ridden out to Whitechapel to greet her and rode immediately behind her through streets swathed with streamers and banners of welcome.[84]

Northumberland was tried for treason on 18 August and executed at Tower Hill on the 22nd. Jane and her husband Guildford were tried on 13 November. Both pleaded guilty, and Jane, who stood before her judges wearing a plain black gown trimmed with black velvet and reading from a prayer book, was sentenced to be burned at the stake or decapitated.[85] Mary was determined to have her revenge on Northumberland, but was inclined to pity Jane, whose mother Frances had always been close to her. It was perhaps Frances who told Mary of Jane's belief that Northumberland had been the source of all her troubles. 'He hath brought me and our stock in most miserable calamity and misery by his exceeding ambition', she was supposed to have said.[86]

Mary's thoughts of clemency were swept aside by Sir Thomas Wyatt's rebellion in January 1554. An evangelical reformer whose forces reached Fleet Street in London before they were defeated, Wyatt aimed to overthrow Mary and replace her with Elizabeth.

On 12 February 1554, Jane and Guildford were executed. With Mary safe on the throne, Elizabeth may have thought that her gestures of support for her half-sister on the eve of her accession might be suitably rewarded.

But if so, she was sadly deceived.

CHAPTER 8

Sisters, Rivals, Queens

ALTHOUGH only 37 when proclaimed queen, Mary had not worn well. 'Of low stature, with a red and white complexion and very thin', as the Venetian ambassador unflatteringly described her, 'her face is round, with a nose rather low and wide.' Wrinkles were forming on her cheeks. Her eyes were large, her gaze piercing, her voice 'rough and loud, almost like a man's, so that when she speaks she is always heard a long way off.'[1]

Regularly ill, her symptoms still included the amenorrhoea, neuralgia and insomnia that had begun when she was 20, to which she had added 'melancholy', heart palpitations, poor appetite, chronic indigestion and increasingly poor vision.[2] As England's first queen regnant, the pressure was on her from the outset and she had never coped well with stress. Once the euphoria of her entry into London was over, her advisers—a mixture of her household retainers, co-religionists and those privy councillors not closely associated with Northumberland or Jane Grey—attempted to push through an unprecedented measure to have her claim to the throne confirmed by Parliament before she was crowned.[3]

Neither the *Royal Book* nor the *Liber Regalis* (the fourteenth-century coronation service book used for all Tudor coronations) made provision for the accession of a woman ruler. Accordingly the Privy Council tried to insist that Edward's 'Device' and last will should first be declared null and void and Henry VIII's will valid before Mary could legitimately be crowned. A further concern was that the default position after her father's break with Rome was that she would become Supreme Head of the Church, whether she liked it or not. Some councillors feared a legal muddle, others an assassination attempt if her status was not first clarified.

The new queen brushed all these objections aside. Her coronation by the bishop of Winchester went ahead at Westminster Abbey on Sunday, 1 October, bypassing Edward's religious settlement by including a full Roman mass.[4] Mary vetted the order of service to ensure that her coronation oath did not mention the new religion. And where Edward's oath had included a promise to observe 'the laws and liberties of this realm', she altered the wording so as to promise to keep 'the *just and licit* laws and liberties'. Anxious, lastly, that the chrism Cranmer had used to anoint her half-brother in 1547 was tainted by schism, Mary arranged for three phials of freshly consecrated unction to be imported from France. The only mishap came at the end of the coronation ceremony, when she was handed two sceptres, 'the one of the king, the other bearing a dove which, by custom, is given to the queen', a curiously contradictory expression of the status of a queen regnant.[5]

Until Mary was crowned, she treated Elizabeth affectionately in public, taking her by the hand as they strolled together, sending for her 'to dinner and supper' and going so far as to greet her gentlewomen with a kiss.[6] In private, however, she was pressing her to convert to Catholicism. On Thursday, 7 September, to gain some wiggle room, Elizabeth had disingenuously resorted to play-acting. Kneeling before Mary in a gallery at Richmond Palace, she begged her in tears to excuse her 'ignorance', saying she 'had never been taught the doctrine of the ancient religion.' She professed herself willing to receive instruction from a priest and even to conform to the mass.[7]

Mary called in the offer the very next day, the feast of the Nativity of the Blessed Virgin. But at the hour appointed for Elizabeth to arrive at the Chapel Royal, she feigned illness. She did eventually arrive, but 'complained loudly all the way to church that her stomach ached, wearing a suffering air.'[8] And the following week, she skipped Sunday mass completely.[9]

Once Mary was crowned, she 'never dined nor supped' with Elizabeth, 'but kept her aloof from her.' Or as the Venetians put it, 'from that time forth, a great change took place in Queen Mary's treatment of her.'[10] Where, before, she had kept up appearances, now she snubbed Elizabeth at every opportunity, exactly replicating her behaviour when her father had forced her to live in a joint household with her younger sibling under the authority of Sir John and Lady Shelton while Anne Boleyn was still alive.

By early December, Elizabeth had been humiliated enough. She pointedly asked to leave Court and return to Ashridge. A few days later, she departed with her baggage train, and no one was fooled when she ostentatiously wrote to Mary asking to borrow copes, chasubles and other items needed for celebrating mass.[11]

By then, Mary had got Parliament to declare her parents' marriage legitimate and uphold Elizabeth's illegitimacy. She had repealed her half-brother's religious settlement and brought the

Church back to where it had stood at her father's death. She intended to go much further than this, abrogating the break with Rome and restoring papal authority, even bringing back the monasteries if she could.

But first, she meant to recreate the dynastic alliance that her parents' marriage had represented. 'Being born of a Spanish mother', said the Venetian ambassador, 'she was always inclined towards that nation, scorning to be English and boasting of her descent from Spain.'[12] Perhaps she remembered the happy days in February 1522 when she was 6 and had taken her cousin Charles V as her 'valentine'. Since he was now a widower, she may again have considered marrying him, until cautioned by his ambassador that he was prematurely aged at 53, and had retired, crippled by gout, to the monastery of Yuste with the prize items from his art collection.

So Mary set her heart on marrying Philip, Charles's son and heir. 26-years-old, fair-haired and handsome, he too had been a widower since 1545 and was already ruling Spain as regent. Soon he would succeed to the sovereignty of Spain, the Low Countries and the Spanish lands in Italy and the New World. Overjoyed at the prospect of adding England to the Spanish empire, Philip ditched his plans to marry the Infanta of Portugal. It was just as well that Mary never knew the degree to which he saw her as an ageing spinster whom he continued to nickname his 'aunt'.[13]

By choosing a husband in the way that she did, Mary split the Privy Council, defying in spirit, if not perhaps quite in the letter, the clause in her father's will that said she should only marry with the 'assent and consent' of the privy councillors he had specifically named. When a parliamentary delegation petitioned her to marry an English nobleman, she declared indignantly that they would not have spoken like that to her father, which was true but missed the point that she was alienating large numbers of her subjects by making Philip her king consort.

Parliament eventually passed the legislation approving the marriage, but stipulated that the 'kingly or regal office' with all 'its dignities, prerogative royal, power, pre-eminences and privileges' remained firmly vested in Mary alone.[14] Parliament also consistently refused to allow Philip a coronation, which he regarded as a snub.

◆　◆　◆

It was Mary's choice of husband that sparked Wyatt's rebellion, which appealed to the Londoners to rise up and replace her with Elizabeth. Four concerted revolts were planned in different parts of the country, but when news of the conspiracy leaked out, the rebels were not ready. Only Sir Thomas Wyatt succeeded in mobilizing his Kentish forces, which surrendered on 7 February 1554, when the Earl of Pembroke's cavalry cornered them.

Ten days later, Mary summoned her half-sister to Whitehall. Fearing the worst now that Wyatt was in the Tower, Elizabeth took her time, claiming 'such a cold and headache that I have never felt the like.'[15]

She arrived on the 23rd, 'dressed all in white and followed by a great company of the queen's people and her own'. Always keen to show herself to the citizens and win their support—for there were more Protestants in London than anywhere else in the kingdom— she travelled in an open horse litter.[16]

For three weeks, Mary kept Elizabeth on tenterhooks, attended by only twelve servants in a closely guarded quarter of the palace.[17] She suspected her of complicity in the revolt after her spies intercepted a courier carrying a bundle of despatches from the French ambassador, Antoine de Noailles, that incriminated her.[18]

According to the intercepted documents, one of Wyatt's chief co-conspirators, Sir James Croft, had confided to de Noailles that he was 'very familiar' with Elizabeth and her servants. He intended, he said, to visit Ashridge ahead of the rising to warn her to move further away from London into the countryside—and it seems he had done so. Francis Russell, one of Jane Grey's staunchest supporters, also admitted carrying a letter from Wyatt to Ashridge. Most suspiciously of all, a copy of Elizabeth's letter explaining her delay in answering Mary's summons to return to Court after the rising had found its way straight into de Noailles's postbag.[19]

The only doubt in Mary's mind, a fatal one as it afterwards turned out, was whether Wyatt's collusion with Elizabeth was directly with her, or indirectly with Thomas Parry and John Ashley. Probably Ashley had been the main point of contact, since shortly after Wyatt's forces were defeated, he fled with Sir John Cheke to Padua.[20]

On Friday, 16 March, the day after Wyatt's conviction for high treason, the Council came to Elizabeth and charged her as an accessory in the revolt.[21] Next day, two privy councillors arrived to escort her to the Tower by river and not through the streets, where her arrest would attract attention. Fearing for her life and determined to play for time, she begged to be allowed to speak to Mary, and if this was not permitted, to write to her. She was grudgingly allowed to write.[22]

In composing what has been called 'the letter of her life',[23] Elizabeth began by quoting the first oration of Isocrates to Nicocles: 'If any ever did try this old saying that a king's word was more than another man's oath, I most humbly beseech Your Majesty to verify it in me.'

She appealed to Mary's conscience to 'take some better way with me than to make me condemned in all men's sight afore my desert known', and she asked to 'answer afore yourself and not suffer me to trust your councillors—yea, and that afore I go to the Tower (if it be possible), if not afore I be further condemned.'

In a cutting reference to the Seymour affair, she said, 'I heard my Lord of Somerset say that if his brother had been suffered to speak with him, he had never suffered, but the persuasions were made to him so great that he was brought in belief that he could not live safely if the Admiral lived, and that made him give his consent to his death.'

Not, she added, that the cases were alike (although of course they were). 'Though these persons are not to be compared to Your Majesty, yet I pray God [that] evil persuasions persuade not one sister against the other.' She denied that she had received letters from Wyatt or given any copies of her own correspondence to de Noailles. 'He [Wyatt] might peradventure write me a letter, but on my faith I never received any from him, and as for the copy of my letter sent to the French king, I pray God confound me eternally if ever I sent him word, message, token or letter by any means, and to this my truth I will stand in to my death.'

In a postscript she added, 'I humbly crave but only one word of answer from yourself', signing herself 'Your Highness's most faithful subject that hath been from the beginning and will be to my end. Elizabeth'. Where space was left on the page, she drew eleven diagonal lines to fill the gap and ensure that no forged additions could be made. And after her name, she drew—as she invariably did after she became mistress of her own household—what looks

FIGURE 14 A view of London Bridge as it appeared in c.1632, by the Dutch artist Claude de Jongh. The narrow openings between the stone pillars are clearly visible, and it was the hazards caused by the strong currents swirling through the gaps at high tide that delayed Elizabeth's passage to the Tower in March 1554, so saving her life.

extraordinarily like a looped portcullis, the Beaufort badge adopted by Henry VII as a symbol of royalty, which Margaret Beaufort, her great-grandmother, had festooned over the stone-work and woodwork of her Collyweston palace that now belonged to Elizabeth.[24]

Although Mary ignored the letter, it still helped to save Elizabeth's life. While she was writing it and the queen's bargemen were standing by for the short journey to the Tower, the spring tide rose so high, 'it was no longer possible to pass under London Bridge, and they had to wait till the morrow.'[25] The bridge was impassable at high tide, since traffic could only go through the narrow openings between its twenty stone pillars. So hazardous was it for boats to pass between the pillars given the swirling currents and the narrowness of the gaps, many safety-conscious passengers routinely disembarked before the bridge even at low tide, walking to the other side of the bridge before continuing their journey.

By the time Elizabeth disembarked at Tower Wharf on the morning of the 18th, the Privy Council could no longer agree on what to do with her. She entered the Tower as a prisoner across the draw-bridge beside the Byward Tower, watched by the guard. As she passed by the Bloody Tower on her way to the royal apartments in the inner ward, she would have caught sight of the scaffold on which Jane Grey had been executed on the other side of the court.[26]

Imprisoned in the very same rooms where her mother had been kept for a fortnight before her execution, Elizabeth was searchingly interrogated. Her inquisitors chiefly wished to know why she had made preparations, as it seemed on Croft's advice, to move on the eve of Wyatt's revolt to her property at Donnington Castle in Berkshire, where the keeper was none other than Thomas

Cawarden, Wyatt's friend and Elizabeth's own 'loving friend'.[27] The castle commanded the main road to Marlborough and the west, which just happened to be the route to Herefordshire and the Welsh border, where Croft planned to lead a rising coordinated with Wyatt's.

In fending off her accusers, Elizabeth used the same barracking techniques she had turned on Sir Robert Tyrwhit during the Seymour affair, while relying on disunity in the Privy Council to blunt the attack on her.[28]

Egged on by the Spanish ambassador, Mary was seriously weighing up whether or not to put her sibling on trial for treason. But she could never prove that Elizabeth had personally endorsed Wyatt's conspiracy or ordered the proposed move to Donnington Castle. With the London juries sympathetic to Wyatt's cause and refusing to convict several of his known accomplices—in one spectacular case returning a verdict of not guilty that flew in the face of the evidence—the Privy Council's divisions enabled Elizabeth to secure her release, albeit on strict conditions.

Just after midday on Saturday, 19 May, the eve of Whitsuntide 1554 and two terrifying months after she had first entered the Tower, the Marquis of Winchester and Sir John Gage took Elizabeth by river to Richmond. On arrival, she was held under guard for a week before being taken on to Windsor and from there to Woodstock in Oxfordshire, where she was kept under house arrest with as few attendants as possible.[29] Sir Henry Bedingfield, a Catholic loyalist whom Mary had made constable of the Tower and would soon promote to captain of the guard, was made her gaoler, receiving his instructions, signed by the queen, on 26 May.[30]

Bedingfield, a fussy, pedantic Norfolk man who worried about the dangers of not discharging his duties and was not above

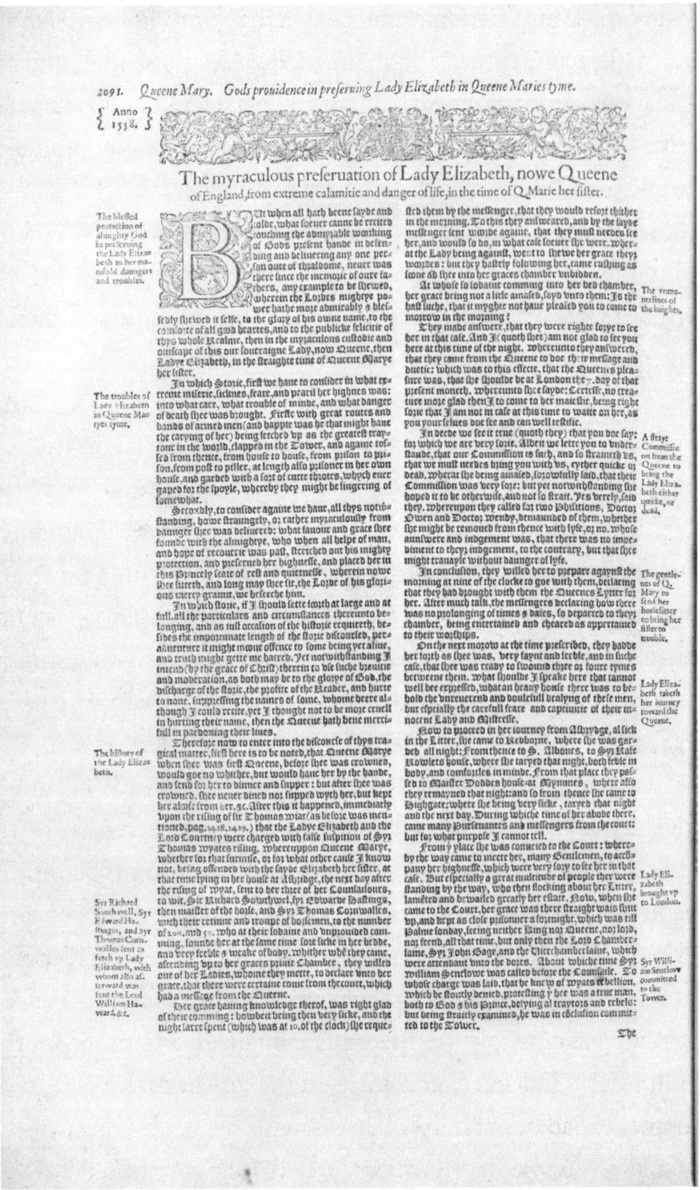

2091. *Queene Mary. Gods prouidence in preseruing Lady Elizabeth in Queene Maries tyme.*

Anno 1558.

The myraculous preseruation of Lady Elizabeth, nowe Queene of England, from extreme calamitie and danger of life, in the time of Q. Marie her sister.

FIGURE 15 The opening page of *The myraculous preservation of Lady Elizabeth, nowe Queene of England, from extreme calamatie and danger of life, in the time of Q. Marie her sister.* First included in John Foxe's *Acts and Monuments* (or 'Book of Martyrs') in 1563 and subsequently expanded, this version is from the 1583 edition and much of the information was supplied by eyewitnesses.

spying on those in his charge, struggled to impose his will on his royal prisoner. Elizabeth gave him a hard time, demanding an English Bible and insisting on saying the litany in English and not Latin on the grounds that the vernacular litany 'was set forth in the king my Father his days'.[31] But when ordered outright to stop, she gave in and conformed to Catholicism by regularly attending mass.[32]

Even then, Bedingfield was not satisfied, complaining that she withdrew for two or three hours a day 'under colour of wishing to pray', but could well have been plotting.

And her servants were vociferously defiant. Infuriated by Elizabeth Sandes, one of Elizabeth's gentlewomen and a strident Protestant, who was repeatedly absent from mass, Bedingfield expelled her from the household. He had no compunction either about reporting a male servant to the Privy Council and sending for a priest to threaten another servant with what was tantamount to a heresy trial.[33]

◆　　◆　　◆

After almost a year of playing cat and mouse at Woodstock, Elizabeth was commanded to await Mary's pleasure at Hampton Court. Bedingfield brought her the news on 17 April 1555, and somewhere between the 24th and the 29th she entered the palace by a back door with only three or four gentlewomen, still under guard and occupying the Prince's Lodging that her father had rebuilt for her half-brother, except the gallery leading to the royal apartments had been sealed off.[34]

By then, Mary's marriage to Philip had been solemnized at Winchester and Cardinal Pole had arrived from exile in Rome and absolved the realm from sin. A younger son of Mary's old governess, the Countess of Salisbury, Pole was made archbishop of Canterbury in place of Cranmer, who was in the Tower. He reunited England with the papacy, assiduously helping Mary to undo the work of Somerset's iconoclasts. He also helped the queen to restore a handful of monasteries, mainly those closely associated with her mother, Katherine of Aragon.

Against Philip's advice and better judgement, Mary encouraged Pole to create the equivalent of an English Inquisition, reinforced by Spanish Dominicans, to root out heresy and compel Protestants to attend confession and mass at least once a year. Unflinching and determined, Pole was assisted by Bishop Bonner of London, a man who deplored the laxity of Tudor prisons and kept suspects locked up in his coal-house. Around 284 victims, including Cranmer, were burned at the stake for their heretical beliefs in just under four years.[35]

It is usually supposed that Elizabeth was brought to Hampton Court because—with her servants' connivance—she had smuggled the astrologer John Dee into the house at Woodstock to cast horoscopes. The destinies she had tried to have foreseen were her own, Philip's and Mary's. Casting a royal horoscope was a dangerous business—Henry VIII had regarded it as tantamount to high treason.

But Mary had not yet found out about the horoscopes when the order was given for Elizabeth to come to Hampton Court. In fact, the warrant for Dee's arrest was not issued by the Privy Council until 28 May.[36]

Elizabeth wanted the horoscopes because rumours were rife that Mary, after just eight months of marriage, was in an advanced state of pregnancy. Said to be 'near her time' as early as the end of March, she had chosen Hampton Court as the place where she would take to her lying-in chamber. So confident was she that God was on her side, she had shown herself from a window of her apartments to Philip and his fellow Knights of the Garter as they processed in their robes to Chapel on St George's Day (23 April), contrary to the strict seclusion demanded of an expectant queen by the *Royal Book*.[37]

Mary, it seems, had sent for Elizabeth in order to gloat. Once a living child of whichever sex was born, her half-sister would no longer be next in line for the succession and the Anglo-Spanish dynastic union would be permanent. So confident was Mary about her pregnancy that, on 16 May, she and Philip began signing open letters announcing 'the happy delivery of a prince' and appointing special messengers to deliver them.[38] The parallel with Anne Boleyn when she gave birth to Elizabeth is uncanny.

Except that in Mary's case it was far worse, since no child was born at all. Mary's turned out to be a false pregnancy, complete with a swelling of the breasts and lactation, probably caused by a prolactinoma, a non-cancerous tumour of the pituitary gland. This results in too much of a hormone called prolactin in the blood, triggering amenorrhoea in the earlier stages and eventually pseudo-pregnancy, and which, as the tumour expands and starts to press on the surrounding structures such as the optic nerve, accounts for Mary's other symptoms, notably migraines, vomiting, depression and loss of vision.[39]

Imagining the birth of her child to be imminent, Mary briefly came to think her sibling posed a much reduced threat. While Elizabeth was still at Hampton Court and about a week after Mary and Philip had signed the letters, the queen sent for her on an impulse at 10 p.m. in an attempt to patch up their differences. Led across the privy garden and up a staircase by Susan Tonge to

Mary's bedchamber, Elizabeth knelt before the queen and protested her loyalty.

But when Mary suddenly upbraided her over her religion, it was clear no reconciliation would be possible. The only positive outcome was that Philip, observing the scene from behind the arras, decided that his sister-in-law was a dynastic asset and therefore best kept alive.[40] According to the Venetians, Elizabeth had been making a determined effort at Hampton Court to ingratiate herself with the Spaniards in Philip's entourage and this was paying off.[41]

◆　◆　◆

When in August it became clear that Mary's pregnancy was a phantom, the royal couple returned to Whitehall scarcely on speaking terms. On 4 September, Philip sailed from Dover to Calais on his way to Brussels.[42] His departure marked the turning point of the reign, for he would not return until March 1557, and only then for three and a half months to drag England into an unpopular war against France.

Realizing she had been all but deserted, Mary succumbed to fits of hysterics, on one occasion haranguing Philip's portrait hanging in the Privy Chamber before kicking it out of the room.[43] In particular, the royal couple disagreed over what to do with Elizabeth. Now 22, she was tall and shapely, with shining red-gold hair and long, slim-fingered hands. Even if her critics judged her complexion to be 'sallow' like her mother's, she had Anne Boleyn's dark eyes and a decidedly royal look. Philip, himself notorious as a womanizer, was not slow to see the potential.[44]

Mary's instinct was to oust Elizabeth from the succession in favour of her cousin Lady Margaret Douglas, Countess of Lennox. The daughter of Henry VIII's elder sister Margaret by her second marriage to the Earl of Angus, Douglas was one of the queen's closest and oldest friends and the staunchest of Catholics. Already Mary had showered Douglas with gifts of jewels, tapestries and cash, giving her clothes from the royal wardrobe and allocating her spacious apartments at the royal palaces.⁴⁵ She was even allowed to order her meals directly from Mary's private kitchen.⁴⁶ The Spanish ambassador knew that before marrying Philip and once afterwards, Mary had urged that Douglas be named as her successor 'if God were to call her without giving her heirs of her body'.⁴⁷

Philip, for his part, understood that excluding Elizabeth from the succession would involve the difficult task of persuading the Privy Council and Parliament to set aside her father's will. He also had to contend with his own father, Charles V, who—as one of his final acts before he abdicated—wanted to see her safely married off to a nonentity. One candidate was Emmanuel Philibert, Prince of Piedmont and titular Duke of Savoy, who had already made a visit to England from the Low Countries to inspect her. Another was the Archduke Ferdinand of Austria.⁴⁸

Philip, from the outset, expressed a clear preference for Philibert. A landless aristocrat with royal pretensions whose father had lost his family's patrimony in supporting Charles against the French, the duke of Savoy was a close ally of Spain, a loyal Catholic, good at languages and not too powerful to appear a threat to the English. But either candidate would ensure that England remained a Spanish–Habsburg dependency should Mary fail to produce a child.⁴⁹

◆　◆　◆

Shortly before Philip left for Brussels, Elizabeth was allowed back to Hatfield and Ashridge with her household restored to her. Only her chaplain Edmund Allen, who had taken a wife and left for the Continent, and Elizabeth Sandes, who had fled to Geneva, were missing. With Philip effectively shielding his sister-in-law from Mary, even John Ashley felt it safe to return from Padua.

Seeing for the first time a very real prospect that she could succeed to the throne if her elder sibling failed to bear a child or died, Elizabeth asked Thomas Parry to seek advice from William Cecil about how she should style herself and to send her word secretly in writing.[50] Addressed as 'the Lady Elizabeth' after she was stripped of her royal title by her father after her mother's trial and execution, she clearly wanted something more impressive, if possible to recover her original title of 'Princess'.

Exactly what Cecil came up with is unknown, but eighteen months later Elizabeth granted him a lease of land from a portion of her Northamptonshire estates once belonging to her great-grandmother. The lease was signed 'Elizabeth' and sealed with a personal seal, never previously used as it appears, bearing a Tudor rose and the inscription 'The seal of Elizabeth, King Edward's Sister' in Latin. Curious as it may seem to style herself after her dead brother, it may well be that this was Cecil's ingenious solution as to how to identify her as a princess without using that word.[51]

If anyone knew how to negotiate his way around the backstairs of Mary's Court, it was Cecil. Far from retiring to his estates at Stamford in Lincolnshire or fleeing into exile in Switzerland or Germany like so many of his fellow Protestants after Jane Grey's execution, he stuck close to London and Westminster, seeking to salvage his Court networks. When, in July 1554, Philip had landed at Southampton for his marriage to Mary, Cecil had laid on temporary lodgings for the king's secretary, Gonzalo Pérez, at his own London house. Then, in November, he was one of a party sent to meet Cardinal Pole in Brussels and escort him back to England. He used the occasion to ingratiate himself with Pole despite their religious differences and they sometimes dined together at Lambeth Palace.[52]

Like Elizabeth, Cecil was playing a long game. On New Year's Day in 1555, he sent a gift of gold to the queen, which he valued in his accounts at £10. And on Easter Day 1556, he and his whole family would make their confessions to a priest and attend a Paschal high mass in their parish church at Wimbledon, complete with tapers and holy oil. Cecil made a special journey by boat to London to purchase supplies of wine, wafers, wax, oil and cream for the mass. He even began learning Spanish ready for a possible assignment as a diplomat.[53]

Both Elizabeth and Cecil were the sort of Protestants whom John Calvin had begun to dismiss contemptuously as 'Nicodemites'—for in St John's Gospel it was said that Nicodemus, for fear, had visited Christ only by night. Both dissembled their true beliefs and conformed (however reluctantly) to the mass when under pressure, preferring to live and fight another day rather than fleeing into exile or joining the Protestant martyrs at the stake.[54]

Roger Ascham was another Nicodemite, and once Elizabeth was safely back at Hatfield and Ashridge, she was allowed occasional visits from him to read the orations of Demosthenes with her. In 1554, Mary had made Ascham her Latin secretary—it was he who drafted some of the letters announcing the birth of a prince during the queen's phantom pregnancy.[55] Like Cecil, Ascham sometimes dined with Pole, when they discussed the possible whereabouts of a missing work by Cicero, *De Republica*, known only from quotations made from it by St Augustine. Praising Pole's kindness to the skies, Ascham presented the cardinal-archbishop with a handsome copy of Jeronimo Osorio's treatise on civic and Christian nobility, a book he was championing at the time.[56]

As Ascham enthused to Johann Sturm after his return to Hatfield, 'Elizabeth and I read together in Greek the orations of Aeschines and Demosthenes.' She 'first reads it to me' and immediately she understands not only the language and the meaning, 'but also the whole nature of the argument, the decrees of the people, the manners and the customs of the city: she is so intelligent you would be simply amazed.'[57]

Once more Ascham made his inflated claims to broadcast his own talents as a teacher.[58] Blinded by his ego, he overlooks the fact that for Elizabeth to have recalled him after his earlier disgrace, she must already have come to see herself as a queen-in-waiting. The sole purpose of reading Demosthenes, by far the most difficult author she had so far tackled, was to train a future ruler or privy councillor to make speeches 'aptly' when addressing a great audience. An author whose work was considered to be the finest training for pure eloquence rather than for promoting religion and moral virtue, Demosthenes represented a traditionally masculine virtue—the art of public oratory—which in a woman was reserved to those in line for the succession to kingdoms.[59]

◆　◆　◆

In the end, it was almost entirely due to Philip that Elizabeth was able to use the skills she had learned from Ascham and one day address her Privy Council and Parliament as queen of England. Philip had first shielded her from Mary's vengeance at Hampton Court. He saved her again when, on 18 March 1556, another conspiracy to put her on the throne was discovered.[60]

Clumsily cobbled together by a Berkshire gentleman with ideas above his station, Christopher Ashton, and a military man, Sir Harry Dudley, fourth cousin of the former Duke of Northumberland, the plotters aimed to steal £50,000 in bars of Spanish silver that were stored in the Exchequer at Westminster to fund an army of mercenaries and Protestant exiles who would invade England, drive out the Spaniards and depose Mary.[61] Unmasked when one of them lost his nerve and betrayed the plot, the conspirators turned out to be the pawns of Antoine de Noailles, the French ambassador, who wrote frantically home asking to be recalled before he was put in the Tower himself.[62]

Part of the plot involved betraying Calais to the French, and Mary was determined to put all those implicated in it on trial for treason. As with Wyatt's revolt, the trail led straight to Elizabeth's household, and as soon as de Noailles left the country in May, Mary decided to strike.

Kat Ashley was arrested at Hatfield and put in the Tower, as was Elizabeth's Italian tutor Giovanni Battista Castiglione and three other female servants.[63] Soon, Francis Verney and Henry Peckham, two of the gentlemen-servants, had been arrested too, and an armed guard stationed around Hatfield. A search of Elizabeth's London house, Somerset Place in the Strand, even led to the discovery of a chest crammed full of imported Protestant books and libels attacking the king and queen.[64]

Verney and Peckham were found to be in the plot up to their necks. Both were convicted of treason.[65] But however much Mary wanted to put Elizabeth on trial for her life, she felt she could not do so without consulting Philip. The Venetian ambassadors in London and Brussels recorded her every move. On 1 June, she sent her confidential courier, Francesco Piamontese, in haste to Brussels, since 'nothing is done, nor does anything take place, without having the King's opinion about it, and hearing his will.'[66] When the courier returned, Mary discovered, humiliatingly, that her husband wanted Elizabeth's name kept out of the trials and reprisals and that the investigations into her conduct were to be dropped.[67]

On 8 June, Mary sent two of her most trusted inner councillors to Hatfield to withdraw the guard placed on her sibling and inform her that Kat, Verney and Peckham in their confessions had implicated her in the conspiracy. The councillors were probably lying— making this an act of deliberate spite on Mary's part, since in a confidential memorandum another privy councillor, writing anonymously, insisted that Elizabeth's involvement was hard to credit. She was, he said, known 'to be of too much honour, wisdom, truth and respect to duty and honesty' to be complicit. 'Who', he asked, 'can let [i.e. prevent] knaves to say... we hope this of My Lady Elizabeth or of this Lord or this man?'

At the very least, the Privy Council was split again.[68] But even if Elizabeth *had* dabbled in treason in the hope of deposing her sister and gaining the throne, it no longer mattered, since Philip had decided that she was to be deemed innocent.

Thus it was that the two councillors went on to explain to her that, on Philip's advice, Mary had decided—it was clearly a decision made through gritted teeth—that she was cleared of all suspicion, in proof of which she was to receive a token, a diamond (said the Venetians) worth as much as 400 ducats.

All the same (and this Philip may not have approved) Mary took the opportunity to remodel Elizabeth's household again, putting it under the control of Sir Thomas Pope, a Catholic privy councillor and the founder of Trinity College, Oxford.[69]

Fortunately for Elizabeth, Sir Thomas was a more agreeable gaoler than Bedingfield. Nor, since he made no secret of how much he disliked his new role, did the change last long. On 19 October, after just four months, Mary discharged Pope and released Kat from the Tower, although she was strictly forbidden to return to Hatfield.

The reason for the sudden reversal was that Elizabeth was to go to Court for Christmas.[70] On 28 November, she and her retinue rode in their finery through the London streets to Somerset Place, her gentlemen-servants all arrayed in velvet coats and gold livery chains, behind them some 200 others in red coats cut and trimmed with black.[71]

Three days later she went to Court and met Mary and Pole, who graciously received her. Except that something went wrong, and on 3 December she unexpectedly retraced her steps to Somerset Place and from there to Hatfield.[72]

The explanation came when the Venetian ambassador to France met Henry II of France at Poissy shortly before Christmas. The king told him that Mary had sent for Elizabeth to inform her that Philip wished her to marry Emmanuel Philibert without further delay. She had refused, purportedly retorting that 'the afflictions suffered by her were such that they had...ridded her of any wish for a husband'. Bursting into tears, she declared that she would rather die than have a husband thrust upon her.[73]

By now, the marriage proposal was the keystone of Philip's plans to secure England as a Spanish dependency should his wife die childless. Mary still violently opposed it. But he overruled her.[74]

If the marriage went ahead, Philip meant to have Parliament confirm Elizabeth as the lawful successor, whereas Mary had come to think that, if her half-sister took the throne, she would, as an act of revenge, restore the break with Rome and make England as Protestant again as it had been under Edward, and Philibert would be too weak a man to stop her.[75]

Mary had now come to hate Elizabeth so much, she was said to have begun claiming her half-sister was not, after all, Henry VIII's daughter. Did she not look far too much like Mark Smeaton, one of Anne Boleyn's alleged lovers, 'who was a very handsome man?'[76]

And yet Mary, struggling to come to terms with her own contradictory feelings, believed that her duty lay in obeying her husband. Faced with Elizabeth's refusal to marry the duke, she threatened again to exclude her from the succession.[77] But she had the Privy Council to contend with. If she wanted Elizabeth disinherited, a majority of councillors led by Lord Paget did not.

A political crisis erupted in March 1557, when Philip returned to England to force his wife into joining Spain in a war against France and to bludgeon Elizabeth into marrying Philibert. He succeeded in the first of these aims and failed in the second. When war was declared on 7 June, it began well, but raged in four separate theatres and was universally unpopular despite a spectacular victory at St Quentin in which English troops played a supporting role.

Elizabeth, meanwhile, dug in her heels and refused to be told whom to marry, even when Philip brought his cousins, the Duchesses of Lorraine and Parma, to London in a clumsy attempt to twist her arm. Arriving at Whitehall while Mary was at mass, the duchesses were greeted by Philip and entertained lavishly for a month.[78]

They failed abysmally to work their magic on Elizabeth, whose resistance the French ambassador had considerably stiffened by sending a message warning her of a possible kidnap attempt. She said she would die before she would allow herself either to be kidnapped or to be forced into marriage.[79]

The last residue of mutual trust between Philip and Mary collapsed when Philip made his second and final departure for Brussels on 6 July after a stay of just three and a half months. By then, the queen's depression over her inability to conceive a child had brought her to the verge of despair.[80] Matters descended into farce when, in January 1558, she asked Pole to write to Philip to assure him that she was pregnant again.[81] In February, she believed she might be delivered later that month, and in March she made her will, directing that the throne was go to 'the heirs, issue and fruit of my body according to the laws of the realm', making Philip guardian of both the child and the realm.[82]

The humiliation of Mary's second phantom pregnancy was, however, eclipsed by the catastrophe on New Year's Day, when the Duke of Guise, the leader of the French armies, led a masterful attack on Calais. A severe frost had made it possible for his troops almost literally to walk on water. The surrounding forts were taken after a brief bombardment and, on the 24th, Henry II made a triumphal entry into the town to the sounds of the anthem 'When Israel came out of Egypt'.

Calais was the last of Henry VIII's continental possessions. The disaster paralysed Mary's regime. As even Philip's diehard supporters slunk away, the government slowly disintegrated. Pole alone continued to enjoy the king's confidence. When Mary fell grievously ill in October and died in the early morning of Thursday, 17 November, she was mourned only by her innermost Catholic circle and the fact that Pole followed her to the grave within a few hours seemed to the Protestants to be an act of divine providence.

On hearing that his wife's health was rapidly declining, Philip had sent the Count of Feria, one of his leading councillors and the captain of the Spanish guard, to salvage what Spanish interests he could. Elizabeth, by then, had moved to Brocket Hall, the home of one of her tenants, some two and a half miles to the north of Hatfield, a house more easily defended and from where her cofferer Thomas Parry was working night and day, coordinating her campaign to secure the throne.[83]

Arriving in London on 9 November, Feria had gone next day to Brocket Hall. He found Elizabeth, as he wrote in his report to Philip, to be 'a very vain and clever woman. She must have been thoroughly schooled in the manner in which her father conducted his affairs, and I am very much afraid that she will not be well-disposed in matters of religion'. He then added, 'I see her inclined to govern through men who are believed to be heretics and I am told that all the women around her definitely are.'[84]

Even as Parry was ordering troops from the frontier garrison at Berwick upon Tweed to march with all speed to Brocket Hall, Elizabeth had made it very clear that she was quite unflustered about her prospects of accession. 'She puts great store by the people and is very confident that they are on her side', Feria had continued to Philip. 'She declares that it was the people who put her in her present position and she will not acknowledge that Your Majesty or the nobility of this realm had any part in it'.[85]

Elizabeth meant to win the throne without Philip's help. Her right and title were set out in her father's will. And miraculously the cards fell into her hand. For even as Mary lay dying, the Privy Council, for the first time united in its wariness of Philip after the loss of Calais, sent a delegation to urge her to recognize her half-sister as her successor. She consented as long as Elizabeth agreed to preserve the Catholic religion and pay Mary's debts.[86]

Elizabeth responded to this request in exactly the way her father would have done in the same situation. She said she would, and reneged once she was crowned.[87] As Feria saw clearly, 'She is determined to be governed by no one.'[88]

CHAPTER 9

Uncharted Waters

Eᴌɪᴢᴀʙᴇᴛʜ was proclaimed queen of England by the heralds in London between 11 a.m. and noon on the day her half-sister died. Standing beside them was Francis Russell, who had carried a letter to Ashridge on the eve of Wyatt's revolt.[1] A committed Protestant and a close ally of William Cecil, Russell had succeeded his father as Earl of Bedford in 1555 and was about to become one of the linchpins of the new regime.

Cecil had been with the 25-year-old Elizabeth at Hatfield on the day Mary died, already functioning as the new queen's Secretary of State, even though he would not officially be appointed to the post for another three days. His jottings show how fast and thorough was his grasp of what needed to be done to secure the Tower and its munitions and treasury, the ports, the border with Scotland and the coinage. He sent couriers to Philip and the other European powers with news of Mary's death, began making arrangements for her funeral and for Elizabeth's coronation, and took the necessary steps to continue the authority of the judges and certain key officers. He gave orders for the engraving of a new great seal, for the opening of peace talks with France and finally 'to consider the condition of the preacher at Paul's Cross that no occasion be given to him to stir any dispute touching the governance of the realm'.[2]

What followed amounted to a comprehensive remodelling of every aspect of Court and government—it only mildly exaggerates to make a comparison with the Bolshevik revolution in 1917. A whole new breed of courtiers and officials linked to the networks that had survived from Katherine Parr's household and the circle around Cecil and Sir John Cheke in Edward's reign took over power. Many had declared themselves for Lady Jane Grey, been involved in Wyatt's revolt or the Ashton–Dudley conspiracy, or else gone into exile in Switzerland or Germany in Mary's reign. Several were linked to Thomas Parry, now made treasurer of the queen's household and a privy councillor, or had cut their teeth like Cecil in the service of Protector Somerset or the Duke of Northumberland. Others were Elizabeth's kinsmen on her mother's side, such as Sir Richard Sackville, her second cousin, and William, Lord Howard of Effingham, her great-uncle.[3]

Only Cheke himself was missing from the roll call. Suspected of being the main impresario of the campaign of Protestant exile propaganda against Philip and Mary and (wrongly) said to be the author of the very worst of the libels found in a chest at Elizabeth's house at Somerset Place, he had been kidnapped on the road between Antwerp and Malines by Mary's agents in May 1556 and forced to make a humiliating recantation on pain of being burned for heresy. He died a year later.[4]

A comparison between the coronation list of Elizabeth's household and the funeral list of Mary's shows how drastic a turnover occurred. The cleanest sweep was among the ladies and gentlewomen of the Privy Chamber, where devoted Catholics like Susan Tonge, Lady Jerningham, Frideswide Strelley and Jane Dormer were displaced by women with advanced reformist or evangelical sympathies, notably Kat Ashley (now returned in triumph), Blanche Parry, Katherine Carey, Anne Carey, Lettice Knollys and Mary Sidney.[5]

Mary Sidney was Northumberland's eldest daughter and the wife of Sir Henry Sidney, a former gentleman of Edward's Privy Chamber who had been present with the young king's physicians when he died. It was she who had brought the news to Jane Grey that she was to be queen.

The Careys and Lettice Knollys were among Elizabeth's nearest kinswomen, whom she was determined to rehabilitate. Katherine Carey, Mary Boleyn's daughter, was the wife of Sir Francis Knollys, who had attended the Eucharistic debates in 1551 at the houses of Cecil and Richard Moryson.[6] When she fled with her husband to Basle and Frankfurt after Jane Grey's execution, Elizabeth wrote her a sorrowful letter of farewell signed 'Your loving cousin and ready friend, *Cor rotto* [i.e. broken heart]'. Anne Carey was Katherine's sister-in-law, the wife of Henry Carey, Mary Boleyn's son, whom Elizabeth elevated to the peerage as Lord Hunsdon and to whom she granted lands worth in excess of £4,000 a year. Lettice Knollys was the eldest daughter of Katherine and Sir Francis, and may have served Elizabeth at Hatfield while her parents were in exile.[7]

For her coronation at Westminster Abbey on Sunday, 15 January 1559, Elizabeth had the cloth of gold and ermine robes worn by her half-sister in 1553 altered by ordering a new, more tightly fitted bodice and pair of sleeves from her tailor. Since she spent a small fortune on her wardrobe for the occasion, it is unlikely that by recycling these robes she had economy in mind. It is sometimes said that she wore Mary's robes as a gesture of solidarity with her sibling. Far more likely is it, given the rivalry between them, that she was dancing on Mary's grave.[8]

In compliance with the *Liber Regalis*, the anointing went ahead according to traditional Catholic forms, but Elizabeth tweaked the coronation mass to signal some of the religious changes that were coming. The Epistle and Gospel were read in English as well as in Latin. The celebrant, George Carew, the Dean of the Chapel Royal, did not elevate the host and the queen took communion in both the bread and the wine. The last, for the moment, was known only to Carew and herself since, in accordance with the *Liber*, she took communion inside a 'traverse' or temporary closet surrounded by curtains.[9]

◆　　◆　　◆

Once crowned, Elizabeth might have supposed that her authority would automatically be accepted, but as an unmarried woman without a husband in view she found herself sailing in uncharted waters. On 25 January 1559, her first Parliament opened with a sermon preached by Richard Cox, Edward's tutor and one of several draftsmen of the 1552 Book of Common Prayer, who had also played a prominent role in proclaiming Jane Grey.[10]

Chosen by Cecil to preach to the assembled Lords and Commons on the need for reform, an occasion on which he held forth for an hour and a half, Cox signalled a faster pace of change than Elizabeth herself envisaged, calling on her to begin without delay a fresh campaign against idolatry and superstition, which she was bound to do because God had made her queen.[11] Never known for his tact, Cox was wrong-footed, perhaps unaware that Elizabeth's leading councillors and retainers were more Protestant than she was. Or if he *did* know of the mismatch, then clearly he expected the young queen to suppress her personal preferences in favour of their yearnings. After all, she was 'only' a woman and (as the Protestants believed) it was largely through their efforts that she had gained the throne.

Cecil, reading the signals, was determined to move quickly, returning doctrines consistent with the *Consensus Tigurinus* to the restored Church of England before Elizabeth changed her mind and backtracked. In a paper entitled the 'Device for the Alteration of Religion', he concluded that a working party of learned men should be convened to 'bring a Plat or Book hereof [i.e. for the "alteration of religion"] ready drawn to her Highness'. Names suggested were a handpicked selection of key members of his coterie, whose support for a lightly revised 1552 Book of Common Prayer was all but guaranteed.[12] And no alternatives to this 'Plat or Book' were to be offered to the queen.

Cecil dealt ruthlessly with the Catholic opposition in the House of Lords, which might otherwise have sought concessions from a young and inexperienced queen. The Earl of Bedford made the lay lords graphically aware of the dire implications of the Marian reunion with Rome for those who had purchased ex-monastic lands. And to remove the ex-Marian bishops from the arena, Cecil and his brother-in-law, Nicholas Bacon, organized a theological disputation at Westminster Abbey at which Cox was one of the leading spokesmen. After Catholic traditions not written in Scripture were excluded from the terms of reference of the debate, the

Elizabeth Regina.

FIGURE 16   Elizabeth kneeling in prayer, with the sceptre and the sword of justice on the floor beside her. A scene in which the queen is depicted in what may be the artist's imagination of her 'closet' or secret oratory at one of her palaces. Off the 'closet' was a smaller room fitted with a kneeling desk for the queen. This image first appeared in 1569.

Catholic bishops walked out, enabling Cecil to imprison them for contempt.[13]

Elizabeth's own religious creed remained close to the moderate beliefs of Katherine Parr and Edmund Allen, her chaplain in Edward's reign—whom Cecil prudently nominated for the bishopric of Rochester.[14] She visibly hankered after the more ambiguously traditionalist 1549 Prayer Book and had started using this version of the liturgy in the Chapel Royal before pressure from her own supporters forced her to abandon it. Subconsciously, she seems to have associated the 1552 alternative with Edward's 'Device for the Succession', which had made Jane Grey queen and excluded herself.[15]

Once committed to the 1552 Book of Common Prayer, Elizabeth sought to dilute its practical effects by stealth. A last-minute clause was inserted into the Act of Uniformity, stating that until she decided otherwise, the vestments of the clergy and ornaments of the chancel should be those of 1549, which were still largely those of the mass.[16]

To her dismay, she found that Matthew Parker—whom she made archbishop of Canterbury, believing him to be a natural ally—circumvented her. Colluding with Cox and Cecil, Parker contrived that the Injunctions drawn up for a general visitation of the dioceses later in 1559 specified clerical dress as worn in 1552 and ordered 'idolatries' such as images, paintings and candlesticks to be stripped out of the parish churches, 'to the intent that all superstition and hypocrisy… may vanish'.[17]

Elizabeth ostentatiously reinstated the crucifix and candlesticks in her Chapel Royal in the autumn of 1559 after the iconoclasts removed them. Thereafter, she expressed her 'old' (some say 'odd') sort of Protestantism in a variety of different ways. High on her list was her scathing disapproval of the clergy's right to marry. She particularly loathed married bishops, believing that their low-born wives considered themselves to be noblewomen. And although preaching the Word of God lay at the heart of the Protestant view of salvation, she considered regular sermons to be unnecessary.[18]

After her early skirmishes over the settlement's small print, Elizabeth maintained a vice-like grip on the Church of England and on the pace of change. Unlike her father during his anti-papal campaign, she demanded only outward conformity to the new settlement. As a former 'Nicodemite' herself, prying into the private beliefs of her subjects as long as they attended church regularly was not on her agenda. As Francis Bacon later said of her, it was not her custom to 'make windows into men's souls', although he added the crucial rider, unless dissent 'did overflow into overt and express acts and affirmations.'[19]

Unlike in Edward's reign, when Cranmer, Cheke, Cecil, Northumberland and the young Josiah's other 'godly councillors' debated preaching and the conversion of the nation, Elizabeth after 1559 excluded her privy councillors from almost every matter concerning the 'further reformation' of religion. Like her father, she interpreted the royal supremacy to mean sacral monarchy by another name. When Parker's successor at Canterbury, Edmund Grindal, clashed with her in 1577 over his support for the puritan campaign of sermon-centred piety, she suspended him for daring to suggest that he owed allegiance to God before the queen.

◆   ◆   ◆

Equally resoundingly, Elizabeth rejected a Calvinist extension of the argument first floated by Roger Ascham that she was an 'exceptional' woman whom God had destined for higher things.

In a clumsy attempt to justify and exalt her position as an unmarried female ruler, several former Marian exiles, among them John Aylmer, Jane Grey's former schoolmaster, declared that the new queen had come to her position as a second 'Deborah'.[20] The most celebrated woman prophet in the Old Testament, Deborah, a judge and virtual king in Israel, had delivered the people from the 'yoke' and 'idolatry' of the Canaanites through her 'extraordinary' faith and courage.[21]

Elizabeth's reaction is not recorded when she first discovered that 'Deborah' had been chosen as an icon of female rule by the City of London's guildsmen in their pageants on the eve of her coronation. Since the costumes for these pageants had been lent by the queen's Master of the Revels, it is often assumed that Elizabeth had personally overseen and approved the pageants or their scripts, but this is highly questionable. The Revels Office and royal Office of Works routinely cooperated with the city guilds over loan of costumes, interior decoration, carpentry and the construction of temporary edifices without reference to the monarch or lord chamberlain.[22]

In any case, *after* the coronation, Elizabeth repudiated the suggestion that she was a second 'Deborah'. In April 1559, John Knox joined in the debate, claiming that Elizabeth's female rule—like Deborah's—was the result of a 'miracle' or an 'extraordinary dispensation of God's great mercy'.[23] In taking this line, Knox sought to wriggle free of the consequences of his bad timing in publishing a book entitled *The First Blast of the Trumpet against the Monstrous Regiment of Women* in the spring of 1558, where he had argued the opposite, saying that a woman ruler was a 'monster in nature' and unfit to rule. A diatribe against female rule in general, *The First Blast* had gone on specifically to attack Mary Tudor in England and the regent Marie de Guise, mother of Mary Queen of Scots, in Scotland, openly inciting the subjects of both kingdoms to depose them for their 'inordinate pride and tyranny'.[24]

In the spring of 1559, a red-faced Knox was corresponding with Cecil from Dieppe in the hope of making amends and so resuming the career in London he had begun under Edward. His solution was to reshape his arguments in line with Calvin's opinion that female monarchy, in exceptional instances, was ordained by the 'peculiar providence' of God. Women's rule, according to Calvin, deviated from the 'proper order of nature', but exceptionally there were special women—of course, he meant only Protestant women—who were 'raised up by divine authority' to rule in order to become the 'nursing mothers' of the Church.[25] In his *First Blast*, Knox had already framed the case of Deborah as an 'extraordinary' exception to the general prohibition of female rule, an act of God's 'inscrutable wisdom' that, at a key moment in biblical history, had allowed a 'godly' woman to be set to rule over men.[26]

Elizabeth, however, never accepted that her monarchy was the result of a 'miracle' or an 'extraordinary dispensation of God's great mercy'. She refused to allow a religious test, rather than hereditary right, to set the standard against which the legitimacy of her rule should be judged. Her reasons were not feminist, but dynastic. Her case was summarized in 1563 or 1566 by Thomas Norton, another of Cecil's coterie. If her title were to be established 'by God's special and immediate ordinance' without any regard to her hereditary right and title, she had insisted, it 'setteth all her subjects at liberty, who acknowledge no such extraordinary calling.' Indeed, 'the pope and papists may as easily say that the queen ought not to be queen though she have right.'[27]

◆   ◆   ◆

FIGURE 17   View of Windsor Castle as it appeared in 1582. Substantially constructed mainly during the reigns of Henry III and Edward III, the royal apartments had been modernized by Edward IV, and Henry VII added a new tower and gallery. The castle was the most secure of all the Tudor royal palaces. Although not one of her favourite residences, Elizabeth would retreat to it whenever she felt herself to be in danger.

Confronted by an increasing challenge—not least from Cecil and his fellow privy councillors in and after 1563—that she should marry and settle the succession, Elizabeth found herself living out the very dilemma that her father had flagged up in the preface to *A Glasse of the Truthe* during his first divorce campaign in 1531. If a woman 'shall chance to rule', he had written, 'she cannot continue long without a husband, which by God's law must then be her governor and head, and so finally shall direct the realm.'[28]

Unless from a Nordic or a North German state (and a Lutheran), a foreign prince whom Elizabeth might consider marrying would inevitably be a Catholic as well as a foreigner. She would never forget what had happened to her half-sister after she had married Philip—her Privy Council was divided, the realm scarred by revolt and xenophobia, then finally dragged into an unpopular war, culminating in the catastrophic loss of Calais. The prospect of an absentee husband, such as Philip had become, was a further complication.

Just as powerful an objection was that marriage with one of her subjects would transform a ruling queen's relationship with her nobles, councillors and people. Elizabeth must have heard the disturbing reports of Jane Grey's experience after she had been proclaimed queen. Her husband, Guildford Dudley, had demanded to be king. A furious row had erupted between the young couple at the Tower, shortly after Jane was handed the crown jewels. Married in haste to a man she barely knew, Jane spiritedly told Guildford he could only be a duke. His response was to refuse to sleep with her which, had the reign lasted longer and Guildford persisted in his attempt to extort the kingship, would have prevented her from having a child and settling the succession.[29] A very similar demand for the kingship would throw Scotland into turmoil and revolt when Mary Queen of Scots married Lord Darnley in 1565, leading within two years to his brutal assassination, followed by her forced abdication and flight to exile in England.[30]

The one man with whom Elizabeth fell in love as queen and whom she would almost certainly have married if the circumstances had been right, Robert Dudley, may have come closest to the truth about her. In 1566, conversing with the nephew and secretary of the French ambassador, who had asked him whether he thought she was more likely to marry abroad or at home, Dudley confided that his 'true opinion was that she would never marry'.

Claiming that he knew Elizabeth 'as well as or better than anyone else of her close acquaintance, for they had first become friends before she was eight years old', Dudley added that 'both then and later (when she was old enough to marry) she said she had never wished to do so.'

The difficulty is that Dudley was at pains to qualify his remarks by observing that, 'if by chance she should change her mind... he was practically assured that she would choose no one else but him, as she had done him the honour of telling him so quite openly on more than one occasion'.[31] Was this true, or were all his remarks part of a wider diplomatic smokescreen?

Already identified as one of Elizabeth's inner circle on the eve of her accession, Dudley had been among the witnesses to the surrender of Philip and Mary's great seal at Hatfield on the day after Mary's death, when he was appointed Master of the Horse. Within weeks of her coronation, he was Elizabeth's most glittering Court favourite, a position he would hold until his death in 1588. Despite opposition from Cecil and the Earl of Bedford, who feared what might happen if she married Dudley, she admitted him as a Knight of the Garter in 1559, created him a privy councillor in 1562 and Earl of Leicester in 1564.

Their relationship caused a scandal. The Count of Feria, who married Jane Dormer and was making ready to return with her to Spain, claimed in April 1559 that Dudley 'does whatever he likes with affairs, and it is even said that Her Majesty visits him in his chamber day and night'.[32] Cecil was said to have threatened to resign, since Elizabeth would only listen to Dudley and was even making gestures of affection towards him in public. Rumours were rife that she was waiting for Dudley's wife, Amy, to die, and that Dudley meant to poison her.

In desperation, Kat Ashley fell at her mistress's feet, begging her 'in God's name to marry and put an end to all these disreputable rumours'.[33]

A furore broke out on 8 September 1560, when Amy was found lying dead at the foot of a small stone spiral staircase while lodged at Cumnor Place, near Oxford, her neck broken but her headdress curiously intact. According to the coroner's report, she had two serious head wounds, one of them two inches deep. The coroner's jury reached a verdict of accidental death, but it turned out that the foreman had once been Elizabeth's servant and that Dudley knew another juror personally. Thomas Blount, Dudley's agent, had allegedly dined with two other jurors before they reached their verdict.[34]

Nothing could be proved and Dudley was probably innocent since he strained every nerve to discover the true cause of his wife's death in an effort to save his reputation. Except he could never overcome the fact that when Amy died, he had not visited her for over a year, and on his few previous visits, he was commanded by Elizabeth to go dressed 'all in black' and 'to say [on his return] that he did nothing with her'.[35]

When Elizabeth came to realize that she would never be able to marry the man she loved and keep her throne, her survival instinct kicked in. Despite allowing nothing to be said against Dudley in her hearing, she decided that marrying him was too risky. Thereafter, her love for him was a powerful emotional barrier preventing her from marrying anyone else.

Of the half dozen or so credible candidates for her hand, the Archduke Charles of Austria, seriously in contention between 1563 and 1567, was the most plausible. But the negotiations collapsed when he insisted on hearing mass regularly in his private apartments, a demand which split the Privy Council. Elizabeth was left in no doubt that a marriage on these terms would be as unpopular as her half-sister's marriage to Philip of Spain.[36]

In 1570–1, the courtship of Henry, Duke of Anjou, Catherine de' Medici's second son and heir presumptive to the French throne, fared no better. Backed by powerful interests at the French Court, it met an indifferent response in England. Always in two minds about it, Elizabeth worried that at 37, and with some eighteen years between them, she was old enough to be the bridegroom's mother and that he would spurn her as she grew older. She only considered him in the first place because she needed some serious muscle in dealing with Spain. When Cecil saw that an entente with France could be achieved by other means, the suit fell into abeyance.[37]

Of the remaining suitors, only Francis, the youngest of Catherine de' Medici's sons who succeeded his brother as Duke of Anjou, seemed to catch her attention. When the negotiations opened in earnest in 1579, she greeted Anjou's agent with a courtesy and coquetry that astonished even seasoned observers. She held lengthy and intimate interviews with the envoy, at which the talk was of love rather than of alliances or treaties. She entertained him at feasts, dances, masques and jousts, and showered him with gifts and love tokens for the duke.

When Anjou himself arrived in England, she played to perfection the role of a woman in love, despite her fear that his unpromising appearance (his face was badly scarred by smallpox) and their twenty-one-year age gap would make him an object of derision. She sported his portrait miniature on her dress or carried it in her prayer book, and sent him letters and a poetic lament on his departure. According to an English account of his final visit in November 1581, she 'drew off a ring from her finger, and put it upon the Duke of Anjou's, upon certain conditions betwixt them two'.[38] According to a Spanish report, she said before witnesses, 'He shall be my husband' and at the same moment turned to him and kissed him on the mouth, 'drawing a ring from her own hand and giving it to him as a pledge'.[39]

Was this Elizabeth's last romance before the menopause? Perhaps, but more likely her outward show of affection was play-acting, an elaborate pretence to clinch a full French alliance and therefore security for the Protestant cause in England and the Low Countries against the menacing threat of Spain. In fact, the scene with the ring had been elaborately staged in response to a message from Henry III and Catherine that they could not allow Elizabeth to draw them into open hostilities with Spain unless she first married Anjou.

◆   ◆   ◆

Under extreme pressure from Cecil and the Privy Council to marry and settle the succession, Elizabeth delivered the most forthright statement as to her intentions that she would ever make before a delegation of both Houses of Parliament in 1566. Invoking once again the first oration of Isocrates to Nicocles, she declared, 'I will never break the word of a prince spoken in [a] public place, for my honour's sake. And therefore I say again, I will marry as soon as I can conveniently, if God take not him away with whom I mind to marry or myself, or else some other great let [i.e. hindrance] happen. I can say no more except the party were present. And I hope to have children, otherwise I would never marry.'[40]

Her views on the succession had been most candidly expressed in 1561 to the Scottish Secretary of State, William Maitland of

Lethington. His mission was to renegotiate a treaty that Cecil had made with France and the Protestant lords in Scotland, which recognized Elizabeth as the rightful queen of England and granted her a right of surveillance over Scotland where religion was concerned. When Mary Queen of Scots returned from France to Holyrood in August 1561 to begin her personal rule, she wanted the treaty (which was agreed behind her back and which she always refused to ratify) amended. As the granddaughter of Henry VIII's elder sister Margaret whose first husband was James IV of Scotland, Mary had a strong residual claim to the English throne, and she wanted it to be recognized. Within two weeks of her return, she sent Maitland south to meet Elizabeth, then on her way back to London from her summer progress.

Elizabeth, who always made it her priority to defend the dynastic ideal, told Maitland that she would consider appointing commissioners to review the treaty, but would never be willing to name her successor. Intriguingly, she declared that Mary had the best possible claim to succeed her if she died childless. 'There protest to you', she avowed, 'in the presence of God [that] I for my part know none better nor that myself would prefer to her or, to be plain with you, that case occurring that might debar her from it.'[41] To Cecil's consternation, it was a view she continued to hold for at least ten more years.

Mary's dynastic credentials were impeccable. What prevented Elizabeth from naming a successor, she confessed to Maitland, was her fear that identifying a successor by name would hasten her own death. 'Princes cannot like their own children', she declared. 'Think you that I could love my own winding-sheet?'[42]

She feared chiefly that a debate on the succession would expose deficiencies in her own claim to the throne. 'I have always abhorred', she said, 'to draw in question the title of the crown. So many disputes have been already touching it in the mouths of men—some that this marriage was unlawful, some that someone was a bastard, some other to and fro as they favoured or misliked.' She then claimed that when she had received her coronation ring in Westminster Abbey and sworn her coronation oath, she had effectively 'married' her realm, with the inference that this stood in the way of her taking a husband.

Her killer argument—the one she described as 'most weighty of all'—was that any attempt to name a successor would incite conspiracies. She told Maitland how deeply she had been affected by the events of her early life. 'I know', she said, 'the inconstancy of the people of England, how they ever mislike the present government and have their eyes fixed upon that person that is next to succeed'. She then gave Maitland an account of her tribulations in Mary's reign. 'I have', she said, 'good experience of myself in my sister's time—how desirous men were that I should be in place and [how] earnest [they were] to set me up. And if I would have consented, I know what enterprises would have been attempted to bring it to pass.'

And she concluded with a conceit. 'As children dream in their sleep after apples and in the morning, when they awake and find not the apples, they weep, so every man that bear me good will when I was Lady Elizabeth or to whom I showed a good visage, imagineth with himself that immediately after my coming to the crown, every man should be rewarded according to his own fantasy.' Such men finding themselves disappointed, 'it may be that some could be content of new change in hope to be then in better case.'

It all, she reflected wistfully, came down to human psychology: 'No prince's revenues be so great that they are able to satisfy the insatiable cupidity of men.'[43]

◆   ◆   ◆

The tragedy of Henry VIII's children is that, for all their father's valiant attempts to produce legitimate heirs who would perpetuate his dynasty, not one of them managed to have even a single child themselves. Each, except possibly Henry Fitzroy, whose horizons were limited by his illegitimacy, had a chequered upbringing. And once Anne Boleyn arrived on the scene, even Fitzroy would be disappointed over his place in the succession and his marriage.

For Mary, Edward and Elizabeth, the highly disturbing or untimely ends of their respective mothers cast a long shadow over their lives. In Mary's case, despite the kindness of Jane Seymour and the best efforts of Katherine Parr, her mother's divorce and the backlash against Spain came to dominate her life. Elizabeth could only have learned of the terrible fate of Anne Boleyn from the reports of others, but she clearly reflected on it, since one of her most treasured possessions was a ring with a hinged head incorporating miniature enamel portraits of herself and her mother.[44]

Their father's succession settlement turned out to be excessively prescriptive and arguably botched in an attempt to freeze the monarchy and the faith of the Church of England in aspic in 1547. It had been found wanting when, in turn, Edward, Mary and Elizabeth (or most notably in Edward's reign his advisers) sought to interpret Henry's legacy in dramatically different ways. Even Mary's own co-religionists did not believe she had an uncontested right to rule or to marry Philip of Spain without confirmation by Parliament. And the manoeuvres that had made Edward Seymour Lord Protector and Jane Grey queen showed how flimsy were Henry's assumptions that his succession settlement could be made to stick, even when underpinned by legislation.

Of the four children, Elizabeth was the most successful, but also the luckiest. Her encounter as an teenager with Thomas Seymour left her badly bruised, but the experience sharpened her wits and steeled her to weather more dangerous storms than an interrogation from Sir Robert Tyrwhit. She knew better than to incriminate herself directly in Mary's reign, allowing her servants to act non-attributably on her behalf, although without Philip she might on at least two occasions have been put on trial for her life and executed. Her imprisonment in the Tower—and in the very same rooms where her mother had been a captive—was her most terrifying moment. Even as queen it was said that she shuddered when duty obliged her to visit the Tower or pass by it in her barge.

Her 'Nicodemism' was a vital source of strength. Once established as queen, she learned to dissimulate in politics as well as in religion in support of her chief aim, which was to preserve the monarchy and its values largely in the form in which they had been handed down to her from the father she revered. Not for nothing was her motto *Semper eadem* ('Always the Same'). Her sole aspiration for change lay in her conviction that the solution to the Reformation divide lay in a moderate form of Protestantism, although her hope that Catholics could be persuaded to conform to it within a generation proved largely a failure.

Pan-European events in the 1570s and 1580s were not in her favour. As an almost cosmic battle between Catholics and Protestants played out in France, the Low Countries and on the Atlantic Ocean, the old dynastic monarchies became vulnerable to ideological attacks rooted in religious sectarianism.

Against her better judgement, Elizabeth was finally pressured by her privy councillors in 1587 to sign an execution warrant for Mary Queen of Scots, who had been plotting against her. Cecil,

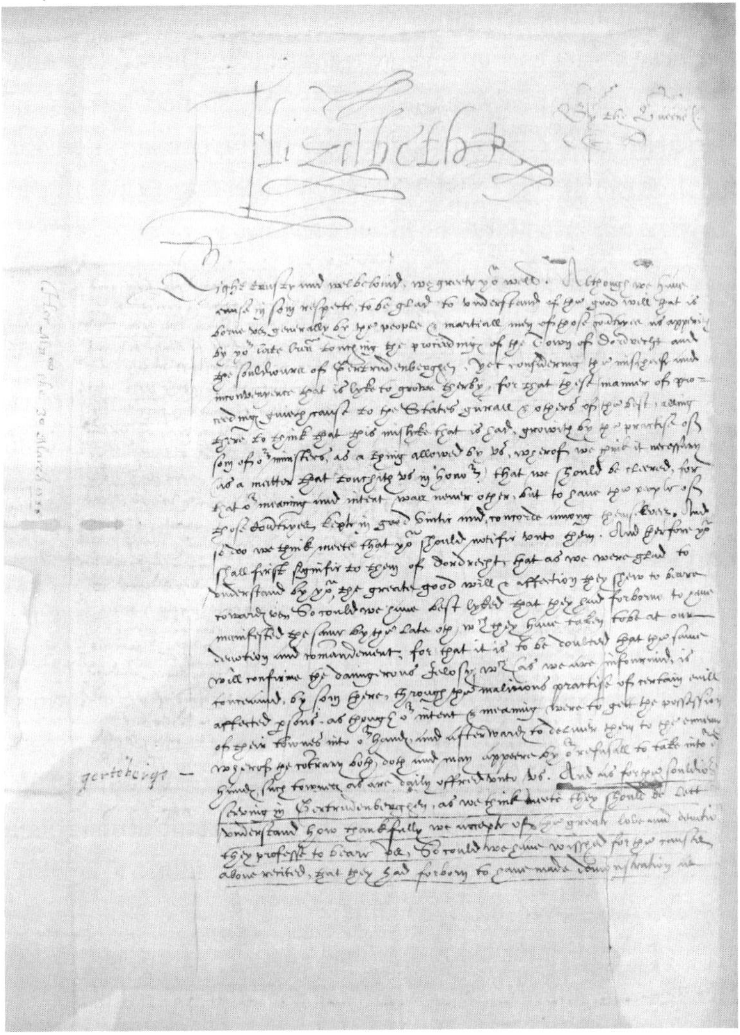

FIGURE 18   A letter signed at the top by Elizabeth using her characteristic sign manual, addressed in 1588 to Peregrine Bertie, Lord Willoughby, Lieutenant-General and Commander in Chief of the English forces against Spain in the Netherlands, some three months before the arrival of the Spanish Armada.

who raised a false alarm that the Spanish Armada had landed a year early in Wales in order to get her to sign, had drafted the warrant in which he called for speedy justice against a woman who was an 'undoubted danger' to Elizabeth and the 'public state of this realm, as well for the cause of the Gospel and the true religion of Christ'.[45]

But the day after signing it, Elizabeth backtracked, sending a messenger to order her secretary, William Davison, not to have the warrant sealed until he had spoken with her again. When they met later, she railed against his 'unseemly haste', with the result that Cecil intervened, directing Davison to hand the warrant (already sealed) to him, and summoning a group of trusted privy councillors to a clandestine meeting in his chamber at the Court at Greenwich. There, Cecil's cabal decided to force Elizabeth's hand and press ahead regardless with the execution, and not to tell her 'until it were done'.[46]

After the unauthorized despatch of the warrant, Elizabeth went through an emotional trauma that proved to be deeper and more enduring than the crisis that would be brought about by the Armada of 1588. By executing a sovereign queen after a public trial in a court of law, she knew that she had fatally attenuated her father's legacy. The execution was a regicide, preparing the way for such future events as the execution of Charles I in 1649 and the deposition of James II in 1688, with the corresponding rise to power of those members of Parliament who called for the deposition or execution of Catholic rulers and the selection and approbation of future monarchs on the basis of criteria that members of Parliament themselves defined.

To a queen who was Henry VIII's daughter, this was abhorrent. The action of Cecil and his fellow privy councillors smacked of republicanism and the sovereignty of elected assemblies like those of Venice or Holland. Likewise, the flip side of Elizabeth's decision not to marry was that, when she died a few months short of her seventieth birthday in March 1603, her dynasty died with her and the succession passed to James VI of Scotland.

The waters were indeed uncharted.

ABBREVIATIONS USED IN THE REFERENCES

In citing manuscripts or printed books, the following abbreviations are used:

APC	*Acts of the Privy Council*, ed. J. R. Dasent, 46 vols (London, 1890–1964)
Baldwin	T. W. Baldwin, *William Shakspere's [sic] Small Latin and Less Greeke*, 2 vols (Urbana, Ill., 1944)
BL	British Library, London
BNF	Bibliothèque Nationale de France, Paris
Bodleian	Bodleian Library, Oxford
Bryson PhD	A. Bryson, '"The Speciall Men in Every Shere". The Edwardian Regime, 1547–1553', unpublished University of St Andrews PhD (St Andrews, 2001)
Chronicle	*The Chronicle of Queen Jane and of Two Years of Queen Mary*, ed. J. G. Nichols, *Camden Society*, Old Series, 48 (1850), pp. 1–196
CPR	*Calendar of Patent Rolls*, 69 vols (London, 1891–1973)
CSPD, Edward	*Calendar of State Papers, Domestic Series, of the Reign of Edward VI, 1547–1553*, ed. C. S. Knighton (London, 1992)
CSPD, Mary	*Calendar of State Papers, Domestic Series, of the Reign of Mary I, 1553–1558*, ed. C. S. Knighton (London, 1998)
CSPF	*Calendar of State Papers Foreign*, 25 vols in 28 parts (London, 1861–1950)
CSPScot	*Calendar of State Papers Relating to Scotland and Mary Queen of Scots, 1547–1603, Preserved in the Public Record*

	Office, the British Museum, and Elsewhere in England, 13 vols (London, 1898–1969)
CSPSp	*Calendar of Letters, Despatches, and State Papers Relating to the Negotiations between England and Spain, Preserved in the Archives at Vienna, Brussels, Simancas and Elsewhere*, 13 vols in 19 parts (London, 1862–1954)
CSPSp, Supp	*Calendar of Letters, Despatches, and State Papers Relating to the Negotiations Between England and Spain, Supplement to Volume I and Volume II* (London, 1868)
CSPSp, Further Supp	*Further Supplement to the Negotiations Between England and Spain*, ed. G. Mattingly (London, 1940)
CSPV	*Calendar of State Papers and Manuscripts relating to English Affairs in the Archives and Collections of Venice and in other Libraries of Northern Italy*, 38 vols (London, 1864–1947)
ECW	*Elizabeth I: Collected Works*, ed. L. S. Marcus, J. Mueller and M. B. Rose (Chicago, 2000)
EHR	*English Historical Review*
Ellis	*Original Letters, Illustrative of British History*, ed. H. Ellis, 3 series, 11 vols (London, 1824–46)
ESW	*Queen Elizabeth I: Selected Works*, ed. S. W. May (New York, 2004)
Fitzroy Inventory	*Inventories of the Wardrobes, Plate, Chapel Stuff etc. of Henry Fitzroy, Duke of Richmond, and of the Wardrobe Stuff at Baynard's Castle of Katherine, Princess Dowager*, ed. J. Nichols, *Camden Society*, Old Series, 61 (1855), pp. 1–55
FF	Ancien Fonds Français
Foedera	*Foedera, Conventiones, Litterae et Cuiuscunque Generis Acta Publica inter Reges Angliae et Alios Quosuis Imperatores, Reges, Pontifices, Principes vel Communitates*, ed. T. Rymer, 20 vols (London, 1726–35)
Foxe	*The first volume of the ecclesiasticall history contayning the actes [and] monumentes of thinges passed in euery*

	kinges time, in this realme, especially in the Churche of England principally to be noted ... Newly recognised and inlarged by the author, 2 vols (London, 1576)
Green	*Letters of Royal and Illustrious Ladies of Great Britain*, ed. M. A. E. Wood, 3 vols (London, 1846)
Hall	*Henry VIII* [an edition of Edward Hall's Chronicle], ed. C. Whibley, 2 vols (London, 1904)
Halliwell	*Letters of the Kings of England*, ed. J. O. Halliwell, 2 vols (London, 1848)
Haynes	*A Collection of State Papers Relating to Affairs in the Reigns of King Henry VIII, King Edward VI, Queen Mary and Queen Elizabeth From the Year 1542 to 1570 ... Left by William Cecil, Lord Burghley* (London, 1740)
HEH	Henry E. Huntington Library, San Marino, California
HJ	*Historical Journal*
HO	*A Collection of Ordinances and Regulations for the Government of the Royal Household* (London, 1790)
JEH	*Journal of Ecclesiastical History*
Lambeth	Lambeth Palace Library
Leland	*Joannis Lelandi antiquarii de rebus Britannicis collectanea. Cum Thomae Hearnii praefatione notis et indice ad editionem primam*, 6 vols (London, 1770)
Lisle Letters	*The Lisle Letters*, ed. M. St. Clare Byrne, 6 vols (Chicago and London, 1981)
Literary Remains	*Literary Remains of King Edward VI*, ed. J. G. Nichols, 2 vols (Roxburghe Club: London, 1857)
Lodge	*Illustrations of British History, Biography and Manners in the Reigns of Henry VIII, Edward VI, Mary, Elizabeth and James I*, ed. E. Lodge, 3 vols (London, 1791)
LP	*Letters and Papers, Foreign and Domestic, of the Reign of Henry VIII*, ed. J. S. Brewer, J. Gairdner and R. H. Brodie, 21 vols in 32 parts, and Addenda (London, 1862–1932)

Machyn	*The Diary of Henry Machyn, Citizen and Merchant-Taylor of London, From A.D. 1550 to A.D. 1563*, ed. J. G. Nichols, *Camden Society*, Old Series, 42 (1848), pp. 1–464
MS	Manuscript
Murphy	B. A. Murphy, *Bastard Prince: Henry VIII's Lost Son* (Stroud, 2001)
NA	National Archives, Kew
ODNB	*The New Oxford Dictionary of National Biography*, ed. Colin Matthew and Brian Harrison, 60 vols (Oxford, 2004)
PPE Elizabeth	*Privy Purse Expenses of Elizabeth of York; Wardrobe Accounts of Edward the Fourth. With a Memoir of Elizabeth of York, and Notes*, ed. N. H. Nicolas (London, 1830)
PPE Mary	*Privy Purse Expenses of the Princess Mary*, ed. F. Madden (London, 1831)
Rawdon Brown	*Four Years at the Court of Henry VIII: Selections of Despatches written by the Venetian Ambassador, Sebastian Giustinian*, ed. Rawdon Brown, 2 vols (London, 1854)
Rogers, Corr.	*The Correspondence of Sir Thomas More*, ed. E. F. Rogers (Princeton, NJ, 1947)
Rutland Papers	*Original Documents Illustrative of the Courts and Times of Henry VII and Henry VIII ... from the Private Archives of His Grace the Duke of Rutland*, ed. W. Jerdan, *Camden Society*, Old Series, 21 (London, 1842), pp. 1–133
Samman PhD	N. Samman, 'The Henrician Court during Cardinal Wolsey's Ascendancy', unpublished University of Wales PhD (Cardiff, 1988)
SR	*Statutes of the Realm*, ed. A. Luders et al., 11 vols (London, 1810–28)
State Papers	*State Papers during the Reign of Henry VIII*, 11 vols (London, 1830–52)

STC	*A Short-Title Catalogue of Books Printed in England, Scotland and Ireland, and of English Books Printed Abroad*, ed. W. A. Jackson, F. S. Ferguson and K. F. Pantzer, 2nd edn, 3 vols (London, 1976–91)
Tytler	*England Under the Reigns of Edward VI and Mary*, ed. P. F. Tytler, 2 vols (London, 1839)
Verney Papers	*Letters and Papers of the Verney Family Down to the End of the Year 1639*, ed. J. Bruce, *Camden Society,* Old Series, 56 (1853), pp. 1–276
Wiesener	*La Jeunesse d'Élisabeth d'Angleterre, 1533–1558* (Paris, 1878)
Wriothesley	*A Chronicle of England during the Reigns of the Tudors, from A.D. 1485 to 1559, by Charles Wriothesley*, ed. W. D. Hamilton, 2 vols, *Camden Society*, New Series, 11 and 20 (1875–77), I, pp. 1–226, II, pp. 1–170

Manuscripts preserved at NA are quoted by the call number there in use. The descriptions of the classes referred to are as follows:

E 36	Exchequer, Treasury of the Receipt, Miscellaneous Books
E 101	Exchequer, King's Remembrancer, Various Accounts
KB 8	Court of King's Bench, Crown Side, Bag of Secrets
KB 9	Court of King's Bench, Ancient Indictments
LC 2	Lord Chamberlain's Department, Special Events
OBS	Obsolete Lists and Indexes
SP 1	State Papers, Henry VIII, General Series
SP 4	State Papers, Henry VIII, Signatures by Stamp
SP 10	State Papers, Domestic, Edward VI
SP 11	State Papers, Domestic, Mary I
SP 12	State Papers, Domestic, Elizabeth I

NOTES ON DATES AND QUOTATIONS

Dates

In giving dates, the Old Style has been retained, but the year is assumed to have begun on 1 January, and not on Lady Day, the feast of the Annunciation (i.e. 25 March), which was by custom the first day of the calendar year in France, Spain and Italy until 1582, in Scotland until 1600, and in England, Wales and Ireland until 1752.

Transcription of primary documents

The spelling and orthography of primary sources in quotations are normally given in modernized form. Modern punctuation and capitalization are provided where there is none in the original manuscript.

Translation from Latin writings

In translations of Latin writings, I have occasionally substituted my own translation where this better matches the sense of the original, avoids an anachronism or is more colloquial.

NOTES AND REFERENCES

Prologue notes

1 Charles Brandon, Duke of Suffolk, who first jousted publicly as a 17-year-old at the tournament to celebrate Arthur's marriage and waited on him the morning after the wedding, testified in 1529 that one of the prince's body servants informed him that Arthur, 'after he had lain with the said Lady Katherine at Shrovetide [8 February 1502] . . . began to decay and was never so lusty in his body and courage from that time unto his death.' BL, Cotton MS Appendix XXVII, fo. 71; *LP*, IV, iii, no. 5774 (13). The identity of the witness is established by Edward, Lord Herbert of Cherbury, *The Life and Raigne of King Henry the Eighth* (London, 1649), p. 243. Herbert had seen the original manuscript before the disastrous fire at Ashburnham House, Westminster, in 1731 that destroyed or severely damaged a quarter of the manuscripts.

2 *The Receyt of the Ladie Kateryne*, ed. G. Kipling, *Early English Text Society*, New Series, 296 (1990), pp. 78–9.

3 T. Vicary, *The English Man's Treasure: with the True Anatomie of Man's Bodie* (London, 1596), pp. 80–2.

4 Both F. Hepburn and T. Penn opt for the 'sweating sickness', but neither cites any evidence that the disease had returned in 1502. Hepburn states mistakenly that the 'sweat' was a form of plague. See F. Hepburn, 'Arthur, Prince of Wales and his Training for Kingship', *The Historian*, 55 (1997), p. 4; T. Penn, *Winter King: The Dawn of Tudor England* (London, 2011), p. 70.

5 A. Dyer, 'The English Sweating Sickness of 1551: An Epidemic Anatomized', *Medical History*, 41 (1997), pp. 362–84; G. Thwaites, M. Taviner and V. Gant, 'The English Sweating Sickness, 1485–1551', *New England Journal of Medicine*, 336 (1997), pp. 580–2; M. Taviner, G. Thwaites and V. Gant, 'The English Sweating Sickness, 1485–1551: A Viral Pulmonary

Disease?', *Medical History*, 42 (1998), pp. 96–8; J. L. Flood, ' "Safer on the Battlefield than in the City": England, the "Sweating Sickness", and the Continent', *Renaissance Studies*, 17 (2003), pp. 147–76; E. Bridson, 'The English "sweate" (*Sudor Anglicus*) and Hantavirus Pulmonary Syndrome', *British Journal of Biomedical Science*, 58 (2001), pp. 1–6. Contemporary descriptions of the disease are found in *STC* nos. 783, 4343, 12766.7; *Chronicles of London*, ed. C. L. Kingsford (Oxford, 1905), p. 193.

6 A. S. MacNalty, 'Sir Thomas More as Public Health Reformer', in *Essential Articles for the Study of Thomas More*, ed. R. S. Sylvester and G. P. Marc'hadour (Hamden, Conn., 1977), p. 128. See also H. Tidy, 'Sweating Sickness and Picardy Sweat', *British Medical Journal* (July 1945, issue 4410), pp. 63–4; L. Roberts, 'Sweating Sickness and Picardy Sweat', *British Medical Journal* (August 1945, issue 4414), p. 196. Although these appear to be MacNalty's sources, neither mentions either 1502 or an outbreak of the 'sweating sickness' in the West Country.

7 W. D. Montagu, 7th Duke of Manchester, *Court and Society from Elizabeth to Anne*, 2 vols (London, 1864), I, pp. 58–61; F. Hepburn, 'The Portraiture of Arthur and Katherine', in *Arthur Tudor, Prince of Wales: Life, Death and Commemoration*, ed. S. Gunn and L. Monckton (Woodbridge, 2009), p. 39.

8 J. Fox, *Sister Queens: Katherine of Aragon and Juana of Castile* (London, 2011), pp. 86–7; K. Brandi, *The Emperor Charles V* (London, 1965), p. 488.

9 D. Starkey, *Six Wives: the Queens of Henry VIII* (London, 2004), pp. 76–7.

10 *CSPSp*, I, no. 327; Montagu, 7th Duke of Manchester, *Court and Society from Elizabeth to Anne*, I, p. 67.

11 *Receyt of the Ladie Kateryne*, p. 80; D. Starkey, *Henry, Virtuous Prince* (London, 2008), pp. 164–5.

12 *Receyt of the Ladie Kateryne*, p. 80.

13 *Receyt of the Ladie Kateryne*, pp. 80–1.

14 *PPE Elizabeth*, pp. 79–80, 85, 95.

15 *PPE Elizabeth*, p. 82; *HO*, p. 125; Starkey, *Henry, Virtuous Prince*, p. 168.

16 *The Great Chronicle of London*, ed. A. H. Thomas and I. D. Thornley (Gloucester, 1983), p. 321.

17 *Materials for the History of the Reign of Henry VII*, ed. W. Campbell, 2 vols (London, 1873–7), II, p. 65.

18 *PPE Elizabeth*, pp. 96–7.

19 *Great Chronicle*, ed. Thomas and Thornley, p. 321.

20 *PPE Elizabeth*, p. 94; Starkey, *Henry, Virtuous Prince*, p. 168.

21 Starkey, *Henry, Virtuous Prince*, pp. 184–256; *Arthur Tudor, Prince of Wales*, ed. Gunn and Monckton, pp. 4–5.

22 *Letters and Papers Illustrative of the Reigns of Richard III and Henry VII*, ed. J. Gairdner, 2 vols (London, 1861–3), I, p. 233; S. Cunningham, 'Loyalty and the Usurper: Recognizances, the Council and Allegiance under Henry VII', *Historical Research*, 82 (2009), pp. 459–81; C. J. Harrison, 'The Petition of Edmund Dudley', *EHR*, 87 (1972), pp. 82–99.

23 S. J. Gunn, 'The Accession of Henry VIII', *Historical Research*, 64 (1991), p. 280.

24 *Great Chronicle*, ed. Thomas and Thornley, pp. 331–2.

25 *Letters and Papers . . . Richard III and Henry VII*, ed. Gairdner, I, pp. 233, 238.

26 *CSPSp*, I, no. 511; Penn, *Winter King*, p. 112.

27 Gunn, 'The Accession of Henry VIII', pp. 278–88.

28 C. S. L. Davies, 'Tudor: What's in a Name?', *History*, 97 (2012), pp. 24–7; H. Pierce, *Margaret Pole, Countess of Salisbury, 1473–1541: Loyalty, Lineage and Leadership* (Cardiff, 2003), p. 10.

29 Starkey, *Virtuous Prince*, pp. 189–92.

30 Gunn, 'Accession of Henry VIII', p. 283; G. Mattingly, *Catherine of Aragon* (London, 1942), pp. 93–5; Starkey, *Virtuous Prince*, pp. 278–81.

31 *Opus Epistolarum Des. Erasmi Roterodami*, ed. P. S. Allen, 12 vols (Oxford, 1906–58), I, no. 215.

32 *Yale Edition of the Complete Works of St. Thomas More*, ed. L. L. Martz, R. S. Sylvester, C. H. Miller et al., 15 vols (New Haven, 1963–97), III, ii, pp. 100–12 (my translation).

Chapter 1 notes

1 Hall, I, pp. 21–2.

2 *HO*, pp. 126–7; *LP*, I, i, no. 670.

3 *HO*, pp. 120–1.

4 Hall, I, p. 22.

5 G. Puttenham, *The Arte of English Poesie* (London, 1589), p. 246.

6 M. Hayward, *Dress at the Court of Henry VIII* (London, 2007), p. 6.

7 Hall, I, pp. 22–7; *LP*, I, i, no. 671.

8 *Great Chronicle*, ed. Thomas and Thornley, pp. 374–5.

9 Hall, I, p. 27.

10 LC 2/1, fos. 159–73 (*LP*, I, i, no. 707).

11 *CSPSp, Supp*, no. 7 (p. 34).

12 A. Boorde, *The Breuiary of helthe for all maner of syckenesses and diseases the whiche may be in man, or woman* (London, 1547), fos. 9, 36v–7v, 128.

13 C. B. Whiteley and K. Kramer, 'A New Explanation for the Reproductive Woes and Midlife Crisis of Henry VIII', *HJ*, 53 (2010), pp. 827–48.

14 Leland, IV, pp. 179–84; *HO*, p. 127.

15 Starkey, *Henry, Virtuous Prince*, pp. 68, 71, 331–2.

16 *LP*, II, ii, no. 3802.

17 *CSPSp, Supp*, nos. 7–9 (pp. 34–44); *LP*, I, i, no. 474; Murphy, pp. 7–8; Samman PhD, p. 175.

18 *LP*, VI, nos. 923–4; S. Thurley, *The Royal Palaces of Tudor England* (New Haven and London, 1993), p. 140; G. W. Bernard, 'The Rise of Sir William Compton, Early Tudor Courtier', *EHR*, 96 (1981), p. 757.

19 Hall, I, p. 143.

20 E 36/215, fo. 225 (*LP*, II, ii, p. 1471). Murphy, pp. 19–20; Samman PhD, p. 148.

21 Hall, I, p. 143; Murphy, pp. 9–18; Samman PhD, p. 147.

22 *LP*, II, ii, nos. 4135–7, 4227, 4396, 4398, 4436.

23 Rawdon Brown, II, pp. 224–5; Hall, I, pp. 170–1; Murphy, pp. 21–4.

24 Murphy, pp. 24–5.

25 OBS 1419.

26 Murphy, pp. 25–6.

27 Murphy, pp. 27–35.

28 *SR* III, pp. 280–1.

29 Davies, 'Tudor: What's in a Name?', p. 25.

30 J. Guy, *A Daughter's Love: Thomas and Margaret More* (London, 2008), pp. 257–8.

31 *PPE Mary*, pp. xxii–xxiii.

32 D. M. Loades, *Mary Tudor: A Life* (Oxford, 1989), p. 29.

33 *ODNB*, s.v. 'Bryan, Sir Francis'.

34 BL, Cotton MS Otho C. X, fo. 234, printed in Ellis, II, ii, pp. 78–83 (quotation from p. 79); Murphy, p. 30.

35 Starkey, *Six Wives*, pp. 167–8.

36 Starkey, *Six Wives*, pp. 168–9.

37 *PPE Mary*, p. xxii.

38 *LP*, III, i, nos. 895–6; Ellis, I, i, p. 175; Starkey, *Six Wives*, pp. 169–71.

39 *PPE Mary*, pp. xx–xxiv; *LP*, II, ii, no. 3429 and p. 1473; *LP*, III, i, no. 970; *LP, Add.*, I, i, no. 259; Starkey, *Six Wives*, pp. 168–9; Loades, *Mary Tudor*, pp. 28–31.

40 *LP*, III, i, no. 895.

41 *LP*, III, ii, no. 2585 (1); *PPE Mary*, pp. xxv–xxvi.

42 *CSPV*, III, no. 167; Starkey, *Six Wives*, p. 171.

43 OBS 1419.

44 KB 9/53; KB 8/5; BL, Harleian MS 283, fo. 72; *LP*, III, i, nos. 1284 (1–5), 1285 (pp. 495–505), 1356; *CSPV*, III, no. 213; Hall, I, pp. 221–6.

45 *LP*, III, i, p. 498. The sum may have been a loan later partially repaid, see *LP*, III, i, p. 501, but is still remarkable.

46 Lord Stafford's grandmother was a sister of Elizabeth Woodville, Edward IV's queen. Ursula Pole's grandfather was Edward IV's brother.

47 *LP*, VIII, no. 263 (p. 101).

Chapter 2 notes

1 *LP*, III, ii, no. 3375 (5).

2 *State Papers*, I, pp. 19–20; *LP*, III, ii, nos. 1437, 1439.

3 *LP*, III, ii, no. 1673.

4 *LP*, III, ii, no. 1669.

5 Hall, I, p. 234.

6 *PPE Mary*, pp. xxvi–xxix; *LP*, III, ii, no. 2585 (2–3).

7 *PPE Mary*, p. xxix.

8 Since no servant was rewarded for delivering Katherine's New Year's gift this year, it follows that it must have been delivered in person. See *PPE Mary*, p. xxix; *LP*, III, ii, no. 2585 (2); Starkey, *Six Wives*, p. 173.

9 *PPE Mary*, p. xxix.

10 *LP*, III, ii, no. 3375 (4).

11 *LP*, III, ii, nos. 2322, 2333 (3, 12); *CSPSp*, II, no. 427; *CSPSp, Further Supp*, pp. 24, 36, 47, 49–50, 56, 62, 112.

12 *CSPSp, Further Supp*, pp. xviii–xxxiv, 24, 36, 47–56, 62–112, 130–49; *LP*, III, ii, no. 2333 (3, 12).

13 *CSPSp, Further Supp*, p. 71; Starkey, *Six Wives*, p. 186.

14 Hall, I, pp. 244–6.

15 *LP*, II, ii, nos. 4467–4471, 4475, 4477.

16 Hall, I, p. 246.

17 *LP*, III, ii, nos. 2288, 2289, 2305, 2306, 2333, 2360; Hall, I, pp. 244–58; *CSPV*, II, nos. 466–7; *Rutland Papers* (1842), pp. 59–100; S. Anglo, *Spectacle, Pageantry, and Early Tudor Policy* (Oxford, 1969), pp. 170–206; Starkey, *Six Wives*, pp. 186–9; Fox, *Sister Queens*, pp. 258–61.

18 Guy, *A Daughter's Love*, pp. 104–5, 116, 164, 169, 170, 191.

19 Anglo, *Spectacle*, p. 197.

20 *CSPSp*, II, no. 437; Anglo, *Spectacle*, pp. 202–5.

21 *CSPSp*, II, no. 425.

22 *CSPSp*, II, nos. 427, 430–4; *LP*, III, ii, nos. 2322, 2333 (3, 6).

23 *LP*, III, ii, p. 1559 (the 'Revels Accounts'); Hall, I, pp. 238–40; E. W. Ives, *The Life and Death of Anne Boleyn, 'The Most Happy'* (Oxford, 2004), pp. 36–9; Anglo, *Spectacle*, pp. 120–1.

24 *LP*, I, ii, no. 3357; *LP*, X, no. 450; Starkey, *Six Wives*, pp. 274–5; Ives, *Life and Death of Anne Boleyn*, pp. 27–9.

25 *LP*, III, ii, p. 1539.

26 *LP*, III, i, no. 317; *LP*, III, ii, no. 2074 (5); *LP*, III, ii, no. 2297 (12), p. 973; *LP*, III, ii, p. 1539 ('the King's Book of Payments'); *LP*, IV, ii, no. 2972, p. 1331.

27 *LP*, III, ii, no. 3358.

28 *Literary Remains*, II, pp. 209–10.

29 *PPE Mary*, p. xxxi; Loades, *Mary Tudor*, p. 31.
30 H. Clifford, *The Life of Jane Dormer*, ed. J. Stevenson (London, 1887), p. 80.
31 Guy, *A Daughter's Love*, pp. 15–16.
32 Pierce, *Margaret Pole*, p. 3.
33 *CSPSp, Further Supp*, p. 74.
34 M. Billingsley, *A Newe booke of copies containing divers sortes of sundry hands, as the English and French secretarie, and bastard secretarie, Italian, Roman, chancery, and court hands* (London, 1620).
35 Ellis, I, ii, p. 20.
36 Guy, *A Daughter's Love*, pp. 59–65, 67–70, 140–3.
37 C. Fantazzi, *Juan Luis Vives: The Education of a Christian Woman, A Sixteenth-Century Manual* (Chicago, 2000), pp. 3–12.
38 Fantazzi, *Vives*, pp. 12–35, 70–1; Foster Watson, *Luis Vives, El Gran Valenciano* (Oxford, 1922), p. 44.
39 Fantazzi, *Vives*, pp. 73–9.
40 Fantazzi, *Vives*, pp. 71–3, 94–109, 125–38; G. Kaufman, 'Juan Luis Vives on the Education of Women', *Journal of Women in Culture and Society*, 3 (1978), pp. 891–6; Starkey, *Six Wives*, pp. 174–9.
41 Watson, *Luis Vives*, p. 45.
42 Fantazzi, *Vives*, p. 13; Kaufman, 'Juan Luis Vives', pp. 895–6; Watson, *Luis Vives*, pp. 41, 45; Baldwin, I, pp. 185–99.
43 *CSPV*, III, no. 1037.

Chapter 3 notes

1 *LP*, IV, i, no. 1371; Murphy, pp. 47–8.
2 Murphy, pp. 48–9.
3 SP 1/55, fo. 12 (*LP*, IV, iii, no. 5807).
4 *LP*, IV, i, no. 1431 (2); Fitzroy Inventory, pp. xii–xiii.
5 Fitzroy Inventory, pp. lxxx–lxxxiv; *LP*, IV, i, no. 1431 (8); Hall, II, pp. 49–50; Murphy, pp. 36–65.
6 Fitzroy Inventory, pp. xvi–xvii.
7 Thurley, *Royal Palaces*, p. 81.
8 *LP*, IV, i, no. 1500.

9 Murphy, p. 56.
10 Murphy, p. 38. See also *LP*, IV, ii, no. 3135.
11 *CSPV*, III, no. 1053; Starkey, *Six Wives*, pp. 198–9.
12 *CSPV*, III, no. 1053.
13 J. J. Scarisbrick, *Henry VIII* (London, 1968), p. 136.
14 Starkey, *Six Wives*, pp. 192–3.
15 *State Papers*, VI, pp. 426–7.
16 *CSPV*, III, no. 1053; *CSPSp*, III, i, no. 120; *CSPSp*, III, ii, no. 37.
17 Starkey, *Six Wives*, p. 198.
18 G. R. Elton, *Policy and Police: the Enforcement of the Reformation in the Age of Thomas Cromwell* (Cambridge, 1972), pp. 176–7.
19 *Records of the Reformation: the Divorce, 1527–1533*, ed. N. Pocock, 2 vols (Oxford, 1870), II, p. 386.
20 M. Levine, *Tudor Dynastic Problems, 1460–1571* (London, 1973), p. 74.
21 J. Guy, 'Thomas Wolsey, Thomas Cromwell, and the Reform of Henrician Government', in *The Reign of Henry VIII: Politics, Patronage and Piety*, ed. D. MacCulloch (London, 1995), pp. 35–57, 227–8, 232–5, 253–9.
22 S. G. Ellis, *Tudor Frontiers and Noble Power: the Making of the British State* (Oxford, 1995), pp. 156–70; J. Guy, *The Cardinal's Court: the Impact of Wolsey in Star Chamber* (Brighton, 1977), pp. 27, 122; Fitzroy Inventory, p. xvii.
23 C. A. J. Skeel, *The Council in the Marches of Wales* (London, 1904), p. 49.
24 *LP*, IV, i, no. 1510; R. R. Reid, *The King's Council in the North* (London, 1921), pp. 101–2; Starkey, *Six Wives*, p. 201. As finally constituted, Richard III's Council of the North was the prince's household without the prince, since the king's son Edward suddenly died, but his household continued.
25 *LP*, IV, i, no. 1514.
26 SP 1/35, fos. 160–2 (*LP*, IV, i, 1515). See also *LP*, IV, i, no. 1530.
27 Murphy, pp. 57–9.
28 *State Papers*, IV, p. 385.
29 Fitzroy Inventory, p. lxxvii (*LP*, IV, i, no. 1431 [4]).
30 *LP*, IV, i, no. 1940; *LP, Add.*, I, i, no. 458.
31 *LP, Add.*, I, i, no. 459.

32 *PPE Mary*, pp. xxxix–xl; *LP*, IV, i, no. 1577 (13); *LP, Add.*, I, i, no. 458.

33 Pierce, *Margaret Pole*, pp. 89–90.

34 *LP*, IV, i, no. 1577 (10).

35 *PPE Mary*, pp. xliv–xlv.

36 *PPE Mary*, p. xxxviii; Starkey, *Six Wives*, p. 201.

37 *State Papers*, pp. 385–6.

38 Murphy, pp. 70–1.

39 Murphy, p. 71.

40 SP 1/55, fo. 13v (*LP*, IV, iii, no. 5806 [2]).

41 *LP*, IV, ii, no. 2081.

42 Rogers, *Corr.*, pp. 403–4.

43 Guy, *A Daughter's Love*, pp. 156–7.

44 Rogers, *Corr.*, pp. 404–5.

45 Rogers, *Corr.*, p. 405.

46 Murphy, p. 71.

47 R. Rex, *The Theology of John Fisher* (Cambridge, 1991), p. 56.

48 *LP*, IV, ii, no. 3135; Fitzroy Inventory, pp. xxxvii–xli; Murphy, pp. 75–6.

49 Fitzroy Inventory, p. xli.

50 SP 1/40, fo. 210; Fitzroy Inventory, p. xxxi.

51 SP 1/46, fos. 169–70 (*LP*, IV, ii, nos. 3860–1); Fitzroy Inventory, pp. xlviii–xlix; Ellis, III, ii, pp. 117–18.

52 *LP*, IV, ii, nos. 2878, 2955–6.

53 *PPE Mary*, p. xli.

54 *PPE Mary*, pp. xli–xlii.

55 BL, Cotton MS, Royal 17 C.XVI; *PPE Mary*, p. cxxviii; Linda Porter, *Mary Tudor: the First Queen* (London, 2007), p. 42.

56 A. Ashbee, 'Groomed for Service: Musicians in the Privy Chamber at the English Court, *c.*1495–1558', *Early Music*, 25 (1997), pp. 188–9; *PPE Mary*, p. cxxxix.

57 *An introductorie for to lerne to rede, to pronounce, and to speake Frenche trewly compyled for the right high, excellent, and most vertuous lady, the lady Mary of Englande* (London, 1533).

58 *LP*, IV, ii, no. 2606; *Négociations Diplomatiques de la France avec la Toscane*, ed. G. Canestrini, 6 vols (Paris, 1859–86), II, pp. 923–6.

59 *CSPSp*, III, ii, no. 39; *LP*, IV, ii, nos. 2505, 2604–5, 2624, 2662–3, 2680, 2684, 2693, 2700, 2704, 2715–16, 2726, 2825, 2827–8, 2833, 2849, 2917, 2948, 2966, 2980, 3080, 3105, 3350, 3353, 3415; *Négociations Diplomatiques de la France avec la Toscane*, II, pp. 986–90.

60 *LP*, IV, ii, no. 3105 (pp. 1411–12).

61 *PPE Mary*, pp. cxxxii–cxxxiii.

62 Loades, *Mary Tudor*, p. 43.

63 *LP*, IV, ii, no. 3080.

64 Ellis, I, ii, p. 19.

65 J. D. M. Derrett, 'Henry Fitzroy and Henry VIII's Scruple of Conscience', *Renaissance News*, 16 (1963), pp. 1–9.

Chapter 4 notes

1 OBS 1419.

2 *LP*, VIII, no. 567.

3 *CSPV*, IV, no. 824.

4 Ives, *Life and Death of Anne Boleyn*, p. 40.

5 G. Cavendish, *The Life of Cardinal Wolsey* and *Metrical Visions*, ed. S. W. Singer, 2 vols (London, 1825), I, p. 58.

6 Cavendish, *Life of Wolsey*, I, pp. 63–6.

7 Starkey, *Six Wives*, pp. 276–7.

8 Cavendish, *Life of Wolsey*, I, p. 66.

9 Halliwell, I, pp. 297–320. In reconstructing the order of these letters, I follow J. Fox, *Jane Boleyn: the Infamous Lady Rochford* (London, 2007), pp. 57–61; Starkey, *Six Wives*, pp. 278–83; Ives, *Life and Death of Anne Boleyn*, pp. 84–8.

10 Halliwell, I, pp. 310, 317–18.

11 Halliwell, I, p. 302.

12 Halliwell, I, p. 310.

13 Halliwell, I, p. 311.

14 Halliwell, I, pp. 302–3.

15 Halliwell, I, pp. 303–4.

16 Halliwell, I, p. 305.

17 Halliwell, I, pp. 305–6.

18 Starkey, *Six Wives*, pp. 282–3.

19 Halliwell, I, pp. 306–7.

20 *LP*, IV, iii, App. 99 (2).

21 Halliwell, I, p. 307.

22 J. Sharkey, 'Between King and Pope: Thomas Wolsey and the Knight Mission', *Historical Research*, 84 (2011), pp. 236–48.

23 Cavendish, *Life of Wolsey*, I, pp. 154–5.

24 J. J. Scarisbrick, *Henry VIII* (London, 1968), pp. 145–6, 154–5.

25 *LP*, IV, ii, nos. 3311, 3353, 3363; *Records of the Reformation*, I, pp. 19–21.

26 *LP*, IV, ii, no. 3400.

27 Scarisbrick, *Henry VIII*, pp. 163–240; C. Fletcher, *Our Man in Rome: Henry VIII and his Italian Ambassador* (London, 2012), pp. 138–93.

28 Halliwell, I, pp. 318–19.

29 E. Surtz and V. M. Murphy, *The Divorce Tracts of Henry VIII* (Angers, 1988), pp. xii–xiii; Rex, *Theology of John Fisher*, pp. 165–70.

30 Surtz and Murphy, *Divorce Tracts*, pp. i–xxxvi.

31 *LP*, IV, ii, no. 5615; Hall, II, pp. 150–4; Fletcher, *Our Man in Rome*, pp. 42–97; Scarisbrick, *Henry VIII*, pp. 224–8.

32 Fletcher, *Our Man in Rome*, p. 97.

33 J. Guy, *The Public Career of Sir Thomas More* (New Haven and London, 1980), pp. 30–3, 97–140.

34 BL, Cotton MS, Cleopatra E.VI, fos. 16–135.

35 Noted on an early draft of the Act of Appeals: BL, Cotton MS, Cleopatra E.VI, fos. 180–4.

36 G. D. Nicholson, 'The Act of Appeals and the English Reformation', in *Law and Government under the Tudors*, ed. Claire Cross, D. M. Loades and J. J. Scarisbrick (Cambridge, 1988), pp. 19–30; J. Guy, 'Thomas Cromwell and the Intellectual Origins of the Henrician Revolution', in *The Tudor Monarchy*, ed. J. Guy (London, 1997), pp. 213–33.

37 Guy, *A Daughter's Love*, p. 195; BNF, MS FF 3014, fos. 78–81v; G. Bapst, *Deux Gentilshommes-Poètes de la Cour de Henry VIII* (Paris, 1891), pp. 25–43; Fletcher, *Our Man in Rome*, pp. 119–87.

38 *CSPSp*, IV, ii, no. 778; Starkey, *Six Wives*, p. 443.

39 *CSPSp*, IV, ii, no. 683.

40 *CSPV*, IV, no. 664.

41 *PPE Mary*, p. liv; *LP*, V, no. 216.

42 *CSPSp*, IV, i, no. 302.

43 *CSPSp*, IV, ii, no. 720.

44 *The History of the King's Works*, ed. H. M. Colvin et al., 7 vols (London, 1963–82), IV, ii, p. 148.

45 Thurley, *Royal Palaces*, pp. 50–2.

46 Hall, II, pp. 218–21; *CSPV*, IV, no. 824; *LP*, V, nos. 1373–4, 1484–5, 1492; *The maner of the tryumphe at Caleys [and] Bulleyn. The second pryntyng, with mo addicio[n]s as it was done in dede* (London, 1532); Starkey, *Six Wives*, pp. 452–61; Anglo, *Spectacle*, pp. 245–6.

47 *CSPV*, IV, no. 824.

48 Fletcher, *Our Man in Rome*, pp. 177–9.

49 Ives, *Life and Death of Anne Boleyn*, p. 161.

50 D. MacCulloch, *Thomas Cranmer* (London and New Haven, 1996), pp. 637–8.

51 Hall, II, pp. 229–42; Ives, *Life and Death of Anne Boleyn*, pp. 173–83.

52 Fox, *Jane Boleyn*, pp. 110–11.

53 *SR*, III, pp. 464–74, 508–9.

54 *State Papers*, I, p. 407.

55 *CSPSp*, IV, ii, no. 1127.

56 *CSPSp*, IV, ii, nos. 1124, 1144, 1158, 1161.

57 Hall, II, pp. 242–4; *LP*, VI, no. 1111; *HO*, pp. 126–7; Bodleian, Folio.Δ.624, facing p. 360 (interleaved note by Thomas Turner from the now-lost manuscript Chronicle of Anthony Anthony).

58 *State Papers*, I, p. 415.

59 William Latymer's *Chronickille of Anne Bulleyne*, ed. Maria Dowling, Camden Society, 4th Series, 39 (1990), p. 63.

60 *CSPSp*, V, i, no. 22.

61 *Lisle Letters*, II, no. 169 (*LP*, VII, no. 509).

62 *LP*, VII, no. 1297 (p. 497).

63 *LP*, VIII, no. 400.

64 *State Papers*, I, p. 426.

Chapter 5 notes

1 SP 1/78, fo. 141 (*LP*, VI, no. 1009).

2 *LP*, VI, no. 1112.

3 *CSPSp*, IV, ii, no. 1127.

4 *LP*, VI, no. 1126.

5 *CSPSp*, IV, ii, no. 1133.

6 *PPE Mary*, pp. lv–lix; *CSPSp*, IV, ii, nos. 1144, 1161.

7 *CSPSp*, IV, ii, nos. 1133, 1161; *CSPSp*, V, i, no. 4.

8 *CSPSp*, IV, ii, no. 1137.

9 *CSPSp*, IV, ii, nos. 1144, 1161, 1164; *CSPSp*, V, i, no. 4.

10 *LP*, VIII, no. 400; *CSPSp*, V, i, no. 17; Loades, *Mary Tudor*, pp. 76–107.

11 *LP*, VI, no. 1558; *CSPSp*, V, i, nos. 10, 26.

12 *LP*, VII, no. 1129.

13 *CSPSp*, V, i, nos. 10, 22, 68.

14 *CSPSp*, V, i, nos. 31–2.

15 *CSPSp*, V, i, no. 86.

16 *CSPSp*, V, i, no. 68.

17 Murphy, pp. 122–4.

18 Murphy, pp. 119–32.

19 Murphy, pp. 132–9.

20 *LP*, X, no. 908.

21 Murphy, pp. 142–3.

22 R. Knecht, *Renaissance Warrior and Patron: the Reign of Francis I* (Cambridge, 1994), p. 300.

23 *LP*, VII, nos. 1257, 1554.

24 *LP*, VIII, no. 263 (p. 104); *Lisle Letters*, V, no. 1086 and pp. 11–12; S. Brigden, *Thomas Wyatt: The Heart's Forest* (London, 2012), pp. 191–9. For a different, probably erroneous identification, see Ives, *Life and Death of Anne Boleyn*, pp. 194–5.

25 Fox, *Jane Boleyn*, pp. 180–1.

26 *LP*, X, no. 54.

27 *LP*, X, no. 141.

28 *LP*, X, no. 351. That Cromwell was correct in his judgement of Francis I is shown by *LP*, X, nos. 35, 190, 228, 279. See also Ives, *Life and Death of Anne Boleyn*, pp. 312–15.

29 *LP*, X, no. 199; *LP*, IX, no. 776.

30 *CSPSp*, V, ii, no. 21.

31 Wriothesley, I, p. 33; *LP*, X, nos. 200, 294; *LP*, XIII, ii, nos. 804 (5), 979 (7); *CSPSp*, V, ii, no. 35; KB 8/11, Pt. 2, m. 7.

32 *CSPSp*, V, ii, no. 21.

33 *CSPSp*, V, ii, no. 29.

34 *LP*, X, no. 351.

35 *LP*, X, no. 908.

36 *Annals of the Reformation and Establishment of Religion*, ed. J. Strype, 3 vols (London, 1725–7), I, p. 433.

37 KB 8/8–9; *LP*, X, nos. 782, 784–5, 798, 838, 876, 908; Hall, II, pp. 268–9; Wriothesley, I, pp. 189–226; Ives, *Life and Death of Anne Boleyn*, pp. 319–56.

38 *LP*, X, no. 926.

39 *LP*, X, no. 915.

40 *SR*, III, pp. 655–62.

41 *CSPSp*, V, ii, no. 9; *LP*, X, nos. 1108, 1110, 1137.

42 *LP*, XI, no. 7.

43 *LP*, X, no. 1110.

44 *LP*, X, no. 1022.

45 *LP*, VII, nos. 1129, 1437; *LP*, X, nos. 133, 1122, 1129; M. Keynes, 'The Aching Head and Increasing Blindness of Queen Mary I', *Journal of Medical Biography*, 8 (2008), pp. 106–8.

46 *LP*, X, no. 1137; *LP*, XI, no. 7.

47 *King's Works*, ed. Colvin, IV, ii, p. 52.

48 *CSPSp*, XI, p. 45. The disease was afterwards 'judged to be the same' as that which killed Edward VI.

49 *CSPSp*, V, ii, no. 71.

50 Murphy, pp. 177–9.

51 SP 1/105, fo. 248v (*LP*, XI, no. 233).

52 SP 1/105, fo. 248v. The fate of Fitzroy's body was confirmed when the tomb was opened in 1841. See J. Ashdown-Hill, 'The Opening of the Tombs of the Dukes of Richmond and Norfolk, Framlingham, April 1841. The Account of the Reverend J. W. Darby', *Ricardian*, 18 (2008), pp. 100–7. I owe this reference to the kindness of Lisa Ford.

53 Murphy, p. 180.

54 *LP*, X, no. 1203.

55 *LP*, X, no. 1204.

56 *LP*, XI, no. 40.

57 *PPE Mary*, p. lxxiv; *LP*, X, no. 1187 (1, 2 [1]).

58 *LP*, XI, no. 1187 (2, [ii]).

59 *LP*, XI, nos. 203; Ellis, II, ii, pp. 78–83.

60 Ellis, II, ii, pp. 80–2.

61 *LP*, XI, no. 312.

62 *PPE Mary*, pp. lxxvii–lxxviii; OBS 1419.

63 *LP*, XI, no. 132.

64 *LP*, XII, ii, no. 911; HEH, MS HM 41955, fos. 127–9.

65 *LP*, XII, ii, no. 970.

66 *LP*, XII, ii, no. 971.

67 J. Loach, *Edward VI* (London, 1999), p. 7.

68 *PPE Mary*, p. lxxx.

69 *LP*, XIV, i, no. 655; Loades, *Mary Tudor*, p. 115.

70 *Literary Remains*, I, pp. xxvi–xxx; Loach, *Edward VI*, pp. 9–10; S. Thurley, 'Henry VIII and the Building of Hampton Court: a Reconstruction of the Tudor Palace', *Architectural History*, 31 (1988), pp. 30–1.

71 *Lisle Letters*, V, no. 1130; Thurley, *Royal Palaces*, pp. 80–1.

72 R. E. Richardson, 'Lady Troy and Blanche Parry: New Evidence about their Lives at the Tudor Court', *Bulletin of the Society for Renaissance Studies*, 26 (2009), pp. 3–15.

73 *LP*, X, no. 1187 (2 [2], 3), which is wrongly dated; *LP*, XIII, ii, no. 1280. See also Loach, *Edward VI*, p. 8; D. Starkey, *Elizabeth: Apprenticeship* (London, 2000), p. 25.

74 Richardson, 'Lady Troy and Blanche Parry', pp. 3–15.

75 Loades, *Mary Tudor*, p. 116.

76 *PPE Mary*, pp. lxxix–xcv; Loach, *Edward VI*, pp. 8–9; C. Skidmore, *Edward VI: the Lost King of England* (London, 2007), pp. 23–9.

77 *LP*, XIV, i, no. 5.

78 *LP*, XV, nos. 822, 850 (6).

79 *LP*, XV, no. 823.

80 *LP*, XVIII, i, no. 873.

81 *LP*, XVIII, ii, no. 39.

82 *LP*, XVIII, ii, no. 39.

83 *LP, Add.*, I, ii, 1636; *Literary Remains*, I, pp. xxxviii–xxxix; Thurley, *Royal Palaces*, pp. 57, 79–82; Skidmore, *Edward VI*, pp. 27–30.

84 *LP*, XIX, i, no. 864.

Chapter 6 notes

1 C. Blair and S. W. Pyhrr, 'The Wilton "Montmorency" Armour: An Italian Armour for Henry VIII', *Metropolitan Museum Journal*, 38, (2003), pp. 95–144.

2 *LP*, XIII, i, no. 995.

3 *LP*, XXI, ii, no. 768.

4 *LP*, XVIII, i, no. 954.

5 S. E. James, *Kateryn Parr: the Making of a Queen* (Aldershot, 1999), pp. 112–15.

6 J. Mueller (ed.), *Katherine Parr: Complete Works and Correspondence* (Chicago, 2011), p. 382.

7 Starkey, *Six Wives*, p. 702.

8 James, *Kateryn Parr*, pp. 22–39, 189–220.

9 Mueller (ed.), *Katherine Parr*, pp. 425–88.

10 James, *Kateryn Parr*, pp. 238–80.

11 E 101/432/12; E 101/424/7; 'Narrative of the Visit of the Duke of Najera', ed. F. Madden, *Archaeologia*, 23 (1831), pp. 344–57; Hayward, *Dress at the Court of Henry VIII*, pp. 185–9; A. J. Carter, 'Mary Tudor's Wardrobe', *Costume*, 18 (1984), pp. 9–28.

12 Hayward, *Dress at the Court of King Henry VIII*, pp. 361–2.

13 E 101/424/7; Hayward, *Dress at the Court of Henry VIII*, pp. 204–6.

14 *SR*, III, pp. 955–8; M. Levine, *Tudor Dynastic Problems* (London, 1973), p. 71; S. E. Lehmberg, *The Later Parliaments of Henry VIII, 1536–1547* (Cambridge, 1977), pp. 193–4.

15 Maria Dowling, 'Scholarship, Politics and the Court of Henry VIII', unpublished London School of Economics PhD (London, 1981), pp. 248–9.

16 *ECW*, pp. 5–6.

17 Starkey, *Elizabeth*, pp. 36–8.

18 *LP*, XIX, i, no. 780.

19 *LP*, XIX, ii, no. 688.

20 *LP*, XIX, i, nos. 979, 1019.

21 *ECW*, p. 5.

22 *LP*, XIX, i, no. 864; Thurley, 'Henry VIII and the Building of Hampton Court', pp. 28–31.

23 *LP*, XIX, ii, no. 688; Starkey, *Elizabeth*, p. 37.

24 *LP*, XIX, ii, nos. 246, 346, 688; Starkey, *Elizabeth*, pp. 37–8.

25 *LP*, XIX, i, no. 864.

26 *Literary Remains*, I, pp. xl–xlvii; *LP*, XIX, i, no. 864; Baldwin, I, pp. 201–2.

27 LC 2/2, fo. 53; *Literary Remains*, I, pp. lvi–lxxv.

28 *Literary Remains*, I, pp. lxx–lxxv.

29 SP 1/195, fo. 201v; *Letters of Roger Ascham*, ed. and trans. A. Vos and M. Hatch (New York, 1989), p. 74.

30 *LP*, XIX, ii, no. 726; Baldwin, I, pp. 200–18, 223–4; Dowling, 'Scholarship, Politics and the Court', pp. 256–7.

31 *LP*, XXI, ii, no. 571.

32 Loach, *Edward VI*, pp. 12–13.

33 *LP*, XIV, ii, no. 697.

34 'The Letters of Richard Scudamore to Sir Philip Hoby, 1549–1555', ed. S. Brigden, *Camden Society*, 4th Series, 39 (1990), p. 78; A. Johnson, 'William Paget and the late-Henrician Polity, 1543–1547', unpublished St Andrews PhD (St Andrews, 2003), pp. 191–202; Dowling, 'Scholarship, Politics and the Court', pp. 249–59.

35 Guy, *A Daughter's Love*, p. 269.

36 Baldwin, I, pp. 200, 257; Dowling, 'Scholarship, Politics and the Court', pp. 251–2; *Letters of Roger Ascham*, p. 63.

37 *LP*, XX, ii, no. 755; *LP*, XXI, i, nos. 50, 59, 370, 452, 518, 576, 770, 802, 867, 886, 900, 978, 988, 1035–6, 1054, 1148, 1206, 1446, 1479; *LP*, XXI, ii, nos. 20, 38, 86, 168, 260, 282, 321, 363–3, 685–7, 737, 745; *Literary Remains*, I, pp. lxxviii–lxxix.

38 *PPE Mary*, p. cii; Hayward, *Dress at the Court of King Henry VIII*, pp. 187, 203.

39 *LP*, XXI, i, nos. 50, 770, 867; *LP*, XXI, ii, nos. 363, 687; *PPE Mary*, pp. 143, 149.

40 *Letters of Roger Ascham*, pp. 115–16.

41 M. Wyatt, *The Italian Encounter with England: A Cultural Politics of Translation* (Cambridge, 2005), p. 125.

42 *Elizabeth's Glass*, ed. M. Shell (Lincoln, Nebraska, 1993), pp. 3–112.

43 Published as *The Mirroure of Golde for the Synfull Soule* (London, 1506).

44 *Foedera*, XV, pp. 112–14.

45 Levine, *Tudor Dynastic Problems*, pp. 74–5.

46 *Foedera*, XV, p. 113.

47 E. W. Ives, 'Henry VIII's Will: A Forensic Conundrum', *Historical Journal*, 35 (1992), pp. 779–804.

48 *CPR, Edward VI*, I, p. 97; Ives, 'Henry VIII's Will', p. 804.

49 Bryson PhD, p. 38.

50 Haynes, p. 82; S. Alford, *Kingship and Politics in the Reign of Edward VI* (Cambridge, 2002), pp. 91–2.

51 Bryson PhD, pp. 81–3.

52 *CSPSp*, IX, p. 340.

53 Alford, *Kingship and Politics*, p. 92.

54 G. W. Bernard, *Power and Politics in Tudor England* (Aldershot, 2000), pp. 139–41; Loach, *Edward VI*, pp. 55–6; Alford, *Kingship and Politics*, pp. 93–4; Bryson PhD, pp. 83–4.

55 Bernard, *Power and Politics*, p. 141.

56 *PPE Mary*, p. cvi–cvii; *CSPSp*, IX, pp. 85, 101, 220, 266, 298; A. Whitelock and D. MacCulloch, 'Princess Mary's Household and the Succession Crisis, July 1553', *HJ*, 50 (2007), pp. 265–87.

57 Ellis, II, ii, pp. 150–1.

58 *Literary Remains*, I, pp. 44–7; Bernard, *Power and Politics*, pp. 135–6; Loach, *Edward VI*, pp. 55–6; Bryson PhD, p. 83.

59 *CSPD, Edward*, p. 49.

60 *CSPSp*, IX, pp. 48–9, 136.

61 LC 2/2, fo. 48v. This household list, giving liveries to Elizabeth's servants for her father's funeral, shows that Richardson is mistaken in claiming that Lady Troy had retired in late 1545 or early 1546. Richardson, 'Lady Troy and Blanche Parry', pp. 3–15.

62 SP 10/6, fo. 16.

63 SP 10/6, fo. 16v. Richardson's account of this passage is misleading, since she maintains it shows that Lady Troy had already been displaced from the household itself, rather than merely displaced from sleeping on a pallet in Elizabeth's bedchamber. Richardson, 'Lady Troy and Blanche Parry', pp. 3–15. Troy's pension, paid by 1552, is from *Household Expenses of the Princess Elizabeth during her Residence at Hatfield, October 1 1551 to September 30 1552*, ed. Viscount Strangford, *Camden Society*, Old Series, 55 (1853), p. 41.

64 SP 10/6, fo. 17.

65 Haynes, p. 83.

66 Haynes, p. 99.

67 Haynes, p. 99.

68 Haynes, pp. 99–100.

69 Haynes, p. 100.

70 Haynes, p. 101.

71 SP 10/2, fo. 84C.

72 Haynes, p. 101.

73 Bryson PhD, p. 86, citing Hatfield House, Cecil MS 150, fo. 86; imperfectly transcribed by Haynes, p. 100.

74 Haynes, pp. 68–70, 95–7.

75 Alford, *Kingship and Politics*, p. 91.

76 Haynes, p. 71.

77 SP 10/6, fos. 16–17.

78 SP 10/6, fos. 51–2, 55–8.

79 Haynes, pp. 94–7.
80 Haynes, pp. 89–90.
81 APC, II, pp. 248–56.
82 *Troubles Connected with the Prayer Book of 1549*, ed. N. Pocock, *Camden Society*, New Series, 37 (1884), pp. 113–18; Bryson PhD, pp. 154–5.

Chapter 7 notes

1 *CSPSp*, IX, p. 445; *CSPSp*, X, p. 6; 'Letters of Richard Scudamore', ed. Brigden, pp. 81–5.
D. E. Hoak, *The King's Council in the Reign of Edward VI* (Cambridge, 1976), pp. 241–58.
2 Hoak, *King's Council*, p. 257.
3 M. L. Bush, *The Government Policy of Protector Somerset* (London, 1975), pp. 119–23; D. MacCulloch, *Tudor Church Militant: Edward VI and the Protestant Reformation* (London, 1999), pp. 57–95.
4 MacCulloch, *Tudor Church Militant*, pp. 77–93.
5 *The Life of the Learned Sir John Cheke, Knight*, ed. J. Strype (London, 1821), pp. 69–86; MacCulloch, *Tudor Church Militant*, pp. 92–3, 167–70; MacCulloch, *Thomas Cranmer*, pp. 454–513.
6 *CSPSp*, IX, pp. 101, 351.
7 *CSPSp*, IX, p. 361; *CSPSp*, X, pp. 5, 80–4; *CSPV*, V, no. 568.
8 *CSPSp*, IX, p. 101.
9 *CSPSp*, IX, p. 444; *CSPSp*, X, pp. 68–9, 205–6.
10 *CSPSp*, X, p. 5.
11 *CSPSp*, IX, p. 407; *CSPSp*, X, pp. 150–1.
12 Ellis, I, ii, pp. 161–3.
13 *CSPSp*, IX, p. 406; *CSPSp*, X, pp. 356–64.
14 *CSPSp*, X, p. 358.
15 Whitelock and MacCulloch, 'Princess Mary's Household and the Succession Crisis', pp. 269–75.
16 *CSPSp*, X, p. 248.
17 *CSPSp*, X, pp. 206, 209–12.
18 Machyn, pp. 4–5.
19 *CSPSp*, X, pp. 258–60.

20 *Literary Remains*, II, p. 308.

21 *Literary Remains*, II, p. 316.

22 Bryson PhD, pp. 89, 183; *Household Expenses of the Princess Elizabeth*, pp. 1–49.

23 Bryson PhD, p. 88.

24 Bryson PhD, p. 183.

25 Starkey, *Elizabeth*, p. 94.

26 *CPR, Edward VI*, III, pp. 238–42; Bryson PhD, p. 183.

27 *CSPSp*, IX, p. 489.

28 *CSPSp*, X, pp. 215–16; SP 4/1 (January 1546), no. 99.

29 *ECW*, p. 35. For the date, see *ESW*, p. 117.

30 Bryson PhD, pp. 204–24.

31 Machyn, p. 16; *CSPSp*, X, p. 493; *Household Expenses of the Princess Elizabeth*, p. 3.

32 Machyn, p. 16.

33 *The Loseley Manuscripts*, ed. A. J. Kempe (London, 1836), pp. 171–3.

34 Richardson, 'Lady Troy and Blanche Parry', pp. 3–15.

35 SP 10/8, fo. 115.

36 S. Alford, *Burghley: William Cecil at the Court of Elizabeth I* (London, 2008), p. 68.

37 Green, III, pp. 220–1; Bryson PhD, p. 184.

38 *ODNB*, s.v. 'Goodacre, Hugh'; A. Bryson and M. Evans, 'Seven Newly-Discovered Letters of Princess Elizabeth' (forthcoming). I am extremely grateful to Dr Alan Bryson for supplying me with copies of their transcripts of these documents ahead of publication.

39 *ODNB*, s.v. 'Allen, Edmund'.

40 S. Doran, 'Elizabeth I's Religion', *JEH*, 51 (2000), pp. 711–12; R. Bowers, 'The Chapel Royal, the First Edwardian Prayer Book, and Elizabeth's Settlement of Religion, 1559', *HJ*, 43 (2000), pp. 320–1.

41 *CSPScot*, I, pp. 257, 289.

42 *Letters of Roger Ascham*, pp. 120–3, 140.

43 *Letters of Roger Ascham*, p. 76, n. 1.

44 *Letters of Roger Ascham*, pp. 75–6; *Literary Remains*, I, pp. lii–liv.

45 *Letters of Roger Ascham*, p. 167.

46 *Letters of Roger Ascham*, p. 167.

47 Baldwin, I, pp. 275–84; *Queen Elizabeth's Englishings*, ed. C. Pemberton, *Early English Text Society*, New Series, 133 (1899), pp. x–xii.

48 *Letters of Roger Ascham*, p. 166; Baldwin, I, pp. 260, 274–6; A. Pollnitz, 'Christian Women or Sovereign Queens? The Schooling of Mary and Elizabeth', in *Tudor Queenship: The Reigns of Mary and Elizabeth*, ed. A. Hunt and A. Whitelock (Basingstoke, 2010), pp. 130–8.

49 *Letters of Roger Ascham*, p. 167.

50 E 101/426/8.

51 Baldwin, I, p. 261.

52 *Isocrates*, ed. G. Norlin, 3 vols (London, 1928), I, pp. 52–3; *ECW*, pp. 41, 95; *Memoirs of Sir James Melville of Halhill, 1535–1617*, ed. A. F. Steuart (London, 1929), p. 258.

53 *Isocrates I*, ed. D. C. Mirhady and Y. L. Too (Austin, TX, 2000), p. 155.

54 *ECW*, p. 35.

55 Machyn, pp. 20–1; *Literary Remains*, I, pp. 80–1; *Literary Remains*, II, pp. 428–63.

56 Baldwin, I, p. 253.

57 Alford, *Kingship and Politics*, pp. 161–73.

58 *Literary Remains*, I, pp. clix–clxiv; BL, Cotton MS, Vespasian F. XIII, fo. 273.

59 *Literary Remains*, II, pp. 310–17; Machyn, pp. 18–20; A. Young, *Tudor and Jacobean Tournaments* (London, 1987), pp. 28–9.

60 *Literary Remains*, I, pp. 80–1.

61 W. K. Jordan, *Edward VI: The Threshold of Power* (London, 1970), p. 403.

62 *Literary Remains*, I, p. 81.

63 E 101/426/8; *Literary Remains*, II, pp. 315, 392; Loach, *Edward VI*, pp. 136–8, 158.

64 E 101/426/8; J. Arnold, *Queen Elizabeth's Wardrobe Unlock'd* (Leeds, 1988), pp. 252–3; Hayward, *Dress at the Court of Henry VIII*, pp. 210–13; *Literary Remains*, I, pp. ccxliii–cclx; Loach, *Edward VI*, p. 138.

65 *CSPSp*, X, p. 249.

66 *CSPSp*, XI, pp. 9, 16–17, 35, 40, 45–6; Loach, *Edward VI*, pp. 159–62. A case for tuberculosis is made by G. Holmes, F. Holmes and

J. McMurrough, 'The Death of Young King Edward VI', *New England Journal of Medicine*, 345 (2001), pp. 60–2. I owe this reference to the kindness of Dale Hoak.

67 E. W. Ives, *Lady Jane Grey: A Tudor Mystery* (Oxford, 2009), pp. 137–68.

68 'The *Vitae Mariae Angliae Reginae* of Robert Wingfield of Brantham', ed. and trans. D. MacCulloch, *Camden Society*, 4th Series, 29 (1984), p. 247; D. Hoak, 'The Succession Crisis of 1553', in *Catholic Renewal and Protestant Resistance in Marian England*, ed. E. Evenden and V. Westbrook (forthcoming).

69 *CSPSp*, XI, pp. 40, 45–6, 54; Ives, *Lady Jane Grey*, pp. 144–5.

70 Inner Temple, London, Petyt MS 538, Vol. 47, fo. 317r–v; *Chronicle*, pp. 89–100.

71 Although the French ambassador, Antoine de Noailles, believed that Northumberland was the instigator of the entire conspiracy to exclude Mary, this is not supported by the English evidence. See E. H. Harbison, *Rival Ambassadors at the Court of Queen Mary* (Princeton, 1940), pp. 33–56; Ives, *Lady Jane Grey*, pp. 150–68.

72 *CSPSp*, XI, pp. 54, 66.

73 *Chronicle*, pp. 91–100.

74 Machyn, p. 35; Whitelock and MacCulloch, 'Princess Mary's Household and the Succession Crisis', pp. 265–6.

75 Machyn, p. 35.

76 *The Accession, Coronation and Marriage of Mary Tudor as related in Four Manuscripts of the Escorial*, ed. C. V. Malfatti (Barcelona: Sociedad Alianza de Artes Graficas, 1956), p. 48.

77 *Letters of Roger Ascham*, p. 145; J. Guy, 'The Story of Lady Jane Grey', in *Painting History: Delaroche and Lady Jane Grey*, ed. S. Bann and L. Whiteley (London, 2010), pp. 9–15.

78 *Chronicle*, p. 101.

79 *Accession, Coronation and Marriage of Mary Tudor*, p. 7; Whitelock and MacCulloch, 'Princess Mary's Household and the Succession Crisis', pp. 266, 276.

80 BL, Harleian MS 416, fos. 30–1v; *Loseley Manuscripts*, pp. 124–6.

81 Bryson PhD, p. 280.

82 Machyn, p. 37.

83 Machyn, p. 37.

84 Machyn, pp. 38–9; Wriothesley, II, pp. 93–4.

85 KB 8/23; *Chronicle*, p. 32.

86 *Chronicle*, p. 25; *Accession, Coronation and Marriage of Mary Tudor*, pp. 45–9.

Chapter 8 notes

1 *CSPV*, V, no. 934; *CSPV*, VI, ii, no. 884.

2 *CSPSp*, XI, pp. 344, 357, 371, 439; *CSPV*, V, no. 934; *CSPV*, VI, ii, no. 884; Keynes, 'Aching Head and Increasing Blindness', pp. 106–8.

3 *CSPSp*, XI, pp. 238–9; A. Hunt, 'The Monarchical Republic of Mary I', *HJ*, 52 (2009), pp. 560–6.

4 Machyn, pp. 45–6.

5 *APC*, II, pp. 30–1; *CSPSp*, XI, pp. 220, 240; *Accession, Coronation and Marriage of Mary Tudor*, p. 34; Hunt, 'Monarchical Republic', pp. 562–5; D. Hoak, 'The Coronations of Edward VI, Mary I and Elizabeth I, and the Transformation of the Tudor Monarchy', in *Westminster Abbey Reformed, 1540–1640*, ed. C. S. Knighton and R. Mortimer (Aldershot, 2003), pp. 136–7.

6 *CSPSp*, XI, p. 151; T. S. Freeman, '"As True a Subiect being Prysoner": John Foxe's Notes on the Imprisonment of Princess Elizabeth, 1554–5', *EHR*, 117 (2002), p. 107.

7 *CSPSp*, XI, p. 220.

8 *CSPSp*, XI, p. 221; Starkey, *Elizabeth*, p. 120.

9 *CSPSp*, XI, p. 240.

10 Freeman, 'John Foxe's Notes', p. 107; *CSPV*, V, no. 934; *CSPC*, VI, ii, no. 884.

11 *CSPSp*, XI, pp. 411, 418, 440.

12 *CSPV*, V, no. 934.

13 D. M. Loades, 'Philip II and the English', in *Felipe II (1598–1988). Europa Dividida: La Monarquía Católica de Felipe II*, ed. J. M. Millán, 2 vols (Madrid, 1998), II, pp. 485–6.

14 *SR*, IV, i, pp. 222–6.

15 Lodge, I, p. 190; *CSPSp*, XII, p. 50.

16 *CSPSp*, XII, p. 125.

17 *CSPSp*, XII, p. 125.

18 Harbison, *Rival Ambassadors*, p. 130.

19 Harbison, *Rival Ambassadors*, pp. 121–30, 337–9; Starkey, *Elizabeth*, pp. 137–8.

20 C. H. Garrett, *The Marian Exiles* (Cambridge, 1966), p. 73.

21 *CSPSp*, XII, pp. 166–7.

22 The correct date is established by *CSPSp*, XII, pp. 166–7; *CSPD, Mary*, p. 53; *ESW*, pp. 126–9.

23 Starkey, *Elizabeth*, p. 139.

24 SP 11/4, fo. 3r–v; *ECW*, pp. 41–2; *Household Expenses of the Princess Elizabeth*, pp. 2, 4–5, 7, 9, 11, 13, 15, 17, 19, 21, 23, 25, 27, 29, 31, 33 *et seq.*

25 *CSPSp*, XII, p. 167.

26 *Chronicle*, p. 70; Machyn, p. 58; *CSPSp*, XII, p. 167; Starkey, *Elizabeth*, pp. 141–2.

27 *Loseley Manuscripts*, p. 172.

28 *CSPSp*, XII, pp. 197–201.

29 Lodge, I, p. 193; Machyn, p. 63 (where the date is wrong).

30 *APC*, V, p. 28.

31 Freeman, 'John Foxe's Notes', p. 115.

32 *CSPSp*, XIII, no. 158.

33 'State Papers Relating to the Custody of the Princess Elizabeth at Woodstock in 1554', *Norfolk Archaeology*, 4 (1855), pp. 133–231; Foxe, II, pp. 1982–6; *CSPSp*, XIII, no. 158; Freeman, 'John Foxe's Notes', pp. 104–16; Starkey, *Elizabeth*, pp. 151–65.

34 Foxe, II, p. 1987; *CSPV*, VI, i, no. 72; Starkey, *Elizabeth*, pp. 178–9.

35 E. Duffy, *Fires of Faith: Catholic England under Mary Tudor* (New Haven and London, 2009), pp. 79–154.

36 'The Compendious Rehearsal of John Dee' in *Johannis, confratris & monachi Glastoniensis, chronica sive historia de rebus Glastoniensibus*, ed. T. Hearne, 2 vols (Oxford, 1726), II, pp. 519–20; Tytler, II, p. 479; *APC*, V, p. 137.

37 *HO*, p. 125; *CSPV*, VI, i, no. 33; Machyn, pp. 84–5.

38 *APC*, V, p. 126; SP 11/5, nos. 28–31.

39 *CSPV*, VI, ii, no. 884; Keynes, 'Aching Head and Increasing Blindness', pp. 108–9.

40 Foxe, II, p. 1987.

41 *CSPV*, VI, ii, no. 884.

42 Wriothesley, II, p. 130.

43 SP 11/7, no. 37 (fo. 71); SP 11/7, no. 66 (fo. 122).

44 *CSPV*, V, no. 934; *CSPV*, VI, ii, no. 884.

45 SP 12/22, fo. 77r–v.

46 SP 12/22, fo. 77v.

47 *CSPSp*, XI, p. 393. Douglas's name was mentioned again in notes for a letter to Philip on the succession in 1558. See *CSPSp*, XIII, no. 417.

48 *CSPSp*, XIII, nos. 111, 164 and pp. xiv–xv; *CSPV*, VI, i, nos. 121, 248, 262, 552, 557, 570; Wiesener, pp. 295–304.

49 *CSPV*, VI, i, no. 67; S. Doran, *Monarchy and Matrimony: The Courtships of Elizabeth I* (London, 1996), p. 19.

50 Bryson and Evans, 'Seven Newly-Discovered Letters of Princess Elizabeth' (forthcoming).

51 Northamptonshire Record Office, Fitzwilliam of Milton Papers, Charter 2286.

52 Alford, *Burghley*, pp. 69–73.

53 BL, Lansdowne MS 118, fo. 70v; Tytler, II, pp. 443–5; Alford, *Burghley*, pp. 71–4.

54 MacCulloch, *Tudor Church Militant*, p. 189.

55 *CSPF*, II, p. 172.

56 *Letters of Roger Ascham*, pp. 209, 255–7.

57 *Letters of Roger Ascham*, pp. 210–11.

58 Baldwin, I, pp. 277–80.

59 M. Peltonen, 'Rhetoric and Citizenship in the Monarchical Republic of Queen Elizabeth I', in *The Monarchical Republic of Early Modern England*, ed. J. F. McDiarmid (Aldershot, 2007), pp. 109–28.

60 Machyn, p. 102.

61 *Verney Papers*, pp. 64–5.

62 Harbison, *Rival Ambassadors*, pp. 270–96; D. M. Loades, *Two Tudor Conspiracies* (Cambridge, 1965), pp. 176–217.

63 Castiglione had previously been thrown into the Tower in May 1555 for allegedly helping to circulate a particularly abusive libel against Philip and Mary that had been written at Emden by one of the Protestant exiles. *CSPV*, VI, i, no. 80; Garrett, *The Marian Exiles*, pp. 116–17.

64 *CSPV*, VI, i, nos. 80, 505, 510; Wiesener, pp. 340–1; Starkey, *Elizabeth*, pp. 195–7.

65 *Verney Papers*, pp. 70–3; Machyn, p. 108.

66 *CSPV*, VI, i, nos. 505–6.

67 Wiesener, pp. 342–3; Starkey, *Elizabeth*, pp. 198–9.

68 Wiesener, p. 343; SP 11/9, fo. 40; *CSPV*, VI, i, no. 510.

69 *CSPV*, VI, i, nos. 510, 514.

70 *CSPV*, VI, i, no. 668.

71 Machyn, p. 120; *CSPV*, VI, ii, no. 743.

72 Machyn, p. 120; *CSPV*, VI, ii, no. 743.

73 *CSPV*, VI, ii, no. 775.

74 Doran, *Monarchy and Matrimony*, p. 19.

75 *CSPV*, VI, ii, no. 884.

76 Clifford, *Life of Jane Dormer*, p. 80.

77 *CSPV*, VI, ii, no. 775.

78 *CSPSp*, XIII, p. 448.

79 Wiesener, p. 358.

80 *CSPV*, VI, ii, no. 884.

81 *CSPSp*, XIII, p. xii.

82 *CSPSp*, XIII, no. 407; *PPE Mary*, p. cxciv.

83 Starkey, *Elizabeth*, pp. 223–4.

84 'The Count of Feria's Despatch to Philip II of 14 November 1558', ed. M. J. Rodríguez-Salgado and S. Adams, *Camden Society*, 4th Series, 29 (1984), p. 331.

85 'The Count of Feria's Despatch', p. 331.

86 *CSPSp*, XIII, no. 498; *CSPV*, VI, iii, no. 1285.

87 Clifford, *Life of Jane Dormer*, pp. 72–3.

88 'The Count of Feria's Despatch', p. 331.

Chapter 9 notes

1 Machyn, p. 178.

2 SP 12/1, fos. 1–5v.

3 W. MacCaffrey, *The Shaping of the Elizabethan Regime* (London, 1969), pp. 27–40; Alford, *Kingship and Politics*, pp. 195–207.

4 Garrett, *The Marian Exiles*, pp. 114–17; CSPV, VI, i, nos. 510.

5 LC 2/4/2, fos. 8–9, 25v–26v; LC 2/4/3, fos. [53v–4], [58v], [59v–63].

6 Garrett, *The Marian Exiles*, pp. 210–13.

7 *ESW*, pp. 124–5; *ODNB*, s.v. 'Dudley [née Knollys], Lettice'.

8 LC 2/4/3, fo. 7; Arnold, *Queen Elizabeth's Wardrobe Unlock'd*, pp. 52–3.

9 Bowers, 'The Chapel Royal, the First Edwardian Prayer Book, and Elizabeth's Settlement of Religion, 1559', pp. 326–8.

10 MacCulloch, *Tudor Church Militant*, pp. 176–7.

11 *CSPV*, VII, no. 15.

12 BL, Cotton MS, Julius F.VI, fos. 167–9v; BL, Additional MS 48035, fos. 141–6v; Alford, *Burghley*, pp. 90–4.

13 N. L. Jones, *Faith by Statute: Parliament and the Settlement of Religion, 1559* (London, 1982), pp. 83–159.

14 B. Usher, *William Cecil and Episcopacy, 1559–1577* (Aldershot, 2003), pp. 7–10.

15 Doran, 'Elizabeth I's Religion', pp. 699–720; Bowers, 'The Chapel Royal, the First Edwardian Prayer Book, and Elizabeth's Settlement of Religion', pp. 317–44; MacCulloch, *Tudor Church Militant*, pp. 191–2, 219.

16 *SR*, IV, i, p. 358; Bowers, 'The Chapel Royal, the First Edwardian Prayer Book, and Elizabeth's Settlement of Religion', pp. 339–40.

17 *Visitation Articles and Injunctions of the Period of the Reformation*, ed. W. H. Frere and W. M. Kennedy, 3 vols (London, 1910), III, pp. 9, 16, 20; *ODNB*, s.v. 'Parker, Matthew'.

18 *CSPScot*, I, pp. 257, 289; *The Zurich Letters*, ed. H. Robinson (2nd edn, Cambridge, 1846), p. 98; P. Collinson, *Archbishop Grindal, 1519–1583* (London, 1979), pp. 97–102; P. Collinson, *Elizabethan Essays* (London, 1994), pp. 87–118.

19 J. Coffey, *Persecution and Toleration in Protestant England, 1558–1689* (London, 2000), p. 82.

20 *An harborovve for faithfull and trevve subiectes agaynst the late blowne blaste, concerninge the gouernme[n]t of wemen* (London, 1559), sigs. B3v, D2v–D3, O4.

21 Judges 4–5.

22 *The Queen's Majesty's Passage and Related Documents*, ed. G. Warkentin (Toronto, 2004), pp. 65–8, 91–4; D. M. Bergeron, 'Elizabeth's Coronation Entry (1559): New Manuscript Evidence', *English Literary Renaissance*, 8 (1978), pp. 3–8; R. C. McCoy, '"The wonderfull spectacle": the Civic Progress of Elizabeth I and the Troublesome Coronation', in *Coronations: Medieval and Early Modern Monarchic Ritual*, ed. J. M. Bak (Berkeley, 1990), pp. 217–27; J. M. Richards, 'Love and a Female Monarch: the Case of Elizabeth Tudor', *Journal of British Studies*, 38 (1999), pp. 144–53; Hoak, 'Coronations of Edward VI, Mary I and Elizabeth I', pp. 140–1.

23 BL, Harleian MS 7004, fo. 2.

24 BL, Additional MS 32091, fos. 167–9; BL, Harleian MS 7004, fos. 1–2; John Knox, *On Rebellion*, ed. R. Mason (Cambridge, 1994), pp. 34–5, 43–4; J. Dawson, 'The Two John Knoxes: England, Scotland and the 1558 Tracts', *JEH*, 42 (1991), pp. 556–76.

25 *Zurich Letters*, ed. Robinson, pp. 76–7.

26 *On Rebellion*, ed. Mason, pp. 34–5.

27 BL, Additional MS 32091, fos. 168v–9. I am indebted to Dr Mark Taviner for discussing the manuscript with me and confirming my reading of its significance. It should be noted that the only unambiguous comparison of herself to Deborah in all of Elizabeth's presumed writings occurs in the so-called 'Spanish Versicles and Prayers' (*ECW*, p. 157). These have repeatedly been shown to be apocryphal and not by Elizabeth. No evidence exists that she had studied Spanish or could write in that language. Not even Jan van der Noot claimed this for her; Baldwin, I, p. 278. The much-vaunted reference to Deborah in HEH, Ellesmere MS 2072, fo. 2a (*ECW*, p. 424) turns out to be an interpolation. The closest Elizabeth came to Knox's view of herself was in her 'Golden Speech', delivered to a grateful delegation of members of the House of Commons in the Council Chamber at Whitehall in 1601,

following her concessions over the issue of monopolies. According to one version of the speech, she asked rhetorically, 'What am I as of myself without the watchful providence of Almighty God, other than a poor silly woman, weak and subject to many imperfections, expecting as you do a future judgement?' But this was to concede no more than that all kings and princes ruled in accordance with God's providence. See *Proceedings in the Parliaments of Elizabeth I*, ed. T. E. Hartley, 4 vols (Leicester, 1981–2002), III, p. 290.

28 *Records of the Reformation*, II, p. 386.

29 *Accession, Coronation and Marriage of Mary Tudor*, p. 48.

30 J. Guy, *'My Heart is My Own': The Life of Mary Queen of Scots* (London, 2004), pp. 215–313.

31 BNF, MS FF 15970, fo. 14r–v; I owe this reference and the translation to the kindness of Dr Simon Adams. See also S. Adams, 'The Dudley Clientèle, 1553–1563', in *The Tudor Nobility*, ed. G. W. Bernard (Manchester, 1992), pp. 241–65.

32 *CSPSp*, XIV, nos. 27, 29.

33 *Queen Elizabeth and Some Foreigners: being a Series of Hitherto Unpublished Letters from the Archives of the Hapsburg Family*, ed. V. von Klarwill (London, 1928), pp. 114–15; C. Skidmore, *Death and the Virgin: Elizabeth, Dudley and the Mysterious Fate of Amy Robsart* (London, 2010), pp. 125–200.

34 Skidmore, *Death and the Virgin*, pp. 203–306.

35 'A "Journall" of Matters of State happened from to time to time as well within and without the realme from and before the death of King Edw. the 6th until the yere 1562', ed. S. Adams, I. W. Archer and G. W. Bernard, *Camden Society*, 5th Series, 22 (2003), p. 66.

36 Doran, *Monarchy and Matrimony*, pp. 73–98.

37 Doran, *Monarchy and Matrimony*, pp, 99–129; MacCaffrey, *The Shaping of the Elizabethan Regime*, pp. 259–62.

38 W. Camden, *The History of the Most Renowned and Victorious Princess Elizabeth, Late Queen of England*, ed. W. T. McCaffrey (Chicago, 1970), p. 135.

39 *CSPSp*, XVI, no. 173; W. T. MacCaffrey, *Queen Elizabeth and the Making of Policy, 1572–1588* (Princeton, 1981), pp. 272–81; Doran, *Monarchy and Matrimony*, pp. 154–94.

40 *Proceedings in the Parliaments of Elizabeth I*, I, p. 147.
41 'Lethington's Account of Negotiations with Elizabeth in September and October 1561', in *A Letter from Mary Queen of Scots to the Duke of Guise, January 1562*, ed. J. H. Pollen (Edinburgh, 1904), Appendix 1, p. 39.
42 'Lethington's Account', p. 41.
43 'Lethington's Account', pp. 41–2.
44 E. W. Ives, 'The Queen and the Painters: Anne Boleyn, Holbein and Tudor Royal Portraits', *Apollo*, 140 (July 1994), pp. 42–3; Ives, *Life and Death of Anne Boleyn*, pp. 42–3.
45 Lambeth, MS 4769.
46 Lambeth, MS 4267, fo. 19; Guy, *'My Heart is My Own': The Life of Mary Queen of Scots*, pp. 460–97.

ILLUSTRATION CREDITS

A. Colour plates

The Bridgeman Art Library

Henry Fitzroy, Duke of Richmond and Somerset, c.1534, by Lucas Horenbout (watercolour and body colour on vellum). The Royal Collection © 2011 Her Majesty Queen Elizabeth II / The Bridgeman Art Library.

Katherine Parr, c.1545, by 'Master John' (oil on panel). The National Portrait Gallery, London / The Bridgeman Art Library.

Elizabeth, c.1551, attrib. William Scrots (oil on panel). The Royal Collection © 2011 Her Majesty Queen Elizabeth II / The Bridgeman Art Library.

Philip and Mary as King and Queen of England, c.1558, by Hans Eworth. Trustees of the Bedford Estate, Woburn Abbey / The Bridgeman Art Library.

Private collection

Henry VIII in old age, engraving by Cornelis Metsys, c.1548.

Sotheby's Picture Library

Portrait of King Edward VI, attrib. William Scrots (oil on panel). Courtesy of Sotheby's Picture Library.

Portrait of Queen Elizabeth I, c.1560, English School (oil on panel). Courtesy of Sotheby's Picture Library.

Yale Center for British Art, Paul Mellon Collection

An Unknown Man (said to be Sir Thomas Seymour), *c.*1543, attrib. Hans Holbein the Younger (gouache and gold). B.1974.2.58.

Portrait of a Lady, possibly Lady Jane Grey, attrib. Levina Teerlinc (body colour on thin card). B.1974.2.59.

An Allegory of the Tudor Succession: The Family of Henry VIII, *c.*1572, by an unknown artist (oil on panel). B.1973.3.7.

Robert Dudley, *c.*1564, by Steven van der Meulen (oil on panel). B1981.25.445.

B. Black and white illustrations

Cambridge University Library

One of Edward VI's schoolroom exercises written during the winter of 1548–49, from *Petit traité à l'encontre de la primauté du pape*, MS Dd.12.59, fo. 1.

Edward VI's Reformation, from John Foxe, *Actes and Monuments of matters most speciall and memorable*, London, 1583, vol. 2, woodcut from p. 1294, shelfmark Young 200. With kind permission of the Syndics of Cambridge University Library.

Bishop Hugh Latimer preaching before Edward VI, from John Foxe, *Actes and Monuments of these latter and perillous dayes*, London, 1563, vol. 2, woodcut from p. 1353, shelfmark Sel.2.15B. With kind permission of the Syndics of Cambridge University Library.

Account of the 'Miraculous Preservation' of the Lady Elizabeth in Mary's reign, from John Foxe, *Actes and Monuments of matters most speciall and memorable*, vol. 2, p. 2091, London, 1583, shelfmark Young 200. With kind permission of the Syndics of Cambridge University Library.

Elizabeth I at Prayer, from Richard Day, *Booke of Christian praiers, collected out of the ancient writers,* woodcut on verso of title page, London, 1608, shelfmark Young.255. With kind permission of the Syndics of Cambridge University Library.

Clare College, University of Cambridge

Windsor Castle (detail) from George Braun, *Civitates Orbis Terrarum,* Cologne and Antwerp, 1582. Courtesy of the Master, Fellows and Scholars of Clare College.

Elizabeth I letter, 1588 (document on loan from an anonymous benefactor), with the kind permission of the benefactor and courtesy of the Master, Fellows and Scholars of Clare College.

The Honourable Society of the Inner Temple

Edward VI's 'My devise for the succession', Inner Temple Library, Petyt MS 538.47, fo. 317 (recto and verso). Courtesy of The Masters of the Bench of the Inner Temple.

The National Archives, Kew

Henry Fitzroy's letter to Henry VIII, 14 January 1527, SP 1/40, fo. 210 (stamped 207).

The Lady Mary's letter to Queen Jane Seymour, 1536, SP 1/104, fo. 223 (stamped 204).

The Lady Elizabeth's letter to Queen Katherine Parr, May 1548, EXT 11/161, fo. 84c.

Private collection

Lady Margaret Beaufort, Countess of Richmond and Derby, from a 19th century engraving.

Edward Stafford, Duke of Buckingham, from a nineteenth-century engraving by R. Ackermann.

Yale Center for British Art, Paul Mellon Collection

View of London Bridge, *c.*1632, by Claude de Jongh (oil on panel). B2005.4.

Other images

Prince Arthur, elder son of Henry VII, from a stained-glass window in the north transept of Great Malvern Priory, attrib. Richard Twygge and Thomas Wodshawe, photo © 2012, John Guy.

The gatehouse at Ludlow Castle, Shropshire, photo © 2011, Julia Fox.

The Old Palace, Hatfield, Hertfordshire, photo © 2012, John Guy.

The tomb of Henry Fitzroy, the Church of St Michael, Framlingham, Suffolk, photo © 2011, Julia Fox.

INDEX